HERE'S WHAT THEY'RE SAYIN' ABOUT . . .

The Partridge Family Album

"Wonderful! This book captures the spirit and magic of *The Partridge Family*! How could any fan live without it?"
—**Shirley Jones (Shirley Partridge)**

"Thank God for this book! I don't remember being there."
—**Danny Bonaduce (Danny Partridge)**

"Very impressive! I found out more things about my television family than I ever knew before!"
—**Brian Forster (Chris Partridge)**

"Joey Green has certainly done his homework! This book is the authoritative Partridge Family reference."
—**Jeremy Gelbwaks (the first Chris Partridge)**

"Exciting and enjoyable! Even for someone like me who was actually there!"
—**Suzanne Crough (Tracy Partridge)**

"Incredible reading! The problem is, I don't remember doing any of it. Not the show, the incredible reading. I guess I'll have to read it again!"
—**Dave Madden (Reuben Kincaid)**

"Come on, get happy! Read *The Partridge Family Album*!"
—**Bernard Slade (Creator)**

"First rate...Candid...Accurate....Amusing. It brings back fond memories."
—**Bob Claver (Producer)**

"This book is the first accurate account of the television and recording phenomenon known as the Partridge Family."
—**Wes Farrell (Music Producer)**

Also by Joey Green

Hellbent on Insanity
(with Bruce Handy and Alan Corcoran)

The Unofficial Gilligan's Island Handbook

The Get Smart Handbook

The Partridge Family Album

Joey Green

Foreword by Shirley Jones

HarperPerennial

A Division of HarperCollins*Publishers*

Designed by Joey Green

Library of Congress Cataloging-in-Publication Data

Green, Joey
    The Partridge family album : the official get happy guide to America's grooviest television family / Joey Green ; foreword by Shirley Jones. — 1st ed.
        p.   cm.
    Includes index.
    ISBN 0-06-095075-7
    1. Partridge family (Television program). I. Title.
    PN1992.77.P266G74   1994
    791.45'75—dc20   94-9281

94 95 96 97 98 PS/RRD 10 9 8 7 6 5 4 3 2 1

For Ashley

Hello world, here's a song that we're singin',
Come on get happy!
A whole lot of lovin' is what we'll be bringin',
We'll make you happy!

Wes Farrell-Danny Janssen • ©1971 Screen Gems-EMI Music Inc.

Contents

Foreword

by Shirley Jones

Depending on which side of the argument you believe, *The Partridge Family* was either the best thing to happen to me or the fatal torpedo to a promising motion picture career. (The role of Shirley Partridge came during a string of major movies and, in fact, after an Academy Award for *Elmer Gantry* with Burt Lancaster.) And so, the good news (or bad, depending on which school of thought you buy) is that people in America know me primarily as Shirley Partridge and not as *Elmer Gantry*'s back-street lover, Lulu Baines . . . or *Carousel*'s Julie . . . or *Oklahoma!*'s Laurie . . . or even *The Music Man*'s Marion, the Librarian.

The Partridge Family happened almost too quickly and easily—without pomp, without fanfare, and without the usual winds of conflict that characterize the sets of most long-term family shows. Except for the short tenure of our first Chris (Jeremy Gelbwaks was replaced by Brian Forster after the first season), the Partridge cast remained intact to the very end. There were the usual and expected personal squeaks that made each of us what we were. Danny Bonaduce was as full of his nine-year-old hell as he was a natural acting talent, and he kept all of us on our toes trying to tie him down to earth. It was Susan Dey's first real job, after some modeling work, and she was vigilantly determined to get it right. Suzanne Crough was a talented twig from a healthy, normal tree. Like his father, David was theatrically gifted, but, also like his father, he was a pushover for the social scene. And David became a television teen idol superstar, virtually the night our pilot premiered. It stunned everyone. Dave Madden, a young stand-up comic from *Laugh-In* and the only adult male on the show, was the happy icing on the cake. He was sweet, he was kind, and he was interminably patient despite all the showbiz hysteria constantly around him. He also developed a sensational fatherly rapport with Danny that worked wonders for us all to the very last day of shooting. And that was the unlikely group (with only two of us being "singers") that would instantly become television's first "rock star family."

But that's about as spicy as the Partridge Family story gets. From beginning to end, it was smooth and banal enough to bore the tabloids.

From the moment I read the pilot script I knew that, "light and fluffy" as it was, it couldn't miss on American television. (It was the only family sitcom with music.) But I really never expected *The Partridge Family* to become a pop culture phenomenon. The country ate it up. Everybody wanted to have a Partridge family. Somehow, it seemed to bridge the big bad generation gap with the simple elixir of music—and bubblegum music at that.

While we are often compared to *The Brady Bunch*, we were basically dissimilar. Unlike Carol Brady, my "typical mother" role never had me leaping in to solve the kids' problems . . . and, in 1970, that was a very progressive idea.

In some ways, it probably still is. And, of course, I don't suspect I will ever unload the "cool mom" badge that follows me everywhere I go. The letters that poured in for years, mostly from kids with less than perfect families, yearned for some touch with what seemed to be the ideal nest. (The truth is I'm still not 100 percent sure if that sort of media influence is desirable. It does offer a glimpse of a positive, healthy home. But at the same time, it may well perpetuate the false hope of finding one exactly like it.)

The idea of working with my own stepson seemed sweet and natural, but it happened by total accident, both of us having read for our parts without the other knowing. Ironically, working together so closely, David and I developed a bond we never would have had in our family life outside the show. As for David's real mother, a talented actress named Evelyn Ward, I'm sure her Partridge impressions are somewhat ambivalent, considering the world still believes that I'm David's mother, off-camera as well as on.

And so, time does its thing, the Partridge-era kids are now parents, their parents are grandparents, and so on and so on. I marvel and smile at "the legs" our funny little family seems to have had and at the regenerated millions who are discovering us for the first time. Yes, *The Partridge Family* is undeniably "light and fluffy," but it also happens to be an enduring, carefree touch of positive and functional television that has clearly become an American cultural icon. And that is an indisputable fact I would offer all the sage and sanguine critics who would tell us something else.

Introduction

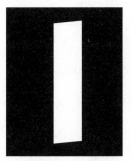 am thoroughly convinced that the Partridge Family was the most influential rock group in recorded history.

Shirley, Keith, Laurie, Danny, Chris, and Tracy came to represent a lifestyle, radically altering the course of music and profoundly influencing the attitudes, manners, and morals of a generation. The Partridge Family brilliantly diluted unpalatable counterculture themes, making long hair, vivid attire, and alternative lifestyles accessible to a wider audience than the Beatles, the Rolling Stones, and Bob Dylan combined could have ever hoped to reach.

On television, the Partridge Family's antics, while seemingly middle-class and bourgeois, actually addressed key social issues and philosophical themes, probing the very foundations of American society. The Partridges, while purportedly naive and innocent, questioned authority, advocated consciousness expansion, and challenged Americans everywhere to "Come On Get Happy!" In episode after episode, they struggle against the evils of co-option, defy stale conventions, advocate non-violence, and rebel against conformity and the status quo—luring a captive adolescent audience into the realm of political and social consciousness.

On the surface, the Partridge Family's songs appear deceptively simple and imitative, but they too were cleverly constructed with lyrics ambitiously tackling issues ranging from social injustice to fragile adolescent emotions. When the Partridge Family sings of idle suburban pleasantries in "Come On Get Happy," they sardonically glorify the intellectual ennui inherent in the suburban dilemma. When they sing "I Think I Love You," they tell us not to let irrational fears shatter our romantic ideals, while warning of the dangerous illusions created by infatuation.

The Partridge Family continually advocated individuality, the freedom of youth, the independence Henry David Thoreau celebrates in *Walden*, and the endless possibilities that life has to offer if we truly yearn to reach for them. Americans couldn't help but extract a new set of values from the dominant philosophical and social themes in the Partridge Family's television series and albums. The Partridge Family would forever alter the American mind.

Here then is the first book to recapture the excitement of the Partridge phenomenon. Here is the Partridge Family as they've never been seen before. On the following pages you'll find all the dates, statistics, and intimately detailed biographies. Here are pages from the fan magazines, critical appraisals, and a complete list of the plots, guest stars, and songs in each *Partridge Family* episode. Here at long last is a look back at the Partridge Family phenomenon to chronicle their genius, rekindle some fond memories, and above all, fan the flames for what would surely be the most celebrated event of the century—a Partridge Family reunion.

—*Joey Green*
Hollywood, California

1

Come On Get Happy

Come On Get Happy

Hello world, here's a song that we're singin',
Come on get happy!
A whole lot of lovin' is what we'll be bringin',
We'll make you happy!

We had a dream, we'd go travelin' together,
We'd spread a little lovin' then we'd keep movin' on.
Somethin' always happens whenever we're together,
We get a happy feelin' when we're singing a song.

Trav'lin' along there's a song that we're singin',
Come on get happy!
A whole lot of lovin' is what we'll be bringin',
We'll make you happy!
We'll make you happy!
We'll make you happy!

I n August of 1969, Bernard Slade, creator of *The Flying Nun*, *Love on a Rooftop*, and *Mr. Deeds Goes to Town*, was under contract to Screen Gems, the television subsidiary of Columbia Pictures, to develop three pilots a year. Inspired by *The Sound of Music*, he decided that "it would be interesting to do a show about a family that sings together." His idea for a new situation comedy, originally titled *Family Business*, centered around the trials and tribulations of a widow with five children who is forced to become a permanent member of her children's rock band when their girl singer gets the mumps.

In keeping with such musical menageries as the Beatles, the Crickets, the Turtles, the Byrds, and the Monkees, Slade named his family group the Partridge Family after a schoolmate. "When I was raised in England, I was on a soccer team," recalls Slade. "The center-half on the team was named Partridge, which I thought was a very unusual name at the time." The Partridges would be loosely modeled after the Cowsills, a genuine musical family rock band from Newport, Rhode Island, that had recorded the number two hit single "The Rain, the Park and Other Things" and the theme song from the rock musical *Hair*.

Initially, Slade considered having the Cowsills, whom he had seen perform on *The Tonight Show Starring Johnny Carson*, play the group. Executive Producer Bob Claver flew to Newport to spend a day with the Cowsill family. "We thought that maybe they could do the show," remembers Claver. "Then we realized that only the little girl would be appropriate."

> "When I was raised in England, I was on a soccer team. The center-half on the team was named Partridge, which I thought was a very unusual name at the time."
>
> —Bernard Slade

"They did better with the characters they got," Bob Cowsill told the *Los Angeles Times* on October 15, 1993. "We had already grown beyond those ages anyway."

"In the back of my mind, the ages [of the children] were chosen to appeal right across the board," says Slade. The five Partridge children would include a male teenager (to attract teenage girls to the show), a female teenager (to lure teenage boys), and three small children (to entice the kids). "And then we figured the adults would like to watch Shirley," Slade adds. The family would live in the fictional town of San Pueblo, California, hold band practice in their garage, wear matching maroon crushed-velvet vests or polyester pants suits in concert, and travel together on a school bus repainted in the colorful geometric style of Piet Mondrian with the motto "Caution Nervous Mother Driving"—a candy-coated version of the psychedelic buses popularized in the Beatles' movie *Magical Mystery Tour*, the Who's song "Magic Bus," and Tom Wolfe's book *The Electric Kool-Aid Acid Test*. "I just thought that would be a great visual thing to have a bus painted that way," recalls Slade. "It was written to be painted psychedelic colors. It was like a sixties thing. I mean, I didn't see it as being squares at all."

Every week the series would feature one or two songs in a rock music video sequence faintly reminiscent of the cinema verité style of the Beatles' film *A Hard Day's Night* and *The Monkees* television series. The Partridge series (to be produced by Screen Gems) would promote the Partridge record albums (to be produced by Columbia's record subsidiary Bell Records), which in turn would promote the series.

Slade insists that he wasn't thinking about the Monkees, the prefabricated, prepackaged, Beatles-inspired rock group with their own television series through which to promote their albums. But Screen Gems, the studio that had produced *The Monkees*, was. The four Monkees had rebelled against their manufactured image, insisting that they be allowed to perform their own music, throwing a monkey wrench into a finely oiled money machine. This time, Screen Gems, while eager to repeat the success of *The Monkees*, wanted to avoid making the same mistakes.

Slade made it clear from the onset of *The Partridge Family* that his group would be nothing but another fabricated television family. Genuine actors would be hired to the play the roles of the family. Studio musicians, aptly credited, would create the Partridge Family's music; the actors would lip-sync to the finished music tracks. The Partridge Family would appeal to the prepubescent audience abandoned by the Beatles and the Monkees. Their music would recapture the lulling harmonies and giddy optimism of the Lovin' Spoonful, the Mamas and the Papas, the Carpenters, and Three Dog Night. Their lyrics would be confined to such heady topics as infatuation, puppy love, and the joys of carefree youth. "*The Monkees* was a copy of the Beatles," explains Bob Claver. "Ours was a family show where they happened to sing."

> "The Monkees was a copy of the Beatles. Ours was a family show where they happened to sing."
> —Bob Claver

The day Slade finished the pilot script, his agent sent it to Shirley Jones. Shirley Mae Jones was born on March 31, 1934, in Smithton, Pennsylvania, where her father ran Jones Brewing Company, makers of Stoney's beer. She entered the Miss America contest after her high school graduation in 1952, became Miss Pittsburgh, and was runner-up for Miss Pennsylvania. With the scholarship she won, she enrolled at the Pitts-

burgh School of Drama and sang with the Pittsburgh Civic Light Company. A year later she met Richard Rodgers and Oscar Hammerstein, who put her in the chorus of *South Pacific* on Broadway and then in the lead of their movie production of *Oklahoma!*, launching her long movie career at the age of twenty. She married actor Jack Cassidy, became stepmother to seven-year-old David Cassidy (who was still living with his mother, actress Evelyn Ward), and, between film roles, had three children: Shaun, Patrick, and Ryan. She starred in *Carousel*, *April Love*, *Never Steal Anything Small*, *Bobbikins*, *Elmer Gantry* (for which she won an Academy Award for her portrayal of prostitute Lulu Baines), *Pepe*, *Two Rode Together*, *The Music Man*, *The Courtship of Eddie's Father*, *A Ticklish Affair*, *Dark Purpose*, *Bedtime Story*, *Fluffy*, *The Secret of My Success*, *The Happy Ending*, and *The Cheyenne Social Club*. She also appeared in theater, including *Maggie Flynn* with husband Jack Cassidy, before her television debut in the NBC world premiere movie *Silent Night, Lonely Night*.

"When I read the script, I was very excited by it because it had music," recalls Jones. "I mean, it was a little bit of everything that was a part of me. And I loved the idea of it being a regular family and yet that little extra added edge of being in show business. I thought that was a great idea and it had never been done, really." She remained stalwart in her conviction that the series would succeed, even when everyone else associated with the show was convinced it would fail. "I thought it had the best chance of success of any pilot script I'd ever read," Jones told the *New York Times* of September 5, 1971. "For a situation comedy, it was written honestly; and the Partridges weren't a fairy-tale, candy-box family."

"I don't remember anyone else being considered [for the role of Shirley Partridge]," recalls Slade. "That was a big coup in those days because Shirley hadn't done television. I do remember getting a call at home from Jane Powell, saying that she had read the script and it was the story of her life, which I thought was a little strange, but I know she wanted to do it."

Bob Claver interviewed 850 children to cast the five Partridge kids, narrowing the group down to ten. He tested two candidates for each role, and, after carefully assessing the chemistry of the performers, created two different families to screen test with Shirley Jones as the mother of both. Jones had no idea that her stepson David Cassidy was being considered for the role of sixteen-year-old Keith Partridge, the eldest of the five children. The only person at Screen Gems aware of their relationship was casting director Rene Valente. She kept quiet until Cassidy became a finalist. The other contender was John David Carson, who later starred in the 1971 Rock Hudson film *Pretty Maids All in a Row*.

"We didn't know we were both up for the parts until we were both actually chosen," recalls Shirley Jones. "When they finally decided that David was the one they wanted, they told him that I was playing the mother and asked how he felt about that. David said, 'That's unbelievable, that's great.' Then they had to ask me before they actually made the choice. They asked, 'How do you get along with David?' and I said, 'Great, that's wonderful news.'"

Born on April 12, 1950, in New York City, David Bruce Cassidy, the son of actor Jack Cassidy and singer-actress Evelyn Ward, was raised in West Orange, New Jersey. His parents were divorced when he was five,

> "For a situation comedy, it was written honestly; and the Partridges weren't a fairy-tale, candy-box family."
> —Shirley Jones

> **"When I first read the script, I thought it was terrible. I was thinking about saying these dumb lines like, 'Gee, Mom, can I borrow the keys to the car?' I just couldn't bring myself to do it."**
> **—David Cassidy**

and he moved to Hollywood when he was eleven. He was expelled from two high schools before completing his education at the private Rexford School in Los Angeles. He lasted one semester at Los Angeles City College, then began playing guitar and drums, writing songs, and performing with the Los Angeles Theater Group. He decided to try acting and moved to New York, landing a costarring role in Allan Sherman's Broadway production of *The Fig Leaves Are Falling*. When it flopped, he returned to Los Angeles, making guest appearances on *Ironside*, *Marcus Welby, M.D.*, *Bonanza*, and *Medical Center*. He started to receive a little fan mail and became the subject of articles in teenybopper magazines like *Fave*, *Flip*, *16*, and *Tiger Beat* with such titles as "David: How to Turn Him On—By the Girls Who Have," "David Needs Your Love," and "David & Those Special Kisses." "When he was tapped for the Partridge role," reported *Newsweek* of August 30, 1971, "no one even knew or cared if he could sing—but he had sung, accompanying himself on guitar, since eleven." His character was named Keith, confesses Slade, because "often I used to choose names that were easy to type."

"When I first read the script, I thought it was terrible," Cassidy told *Rolling Stone* of May 11, 1972. "I was thinking about saying these dumb lines like, 'Gee, Mom, can I borrow the keys to the car?' I just couldn't bring myself to do it." He called his manager, Ruth Aarons, who urged him to read it again. "Well, I'm soft. I read it over—twice—and then I called her back and I said, 'I guess it's not so bad.' Only because I'd gotten used to it."

Seventeen-year-old model Susan Hallock Dey was cast to play Keith's fifteen-year-old teenage sister, Laurie. Born on December 10, 1952, in Pekin, Illinois, Susan Dey is the daughter of a newspaper journalist who moved his family to Mount Kisco, New York, when Susan was three months old. Her mother died from pneumonia when Susan was eight, and her father remarried a few years later. When Susan was fifteen, her stepmother took her to a modeling agency, and Dey was soon posing for *Vogue*, *McCall's*, and *Mademoiselle*. Within a year, her picture had appeared on the covers of *Glamour*, *Bride's*, and *Seventeen*. In 1969 she flew to Los Angeles to audition for *The Partridge Family*, and moved to Los Angeles alone to take the part. "I met Susan Dey in New York," recalls Producer Paul Witt. "She had never really acted before. She had played a duck in a school play." She completed her high school courses at Fox Lane High in Bedford, New York, by mail.

Claver cast Dante Daniel Bonaduce, an eleven-year-old redhead with an impish grin and an uncanny ability to make anything he said sound funny, as the third Partridge child, Danny. Born on August 13, 1959, Bonaduce had acted in commercials and made guest appearances on *Mayberry RFD*, *Bewitched*, *My World and Welcome to It*, *The Ghost and Mrs. Muir*, and *Accidental Family*. Remarked the *New York Times*: "Danny's comic ability is so obvious that one can actually believe television writer Joe Bonaduce's story that 'when I moved out here six years ago I couldn't get a job. I couldn't even get arrested. But everybody we met wanted Danny. Against our will, we finally let him give it a try.'"

"We got very lucky with the casting basically because of Danny Bonaduce, who was just innately talented and funny as a kid," recalls Slade. "I mean, he was a wonderful child actor. When you wanted to get a laugh, you'd always go to that character."

Two other children, newcomers Jeremy Gelbwaks and Suzanne Crough, were cast as the remaining Partridges, Chris and Tracy.

"The characters in the show are named after my children," confesses Slade. "I have a daughter named Laurel and a son named Christopher. Even the dog, actually. We had a dog called Simon. On the show the dog is called Simone because it was a female dog."

Comedian Dave Madden was cast as the Partridge Family's child-hating manager, Reuben Kincaid. Born in Sarnia, Ontario, on December 15, 1933, Madden, the youngest of four children, was sent to live with an aunt and uncle in Terre Haute, Indiana, after his father died. Immobilized by a bicycle accident, he took up magic and later added comedy to his act. He graduated from Otter Creek High, attended Indiana State Teachers College for one semester, and then worked in a bakery. In 1951, he joined the air force, was assigned to Special Services, and was stationed in Tripoli, Libya, where he once performed before the king of Libya. After his discharge, he majored in communications at the University of Miami, performed his comedy routine at fraternity parties and clubs on Miami Beach, and, following graduation, played the Southern night-club circuit for two years, finally moving to Los Angeles. During a club engagement, he was discovered by Frank Sinatra, who called Ed Sullivan and got him booked for three shows. Madden later played Pruett on the short-lived situation comedy *Camp Runamuck*, did voice-overs in commercials, and made guest appearances on several television shows, including *Bewitched* and *Hogan's Heroes*. After touring one summer with a comedy troupe headed by Dan Rowan and Dick Martin, he was hired as a regular in the first season of *Rowan & Martin's Laugh-In*, appearing as the guy who threw confetti in the air. "Dave Madden brings to such dialogue a touch of self-mockery that somehow blunts the edge of meanness," commented *TV Guide* of December 18, 1971. "Madden's looks also tend to dilute the sting. Tall and round-shouldered, with a mop of straw-blond hair, Madden has a lugubrious basset-hound's face. His dour but friendly blue eyes view the world less in anger than in doubtful resignation."

> **"The Partridge Family was the original Milli Vanilli."**
> **—Danny Bonaduce**

The Partridge Family's music would be overseen by music producer Wes Farrell, who also penned the hit singles "Hang on Sloopy" and "Come a Little Bit Closer." Farrell, who had produced the Cowsills and Every Mother's Son, had tried to create television shows around those two rock groups. When Bell Records approached him with the opportunity to produce the Partridge Family, Farrell was "instantly interested," especially after viewing the pilot. "It fit that genre of everybody music, truly

American," recalls Farrell. "I thought David had the charisma to became a major idol. And Shirley had the intelligence and the talent of a professional singer."

Farrell commissioned veteran songwriters, including Tony Romeo (who wrote the Cowsills' "Indian Lake"), Gerry Goffin and Carole King, Barry Mann and Cynthia Weil, Tommy Boyce and Bobby Hart (who wrote the Monkees' hit "Last Train to Clarksville"), Paul Anka, Rupert Holmes, Neil Sedaka and Howard Greenfield, and Irwin Levine and L. Russell Brown (who together wrote Tony Orlando and Dawn's hits "Candida," "Knock Three Times," and "Tie a Yellow Ribbon"), to pen hits for the Partridges. Farrell was given story outlines far in advance of any shooting so he and his songwriters could target the songs to the theme of each show.

He recorded the Partridge albums in Studio 2 of Western Recorders in Los Angeles using session musicians who had also played for the Fifth Dimension, the Carpenters, and the Mamas and the Papas. Session vocalists Tom and John Bahler (former members of the Love Generation, the group responsible for the pop hit "Groovy Summertime") sang the harmonies with Jackie Ward and Ron Hicklin (who also appeared on *Brady Bunch* recordings).

What Was the Message of The Partridge Family?

Shirley Jones (Shirley Partridge):

"I don't think there really was a message. If we had given the show a message I think it would be: there are happy families around. I mean, it isn't just a storybook family. Everybody still thinks it was. I mean, everybody says, 'Ho, ho, ho. That doesn't happen in real families.' But it did. I mean, a lot of the stories that the writers got were right out of my own house. I had three growing boys then, and sometimes the writers would come over on weekends and see what was happening with Little League and this-and-that, and they developed some story ideas from my family. So it did happen that way sometimes. Yeah, it was a little glossy, but for the time, there were families like that."

David Cassidy (Keith Partridge):

"I think that there could be competition, there could be conflict, there could be diversity, but that the family and the love was the glue."

Danny Bonaduce (Danny Partridge):

"I don't think there was one at the time. I think there's been one since. Family television went so far into the toilet that our show ended up having a message of family values. You know, being able to get along well. We did shows on honesty. We did a particular show where I got caught lying and then documented any little white lie anybody would tell, such as Shirley saying, 'I don't want to talk to her, tell her I'm not here' [Episode 84]. That kind of thing. So I would say those kind of good, decent family values."

Brian Forster (Chris Partridge):

"Peace, love, and happiness, and all that kind of thing. It was one of the first family shows that actually had a single mother involved. I thought that was kind of ahead of its time in a sense. Having the musical numbers and the-family-that-sings-together-stays-together theme was really a good way of showing that a family can work together."

Jeremy Gelbwaks (Chris Partridge):

"The show wasn't really about 'a messsage.' You know, it was just a television show about a family and some music. That said, there were some subtexts, like, 'Here's five kids and their mom who get rich and famous singing songs because they love each other and work together.' So it's a fairly optimistic show, I suppose."

Suzanne Crough (Tracy Partridge):

"Family interaction. I mean, there are shows like *The Brady Bunch*, but I don't think those were as realistic as *The Partridge Family*. Coming from a large family myself, I know there's always constant upheaval going on between some sibling or another. But when things start falling apart, they tend to stick together really strong."

Dave Madden (Mr. Kincaid):

"Money. You see, I think the message of all television is money. I mean, we're not talking about art here, are we? We're talking about a commercial venture to make money. Now I'm sure that each show had its own individual message. I think there was some kind of the-family-that-plays-together-stays-together moral to the totality of that show, but I promise you, there was no intent. You could drag many messages out of *The Partridge Family* that just accidentally happened to be there, but if you're looking for a message that *The Partridge Family* was trying to apply, then I think you've skirted the real purpose of doing *The Partridge Family*, and that was to make money."

Bernard Slade (Creator):

"This was made primarily to entertain. It was entertainment. I suppose we dealt with sort of average middle-class family problems. There was certainly no deep meaning. But I don't think there were any television shows that had messages in those days. They were all about getting ratings and staying on [television]. You know, that was it. And playing some sort of mix. Certainly the music, everything was kind of white bread. But that's what it was; it wasn't aspiring to be anything else."

Bob Claver (Executive Producer):

"None. We did messages in individual shows. We'd take something like the episode where Danny falls in love with a Jewish girl [Episode 91]. That kind of stuff we did a lot. Stealing, all kinds of themes. Almost every show had that. As far as overall philosophy, there wasn't one. They were a family that got along, which, in those days, television families did. And we were kind of ahead of our time because we had all kinds of arguments between the kids. I mean, they were forever fighting, and that was unique in those days."

Paul Witt (Producer):

"I can't say we ever sat down and decided on a specific message. There always was an obvious one, such as that a family is central to everyone's life. Even a family that has been diminished by death like the Partridge Family can maintain a very structured family life. Although putting together a group was a way in which they could support themselves, they were a normal family in every other respect. So family values—if there was a message—certainly was the underlying basis of the show.

"When I was a child I had a lot of trouble watching situation comedies because they made my family seem dysfunctional. My parents did fight occasionally. They didn't have answers to all kinds of problems in twenty-three minutes. I would watch some very successful shows, and I used to feel badly. I thought that my parents might be deficient or I was doing something wrong, that we just weren't American because they [television families] seemed so Middle American yet they could solve anything in twenty-three minutes. And you know, in the body of my work, anyway, especially when we dealt with families, we tried not to have them have all the answers all the time. I think *The Partridge Family* was pretty tidy; Shirley generally did solve everything in twenty-three minutes, but it wasn't as easy as it was for the previous generation."

Wes Farrell (Music Producer):

"Very apple pie and the American flag, and all the things that are youthful and possible to a group in a family setting: a lot of human responses, most of it satire, and nothing that engaged in extremes. There was nothing very deep about *The Partridge Family*. I think it brought you along each week to the next stop in their life. They were never stepping into black holes. They were stepping into real life situations. They were easy to interpret, and it was done with a view toward a wholesome outcome."

"David was never meant, nor Shirley for that matter, to sing on the show," insists Claver. "We didn't know David could sing. And it was never a part of hiring him. He was the one who said he could sing, and then we said, 'Well, if you want to go see Wes Farrell and see if you can sing, fine, so much the better.' It had nothing to do with the casting. It was all serendipity. It was very good fortune that it happened. I thought it made the show better and gave it more integrity."

Initially, Farrell intended to use Shirley Jones on the lead vocals, until he discovered that David Cassidy could also sing. "When Bob Claver, [Producer] Paul Witt, and I had our first meeting, I asked them if anybody knew if David could sing," recalls Farrell. "No one knew, so they called David and had him come down to answer the question himself. He sang along with a Crosby, Stills and Nash record, and he had a very promising sound. I thought how nice it would be if this particular piece of the creation were to be real and David Cassidy fronted as the lead singer. So I had all the songs written with him in mind, and it was a process of elimination. Some songs worked, some songs didn't. He was very pliable, he was very interested in what he was doing, he made creating an easy chore because he took easily to direction and ideas, and, for the most part, he embraced, at the time, most of what we did."

> "I'd never heard of bubblegum music. But when I realized this was a singing family, I knew we weren't going to be doing 'You Made Me Love You' or something from La Traviata."
> —Shirley Jones

Susan Dey, Danny Bonaduce, Jeremy Gelbwaks, and Suzanne Crough never sang on the records; they merely lip-synced during each episode. "The Partridge Family was the original Milli Vanilli," says Bonaduce.

"We tried to make the music very basic, rather simple, and not too complex," says Farrell. "Simplicity was really the primary key, and sometimes creating on that level is much harder than something that's complex. We also stayed with you-me situations. When I went to mixes, we did a number of things to bring the presence of what you were seeing closer to you. When you would see Cassidy on camera, we'd push the track, so his lead would come a little closer to you; it becomes more personalized."

"It was right after the success of *The Monkees*, and there would be those obvious comparisons," recalls Paul Witt. "It was a very different sound. It was a bit more bubblegummy, a bit more white bread, less pure rock 'n' roll, more pop, but it was certainly something that was very successful."

"At that point, I didn't know what kind of music they were going to be doing," says Jones. "I'd never heard of bubblegum music. But when I realized this was a singing family, I knew we weren't going to be doing 'You Made Me Love You' or something from *La Traviata*. They developed their own style; it certainly wasn't my style. And then I realized I was just basically going to be a background singer for David, but that was okay with me because I felt the show required that. I mean, it was that kind of family and they needed to have the day's music in order to sell the show and the records."

After the family was assembled, the pilot was shot using a facade of a house on the Columbia Pictures lot in Burbank (now owned by Warner Brothers) and featuring two unreleased songs sung by a studio male vocalist. In the original version of the pilot, Shirley was named Connie Partridge, she dated a man played by Jack Cassidy, and Johnny Cash introduced the Partridge Family at their Caesars Palace debut. The completed pilot, incorporating various changes, was finished in December of 1969.

ABC policy required that the pilot pass an audience research test. "They used to test every show at a place called Preview House," remembers Slade. "It was a joke. I think one of the worst testing pilots was *The Mary Tyler Moore Show*. It got so that I could write to make the needle go up. I mean, it was just insanity. They made terrible mistakes. For a long time, they kept firing actors who were playing villains because they were getting a negative reaction—until they finally figured out villains were supposed to get a negative reaction. I remember watching that needle like I was trying to keep a heart patient alive."

The pilot passed with flying colors and the network gave the go-ahead, but a few months later, when the first six shows were tested, the audience hated them. "The pilot tested well because it skewed toward Danny," recalls Claver. "He was very funny. So we had meetings with the network and they said, 'We have to have that kid in every episode.' I kept saying he would come off as smart-ass instead of amusing. So we made the six shows, and he *was* a smart-ass. And then people didn't like him. It's one thing to be amusing and more mature than your age, and it's another thing to be annoying. So we softened him up and gave the other actors more to do."

Reluctantly, ABC added *The Partridge Family* to its Friday-night lineup, opposite Andy Griffith's *The Headmaster* on CBS, turning the Partridges into sitting ducks (Griffith's shows had always ranked among the ten most popular on television).

To hype the series, the Partridge Family's first single, "I Think I Love You," was released a few weeks before *The Partridge Family* premiered on September 25, 1970, at 8:30 P.M., following the *Brady Bunch* and *Nanny and the Professor*.

"Traveling in a psychedelic bus, which they painted themselves, this strange musical family has as its leader, not their mother, the lovely Miss Jones, but ten-year-old Danny Bonaduce, who plays Danny, the brains of the group," reported Kay Gardella in the *New York Daily News* on September 26, 1970. "It was this red-headed lad who separated the show from other family situations by creatively interpreting his role of the son with the business brains."

Variety of September 30 disagreed: "With the exception of the casting of Shirley Jones as the mother and some 'inside' showbiz lines put in ten-year-old Danny Bonaduce's mouth, *The Partridge Family* looks like it was made for Saturday morning rather than primetime. The premiere's plot line, rather quickly cut to establish the singing family (a la the Cowsills), was beyond belief."

Diana Loercher of the *Christian Science Monitor* chimed in on September 28: "Would that every fatherless, financially distressed American family could successfully take up guitars against a sea of troubles like grin-and-bear-it Shirley Partridge, played by Shirley Jones, and her five winsome moppets, in *The Partridge Family*. The show stacks implausibility upon implausibility from the hit record to the psychedelic bus they tool around in. Danny Bonaduce as the ten-year-old wheeler-dealer provides a few faintly funny moments, but it's all so predictable that the viewer is left with a sense of wasted time and effort, not the least of which was his own."

"By the fifth Nielsen, I knew we had a winner," Claver told the *New York Times*. The fifth Nielsen, reported on October 23, 1970, showed *The Partridge Family* with a 17.5 rating, followed by the *Headmaster* starring Andy Griffith on CBS with a 16.8 rating, and *The Name of the Game* on NBC with a 16.3 rating. *The Partridge Family Album*, the group's first album, released in October 1970, rocketed to number four on the charts. By November "I Think I Love You" hit the number one spot on the charts and the single had sold almost 3.5 million copies (and eventually reached five million). By December *The Partridge Family* was flying high in the Top Ten.

One survey called *The Partridge Family* the highest rated television program among children ages six to eleven years old. Even though 38 percent of *The Partridge Family* viewers were children, the audience breakdown also showed that 28 percent of the audience were women over the age of nineteen, and 19 percent were grown men.

"It's Shirley Jones who makes it all happen," Slade told the *New York Times* of September 5, 1971. "Kids loved *The Monkees* but their parents hated it and the result was no more Monkees. Shirley is our adult point of view, a parent figure who appeals to adults for her beauty and her warmth and her brains."

"The warmth of the unusual relationship between stepmother and stepson filters through to the camera and has contributed to making *The Partridge Family* ABC's top-rated new series," observed *Good Housekeeping* of August 1971. What's more, reported the *New York Times*, Shirley Jones balks at "'the usual mother image of male television writers, the little woman in the kitchen stirring something on the stove and patting the little dear on the head. I refuse to allow my own children to wallow in self-pity, so I won't allow it with my television children. I won't say, "Now Danny, honey, let mother help you. What's your little problem?" The producers were afraid I sounded too harsh with the kids, that the audience wouldn't like it. But the audience loved it.'"

"Shirley Jones in *The Partridge Family* is perhaps the most liberated woman being portrayed on any television program this season," read a

letter to the editor in the *New York Times* in July 1973. "The program may be inane—repetitious and so on—but there at least she is, one mother about whom my son does not assume 'she spends the day shopping.'"

While Jones portrayed a progressive mom on the series, she was notoriously strict on the set with the younger children who played her children on the series. During the first season, she called a meeting of the kids and their mothers, demanding they cease all fighting, backstabbing, and jockeying for position and behave like professional actors.

"I sat everybody down when we found out the show had the highest share consistently," recalls Jones, "and I said, 'Okay, the show's a hit because we have all worked together on this. Nobody has made the show a hit. It's the show that's made the hit. We have to work as a unit. I don't want anybody thinking that they're the star. There is no star. We're a unit, and we work toward and for the show.' And I think it worked that way. We really worked well together. I think that's one of the reasons the show was so successful. We didn't have any ego problems, and that's unusual when you have that many people and certainly children with mothers and fathers. I mean, we had little problems. Kids will be kids. But other than that, we really were good friends; we really enjoyed each other."

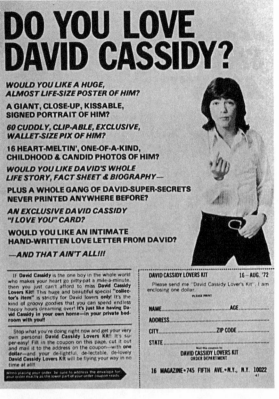

"There are a number of negative things to say about *The Partridge Family*, if you want to jump up and down on a cripple," wrote television critic Cyclops in the *New York Times*. "Shirley Jones is another one of those indomitable widows in which television specializes because its writers usually can't cope with an adult sexual relationship. David Cassidy lapses too often into a callowness and vapidity unbecoming even to a rock star. The little kids that they keep adding to the cast are sweet enough to double the demand for dentists in a single year. And the music is more rocking chair than rock. . . . However: I am grateful to *The Partridge Family* for rescuing Shirley Jones from old Pat Boone movies; she has an affecting presence; she embodies common sense; I like Danny, who is in the continuing tradition of Tom Sawyer, Dennis the Menace, and Abbie Hoffman. Each episode has a not entirely sappy moral that very much resembles what we grope for in our negotiations with our own children."

David Cassidy quickly became a full-fledged idol of the orthodontia set, and by late spring 1971, as the heartthrob of millions of teenage girls who faithfully turned to the pages of *16*, *Tiger Beat*, *Flip*, and *Fave*, he added a series of live concerts to his schedule and was contracted to record a solo album. "We cast him hoping for that," admits Slade. Proclaimed *Newsweek*: "Along with such other contenders for top idol among the bubblegum set such as Bobby Sherman, Donny Osmond and Barry Williams, Cassidy's della Robbia choirboy face, with its demure dimples and fawn-like smile gazes out from fan magazines like *Fave*, *16* and *Flip* surrounded by such bannerlines as 'You know your love for David Cassidy is deep and true,' or 'Why no girl can make him happy,' or 'Would you like to know when I was born, how old I am, my coloring—and *all* my measurements?!!'"

"Who can say why one person is singled out?" pondered Cassidy in the *New York Times*. "Maybe because of the way I talk or look. Possibly because I'm uncomplicated, clean. There's no threat involved."

Explained *Life*: "Small and slender, with fine, delicate features, green eyes of childlike clarity, and hair cut in a modified Jane Fonda shag, he combines the sweet-faced charm of the young Paul McCartney with the androgynous appeal of a squeaky-clean Mick Jagger."

"Part of Cassidy's success is a matter of wonderfully slick packaging," offered *Newsweek*. "*The Partridge Family* format is a subtle compromise and blend of the Cowsills and the Monkees, with the added fantasy of a truly hip mom and real togetherness. His frankly androgynous beauty is perfect for little girls too old to adore daddy but too young to date and form real crushes. His singing is not inspired, but neither is it too bland. It has enough cotton candy, oooh-oooh sweetness to satisfy the kids and avoids the rock menace that would bug the parents. On TV, he's an

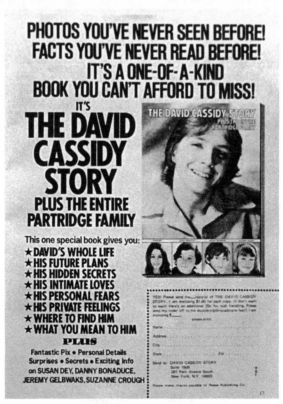

all-American Penrod of the '70s; on stage he struts like some mini–Mick Jagger, a wave of his hand starting the screams—but he doesn't fan it and the hysteria stops just as abruptly as it began."

"The whole phenomenon is rather good-natured," noted *The New Yorker* of June 24, 1972. "The little girls don't take it entirely seriously. Neither does Cassidy."

Yet every morning when Cassidy drove into the Columbia Pictures lot in Burbank, he was greeted by an ever-present throng of girls waiting on the curbstone, hoping to get a glimpse of his face. When he left *The Partridge Family* set on Stage 29 every evening, they would still be waiting. "That's no way for anyone to spend an afternoon," Cassidy told *Life*. "I tell them sometimes, 'Do something, go somewhere, go to the beach.'"

"At first David was overwhelmed with the whole thing, and his ego blew way up," Shirley Jones told *Life*. "And I think he hoped that some of those adoring fans would come a *little* closer to his own age. Now, the boy lives in a fishbowl. He's had to move twice, because they found out where he lived. But he still loves it—and it *is* very exciting."

"David, I thought, handled his success marvelously well," recalls Bob Claver. "You have to remember, at that time he was traveling all over the world on weekends, and he'd have one hundred thousand kids screaming at his concerts, and then he'd come back on Monday and sit there all day to do four straight lines for Danny Bonaduce. That's not easy to do. You have to be very mature to do that. And David was able to handle that very well. He was very, very good about that."

"I never thought of myself as a teenage idol," Cassidy told *TV Guide*

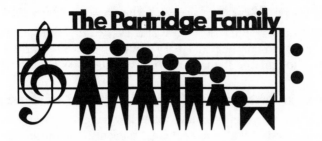

What Attributed to the Success of
The Partridge Family?

Shirley Jones (Shirley Partridge):

"I really think it was the combination. There had really been nothing quite like it. I mean, *The Monkees*, yes, had some music in their show, but that was a different format all together. *The Partridge Family* was based on a true family, the Cowsills. And I think it was intriguing and interesting. It had enough of the show-business edge, and yet we were a real family. And I think that was appealing to everybody. It had David, who appealed to all the teens in America, and the music that appealed to all the teens in America. We had me, who I hope appealed to the mothers and fathers, and I suddenly became everybody's wannabe mother. There was the fantasy, too, and I think that's why it was a big hit."

David Cassidy (Keith Partridge):

"I think timing more than anything. It was a unique time on this planet. I think it struck a chord in people. And it still does. Which is why it's successful today. And I think the creative forces behind the show had a lot to do with it, and certainly people got a sense that the cast cared for one another."

Susan Dey (Laurie Partridge):

"Everyone worked very hard. The show was an immediate hit. The timing was absolutely perfect. I loved the work. The publicity was something entirely different. This was the time of the teen fan magazines. They published whatever they wanted to. No matter how often I would say that I didn't do my own singing on the show, they convinced readers that I did. Just the other day, I was talking to an extra on our show [*L.A. Law*] and I happened to mention that it was not me singing, and he was furious." (in *Playboy*, January 1988)

Danny Bonaduce (Danny Partridge):

"David Cassidy. But I think it was also a very funny show, first of all. I think the music certainly helped. I really don't know. To be honest with you, I've never thought about analyzing *The Partridge Family* before."

Brian Forster (Chris Partridge):

"More than anything, I'd have to say it was David Cassidy, you know, the teen idol and all that kind of thing. I think also the music was really good for its time."

Jeremy Gelbwaks (Chris Partridge):

"A couple of things. I think the large-family sitcom was a new form, especially with the music. People reacted to it because it was something new. And David Cassidy was a heartthob, so all the young girls were watching. Parents could enjoy the interaction between Danny and the adult world. Plus the optimism. There was a lot of upheaval at the time, and this was just sort of an oasis of gentle optimism, where the problems are all solved by the end of the show."

Suzanne Crough (Tracy Partridge):

"I think it was a combination of things. Obviously Shirley Jones was a very popular figure. She had done plenty of things to be acclaimed for. Also, we had David and the girls who enjoyed watching him and hearing him sing—whether or not he ever said anything. I mean, they just had a crush on him. It was a good show and well-cast, and everyone kind of took off in their own direction. So there was somebody for the little boys, they were in love with Susan Dey. And Danny just kind of kept us all entertained. I think it was just a well cast show."

Dave Madden (Mr. Kincaid):

"*The Headmaster* failed. Andy Griffith made his comeback to television with a series called *The Headmaster*. When I heard he was going to be put on opposite us, I went out looking for a day job because I figured it was over. Andy Griffith had left television as a big success, and so I figured when he came back, he would continue to be a big success, which would be the end of *The Partridge Family* and whatever else was on in that time slot. The fact that Andy Griffith chose to do something a little too far afield of what people wanted Andy Griffith to do made that show a disaster. And because that show was a disaster, we were a success. That's what I really think. We survived because they didn't.

"I think there were a certain number of people who watched because they always loved Shirley Jones. They loved her in *Oklahoma!*, they loved her in *Carousel*, and by gosh, now they were going to love her on television. The way that David Cassidy was handled in terms of building his career—and there were an awful lot of young girls who were in love with David Cassidy—was another reason. I suppose once people started watching, they maybe enjoyed the conflict between Danny and me. The fact that a series about a family of rock singers was very unique and a little more believable than *The Monkees* was possibly another very major factor."

Bernard Slade (Creator):

"Partly, I think it could appeal to the whole family. But it's very difficult to zero in on why something is a success because often it's just a good show, it made people laugh, or it was company for them growing up. I think if you had a pretty good pilot and a couple of good episodes to start, most people started to watch as habit viewing. It seemed to me that the good scripts didn't get any better ratings than the ones that weren't so good. If they liked a show, people would sort of stay with it. I mean, it was amazing to me.

"The Partridge Family didn't have a lot of money. We never did a thing where this was a major rock group. They worked out of a garage. In a way, I think that kept it in touch with the audience, and it was also the sort of thing where a kid sitting at home could say, 'Oh, I could do that!' It's right back to the old equivalent of Judy Garland and Mickey Rooney saying, 'My aunt has a barn, let's put on a show!'

"It's how people want life to be. Most people don't have that sort of happy family. For most people it's much more miserable. If you introduced incest into a *Partridge Family* episode, it just wouldn't go. But we all grew up on *Leave It to Beaver* and *Father Knows Best*, and this lovely family lives in this nice house and they have these *little* problems. It's an escape medium."

Bob Claver (Executive Producer):

"I couldn't tell you. I don't think anybody knows. After the fact, you can make up anything. People wanted to watch this group of people, that's all. David had a gentility to him. And I think that was not frightening to the youngsters. There was a sweetness. I mean, there's a gentleness to that kind of physique and look.

"I think that family had a lot of fun. And it would be fun to be in that family. They didn't have fun all the time. But they would stand together when the chips were down. They would come to each other's aid. But they fought, and that was very normal. And that's the part I liked. I hated the idea of these families, for example, *Ozzie and Harriet*, where they never, ever seem to disagree with each other."

Paul Witt *(Producer)*:

"I think we had an adorable bunch of children. I think Shirley is a very appealing woman. Certainly the synergy between music and sitcom at that time was very strong. We were able to grab a kids' audience and grab enough adults so that we were successful. For that kind of show it was a pretty strong ensemble. Susan really developed quickly. David is very, very talented. And Danny was a creative prodigy. He was remarkably funny. Extraordinarily so.

"That period of time in the seventies was a difficult time for a lot of families. There was a lot of rebellion. It was a time of radically changing values, and we were able to create a family that was able to embody certain elements of the time without giving up more traditional values. And I think America's very comfortable with that."

Wes Farrell *(Music Producer)*:

"The television show was a wonderful family situation. It did what kids do. It did what kids are all about. Musically, we looked at it as a stand alone situation. If we could have hit records, we could sell at least twice the amount because of the medium of television."

of May 22, 1971. "I don't *want* to be a teenage idol. I can't go out anymore because I'm recognized wherever I go, so I stay home a lot." Although Cassidy's photograph was featured on the cover of *16 Magazine* for 24 issues in a row, he was not averse to fame. "It's a *nice* inconvenience," he told *TV Guide*. "When you don't have it, you sure wish you did."

Still, a random sampling of children in West Los Angeles showed that almost all viewers under the age of twelve tuned into *The Partridge Family* not for David Cassidy but for Danny Bonaduce. In fact, for young children, David Cassidy ran a poor third to Shirley Jones, who was receiving more fan mail in the teen magazines than any other adult had ever received. "Some of it was very sad," confesses Jones. "A lot of the letters were from broken homes, troubled teens, and kids who wanted me to be their mother. Some, I'm serious, were on a train or airplane to come here and join the family. I had young people camping on my lawn with their knapsacks, waiting for me to come out the door so they could say ,'Take me in, I want you to be my mother.' I also got a lot of letters from parents saying, 'Thank you for a wonderful show' and how much they loved having a family show on the air."

Meanwhile, Screen Gems' merchandizing expert Ed Justin was flooding the market with Partridge Family merchandice, including trading cards, coloring books, paper dolls, comic books, wiggle postcards, children's dresses, paperback mystery novels, dolls, astrological charts, love beads, diaries, posters, bumper stickers, wallets, games, record albums, and lunch boxes. General Foods put photos of the Partridge kids on cereal boxes. For

YOU Can be David's Summer LOVE!

two dollars, fans could purchase a "David Cassidy Love Kit" from *16 Magazine*, containing "a life-size, full-length portrait, an autographed maxiposter three times life-size, a complete biography & childhood photo album, 40 wallet-size photos, a secret love message from David, and a lovers' card with his name and yours." By 1971, the Partridge Family Fan Club, run by Chuck Laufer, owner of several teenybopper magazines, had 100,000 members at $2.25 a head. "During April and May of 1971," reported the *New York Times*, "Screen Gems' royalties from *Partridge Family* bubblegum alone were $59,000."

In April 1971, the Partridge Family's second album, *Up to Date*, containing two Top Ten singles, "I'll Meet You Halfway" and "Doesn't Somebody Want to Be Wanted," climbed to number three on the charts and became the group's best-selling album ever. The frenzy over the Partridge Family reached such proportions after the first season that promoters wanted to book the group for live performances. "It was hysterical," recalled Shirley Jones in the liner notes to the *Up to Date* compact disc. "They thought we were a real singing group! They said, 'Why aren't you playing Las Vegas?' I kept saying, 'You don't understand . . . there is no Partridge Family!'"

"Some young viewers, confusing series life with reality, assume there actually is a group managed by a Reuben Kincaid," reported *TV Guide* of December 18, 1971, "and [Dave] Madden is besieged by kids seeking the Partridges for school dances. 'With all the fan mail I'm getting,' says Madden, 'it takes me hours to clean the Crayola marks off my fingers.'"

"I had no idea *The Partridge Family* was going to be that successful," admits Jones, "and that the music would just revolutionize the music industry there for a while with bubblegum music. I mean, I had no idea this was going to happen. I don't think David did either."

David Cassidy's concert appearances were greeted with all the pandemonium that had accompanied the Beatles' arrival in the United States. "Attendance at a David Cassidy concert is an exercise in incredulity," reported *Life*. "Hordes of girls, average age 11-1/2, with hearts seemingly placed inside their vocal chords, shout themselves into a frenzy." In 1971, Cassidy played 35 concerts on weekends, grossing over one million dollars.

Even *The New Yorker* covered a sold-out David Cassidy concert at the Nassau County Coliseum. "As soon as Cassidy appeared on stage, the little girls in the audience began to scream and take pictures," reported the magazine in its June 24, 1972, issue. "All the cameras were equipped with flash cubes, and all the flash cubes went off one after another, squirting tiny bursts of light in Cassidy's direction. Flash cubes are a new form of visual applause. We admired the girls' ability to do two things at once.... We interviewed Cassidy after the show.... He said that after he'd played the Garden he and his staff had sat around trying to figure out how much G.E. and Sylvania had made on flash cubes during his concert. The figure they came up with was nine thousand dollars."

> *"I was a piece of raw meat. I was being manipulated and was powerless to do anything about it. What I wanted didn't count."*
> —David Cassidy

"I was thrilled that the show was successful," recalls Shirley Jones. "I was afraid for many reasons for the kids, David certainly, because then, of course, all of this started to happen to him, and then they started the whole concert idea of him going out every weekend and doing concerts promoting the albums and then he had to come back to work on Monday on *The Partridge Family*. And you know, that was really round the clock work for him. He was burning a candle at both ends, and I was naturally afraid that this would really wear him down. And he had a hard time during those times. But the show was a hit."

In the show's second season, *The Partridge Family* was pitted against *O'Hara, U.S. Treasury* on CBS and *NBC World Premiere Movies*. "With its strong teenybopper appeal, it's one of those programs that's in the right place at the right time, Fridays being a big night before the set for young kids, babysitters and old folks," commented *Variety* in September 1972. "The season's opener held right to the formula—a bit of heart, a bit of comedy, a bit of insight and a bit of song." Brown-haired Jeremy Gelbwaks, who played Christopher Partridge, was replaced by blond Brian Forster, without any explanation. Forster had appeared in television commercials and made guest appearances on *My Friend Tony*, *The Brady Bunch*, *The Survivors*, and *Family Affair*.

The Partridge Family's third album, *Sound Magazine*, contained the hit single "I Woke Up in Love This Morning," which rose to number thirteen on the charts in August 1971. Commented *Variety*: "*The Partridge Family* goes into its second season still the top TV candidate for cuteness—and that's not bad in a medium inundated with tots who look like Mattel dolls or shrunken society band leaders." The group's fourth album, *Shopping Bag*, contained the hit single "It's One of Those Nights," which rose to number twenty on the charts in January 1972. *TV Guide* reported that one of the first twelve Partridge Family paperback mystery books sold one million copies. "In a single day last fall, reports the *Los Angeles Times*, the four PF record albums on the market sold a total of 200,000 copies at $4.98 each. Six singles by David Cassidy have gone a million or better, with 'I Think I Love You' topping the list at 3,500,000."

David Cassidy, eager to shed his teen idol image and gain acceptance from his peers, posed nude on the cover of *Rolling Stone* in May 1972. In the accompanying cover story, Cassidy exposed his true musical influences and aspirations, admitted to a history of experimentation with drugs, and revealed his growing disenchantment with his teen idol status, bubblegum music, and prepubescent groupies. "I was a piece of raw meat," he told *TV Guide* of June 25, 1977. "I was being manipulated and was powerless to do anything about it. What I wanted didn't count."

"David came in with his own management team intact," recalls Paul Witt. "[His manager] Ruth Aarons was a remarkable woman. His father was in the business, his mother was an actress, his step-mother [is Shirley Jones], his step-father was a director. I mean, this was a kid who had a degree of sophistication and had some very sophisticated people around him. He was his own person."

In January 1973, *The Partridge Family* had a 20.3 share of the audience, placing the series in the Top Twenty. By the following year, the show, moved to Saturday nights to compete against *All in the Family*, sank to number 68 out of 71 network series programs surveyed in 1974 with a 10.6 share of the audience.

"The big news in the return of *The Partridge Family*, now 8 P.M. Saturdays on ABC-TV, is that it introduced Ricky Segall as a regular member of the family's rock group," reported *Variety* of September 19, 1973. "Ricky is four years old and came on with one of the greatest smiles seen on TV in years. But his singing, while undoubtedly precocious for a four-year-old, will hardly produce a craving, and his 'cute' remarks promise to be even more cloying than that of the Partridge kids."

On January 13, 1974, the *New York Times'* Cyclops jumped to the show's defense. "I imagine that some ABC vice president in charge of annoying me pulled the Friday-Saturday switch in hopes that the teeny-bopper passion for David Cassidy, who plays Keith Partridge in the show, would gnaw away at Archie Bunker's popularity. As usual, this kind of creative counterprogramming has ended in disaster, and the culpable vice president should be sentenced to 40 years of Orange Bowl halftimes."

Finally, in May 1974, after a fourteen-year-old fan named Bernadette Wheeler suffered a fatal heart attack at a David Cassidy concert in London, Cassidy, severely shaken, decided to tone down his teen idol image and quit the series. Cassidy called a press conference in England to announce that he was taking time off for a long rest. "I look back at the experience now of the success and everything," Cassidy said in an interview on *Good Night America* on July 4, 1974. "It's over on that phase of my career, and I touched something that very few people touched, and I've reached a level that very few people reach, and I wish everyone could experience that kind of a high. Now, I'm just really into satisfying myself creatively."

Producers Mel Swope and William Bickley reportedly started conducting a quiet search for a replacement for Cassidy, and although Shirley Jones was willing to stay with the show for another season, ABC, citing plummeting ratings, canceled the series.

The Partridge Family has been seen in syndicated reruns ever since, and the group continues to make its influence felt on American culture. Partridge Family songs are still played on radio stations across America. Six Partridge Family albums have gone platinum, and all are available on compact disc. Hanna-Barbera produced an animated cartoon series,

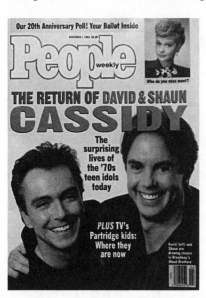

Partridge Family: 2200 AD, featuring the voices of Susan Dey, Danny Bonaduce, Brian Forster, Suzanne Crough, and Dave Madden, which ran on Saturday mornings on CBS from 1974 to 1975. On November 25, 1977, ABC aired The Partridge Family, My Three Sons Thanksgiving Reunion, hosted by Fred MacMurray and Shirley Jones, giving viewers an update on the cast members of the respective series. Andy Williams, Perry Como, and Voice of the Beehive recorded "I Think I Love You," and the Reuben Kincaids, a punk band from Athens, Georgia, was popular on the club circuit in the 1980s.

In 1991, David Cassidy hit the concert circuit again, for the first time in more than fifteen years, with a 35-city tour, performing updated versions of his old hits along with new material, including his 1990 top twenty hit, "Lyin' to Myself." Cassidy, Bonaduce, and Madden appeared on Geraldo on September 23, 1991, with a call-in from Shirley Jones. When Susan Dey hosted Saturday Night Live in 1992, she played Laurie Partridge, Dana Carvey played Keith Partridge, and Mike Myers played Danny Partridge in a sketch featuring a battle of the bands between the Partridge Family and the Brady Bunch. In July 1993, Nick at Night broadcast four episodes of the series every night for a week, culminating with Cassidy hosting his four favorite Partridge Family episodes. After touring seven cities with the Partridge Family bus to promote the series, Cassidy hosted sixteen episodes of The Partridge Family on MTV on Sunday, July 23, 1993. That same week, Jones, Cassidy, and Bonaduce appeared together as guests on the Arsenio Hall Show.

In the Village Voice of August 24, 1993, essayist Ann Powers provided a sociological insight into how *The Partridge Family* speaks for Generation X. "On one level, *The Partridge Family* was about 1960s mores being absorbed into conventional, domesticated America," explained Powers. "The show captured the predicament of 1970s kids, the first to experience rock's rebellion as a hand-me-down."

The cover of *People* featured David Cassidy and half-brother Shaun Cassidy on November 1, 1993. The two Chris Partridges, Jeremy Gelbwaks and Brian Forster, met for the first time on *Nick at Night*'s New Year's Eve broadcast in 1993. On January 10, 1994, MTV ran every episode of *The Partridge Family* in a marathon called "MTV Pile of Partridge," and as of this writing, *The Partridge Family* can be seen every weekday night at 8:00 P.M. on *Nick at Night*.

As for the cast, Shirley Jones performs symphony concerts worldwide and published her autobiography, *Shirley and Marty: An Unlikely Love Story*. David Cassidy has starred on Broadway in *Joseph and the Amazing Technicolor Dreamcoat* and *Blood Brothers*, and published his autobiography, *C'mon, Get Happy: Fear and Loathing on the Partridge Family Bus*. Susan Dey starred as Grace Van Owen on *L.A. Law*. Danny Bonaduce is a popular radio deejay in Chicago on WLUP-FM. Brian Forster is a professional race car driver and instructor in Sebastopol, California. Jeremy Gelbwaks is a computer consultant on interactive television in New Orleans. Suzanne Crough ran a book store in Temecula, California. Dave Madden is a highly successful commercial voice-over talent in Los Angeles.

To this day, Shirley Jones is asked about the whereabouts and health of the Partridge Family. "We became family to these people," she explains. "They can't quite understand that we're not a family. You know, I don't see Danny every day, I don't see Susan every day. We don't talk on the phone every day. To them, we were their family. They want to make sure we're still together even though intellectually they know we weren't a real family. They don't want all of their images torn apart."

2

I Think I Love You

I Think I Love You

I was sleepin', and right in the middle of a good dream,
Like all at once I wake up from something that keeps
knocking at my brain.
Before I go insane, I hold my pillow to my head,
And spring up in my bed, screamin' out the words I dread:
I think I love you.
This morning, I woke up with this feeling,
I didn't know how to deal with, and so I just decided to myself,
I'd hide it to myself and never talk about it,
And didn't I go and shout it when you walked into the room:
I think I love you.

I think I love you, So what am I so afraid of?
I'm afraid that I'm not sure of, A love there is no cure for.
I think I love you, Isn't that what life is made of?
Though it worries me to say, That I never felt this way.

I don't know what I'm up against.
I don't know what it's all about.
I've got so much to figure out.

Believe me, you really don't have to worry,
I only want to make you happy,
And if you say "Hey, go away," I will,
But I think better still I'd better stay around and love you.
Do you think I have a case? Let me ask you to your face:
Do you think you love me?
I think I love you. I think I love you. I think I love you.

or an incredibly close knit and open family, the Partridges oddly never discuss or even allude to the most traumatic and unifying event in their lives: the death of Mr. Partridge.

We never see a photograph of the late Mr. Partridge, learn his first name, or discover the details of his death (although we learn he died suddenly six months before we first meet the fatherless Partridges). No one ever visits Mr. Partridge's grave or reminisces about him. Neither his widow nor his five children have anything to say about him—good or bad. He is buried and forgotten.

Still, Shirley has yet to remarry, implying that she is either still grieving deeply over her loss or has yet to meet a prospective husband who rises to the standards of the man she and her children never mention in 96 episodes of the series.

Perhaps Mr. Partridge's death was so traumatic that Shirley and her children were catapulted into a deep state of denial, repressing and sublimating their grief—until the only way they could release their angst was to form a bubblegum rock band. Clearly, their seemingly vacuous lyrics and feel-good harmonies are a transparent attempt to suppress deeply pent-up hostilities. Or perhaps Mr. Partridge was such an unremarkable father that his disappearance from their lives went completely unnoticed.

Despite their inability to deal with death, the Partridge Family is strongly, if not excessively, united. Unlike most families, the Partridges make decisions democratically, often at the breakfast table or during daily band rehearsals starting at 3 P.M. in the family garage, decorated with stolen street and highway signs (among them Ohio 73, US 40, Texas 73, and Pennsylvania Interstate 76). After each family member expresses an opinion, the group reaches a consensus. They can also communicate remarkably well during band practices and performances without uttering a word, reading each other's faces and moods with psychic accuracy. Of course, the Partridge Family is no ordinary family. Since their only source of income is derived from band performances and album sales, group decisions are vital to their financial security and so Shirley can pay the mortgage on their comfortable suburban home in San Pueblo, California. Each child learns at an early age to put personal needs aside and compromise for the good of the group. The kids still enjoy teasing each other, but only in the spirit of camaraderie. Even their matching stage costumes— those dreamy maroon crushed-velvet vests and pants with the same ruffled white shirts—attest that the family members could only have sacrificed their individuality and pride to overcompensate for a painful loss.

Whether the Partridge Family's togetherness resulted from simply being in the same rock band together or from an inability to adequately deal with the death of Mr. Partridge is unimportant. What matters is that the Partridge Family sticks together like birds of a feather in times of both adversity and happiness. And togetherness is what the Partridge Family is all about.

Shirley

"People aren't as different as we think. We may have different beliefs, but we're all pretty much alike."
—*Shirley Partridge*

Shirley Partridge stood alone as a breakthrough role model for women in the 1970s. As a single mother, she raises her five children through compromise and understanding rather than discipline and a firm hand. She is an exceptionally progressive parent, speaking to her children as if they are adults. She values their opinions, heeds their advice, and lets each make his or her own mistakes. Shirley runs her family like a democracy. While she sits at the head of the table and makes the executive decisions, she encourages each child to join in the discussions and voice his or her opinion—a far cry from the benevolent authoritarian rule common to *The Donna Reed Show, Father Knows Best, Leave It to Beaver*, and *The Brady Bunch*.

Shirley is a liberated woman, but like all good moms, her kids come first. She places her kids' normal life above their professional music career. Shirley Partridge bridges the generation gap between her kids, not merely because she plays the organ and sings in their band, but because she tries to understand their problems as a peer, and lets them make their own decisions and live with the consequences. In return, her children respect

and appreciate her needs, and they genuinely appreciate her as a person. They consider themselves extraordinarily lucky to have such a beautiful and talented mother and often tell her so. Yet, they rarely lend a hand with the household chores. Shirley does all the food shopping, carries all the groceries into the house, cooks all the meals, and folds all the laundry without any help from her kids.

Still, Shirley is indebted to her children for giving her a stimulating career and for helping her earn the income to pay their living expenses and put savings in the bank toward five college educations. Before joining her children's rock group, the widowed Shirley Partridge was working at a bank to support her family.

We learn very little more about her. Her maiden name was Renfrew; her retired parents, Fred and Amanda, live on a farm, occasionally drop in on the Partridges to visit, and are celebrating 44 years of marriage when we first meet them. Shirley's father worked as a plumber, and her children have an Uncle Milton who gave the Partridges a souvenir pillow from Atlantic City depicting a flapper eating a lobster. When she was nine years old, she fell in love with Tommy Miller, who walked her home from school and tried to carve their initials in a tree, but was stopped by a police officer. In high school she tried out for head cheerleader, but lost. Now, Shirley is a member of the PTA and enjoys sewing, knitting, quilting, gardening, painting, and Chinese food. She always seems to be wearing yellow or pink clothes, and she has a penchant for matching pants suits and maxiskirts. We never learn where she was born, raised, educated, or married.

While the identity of Shirley's late husband and the nature of their life together remains a matter of conjecture, Shirley does venture out onto the dating scene, encouraged by her children and reliant upon Laurie for advice. She never falls for any man, but then again, her dating may simply be a ruse to divert suspicions away from the possibility that she and band manager Reuben Kincaid are passionately involved in a clandestine tryst.

Shirley's Love Interests

♥ **Larry Metcalf**—old flame who went off to be an engineer in South America, never married, owns an engineering company, and has a net worth of over $1.5 million [Episode 5]

♥ **Dr. Jim Lucas**—obstetrician who aspires to be a songwriter [Episode 17]

♥ **Dr. Bernie Applebaum**—overly cautious pediatrician; Keith calls him "Captain Cholesterol" [Episodes 27 and 63]

♥ **Paul Bruner**—19-year-old college student [Episode 29]

♥ **Richard Lawrence**—an attorney from San Francisco running for Congress against incumbent Congressman Antonelli; he is a single parent with two daughters, Cathy and Julie. ("I think he's good enough to be a Congressman," Keith tells his mother, "I just don't know if he's good enough for you.") [Episodes 57 and 67]

♥ **Unnamed love interest**—mentioned by Shirley when the Partridges are being pursued by mystery writer Michelangelo Rezo [Episode 74]

♥ **Ambassador Howard Lipton**—U.S. ambassador and reputed ladies' man [Episode 82]

♥ **Captain Chuck "Cuddles" Corwin**—naval officer who was senior class president, a letterman three times, Shirley's date to the senior prom and Muldune's Point [Episode 96]

After all, Mr. Kincaid does spend an inordinate amount of time at the Partridge home, and the two adults do have plenty of opportunities on the road to take their relationship to new plateaus—if Kincaid wouldn't be so timid and Shirley wouldn't be so highly principled.

Then again, if Shirley Partridge, the liberated mother and rock star, ever married again, would her new husband let her continue performing with the group? Or would the group be forced to ask him to join? Or does Shirley Partridge anticipate those dilemmas and intentionally keep her emotional and sexual needs on a very tight leash?

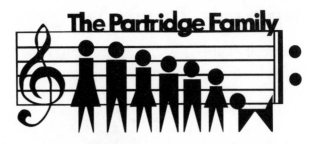

How Would You Describe
Shirley Partridge?

Shirley Jones (Shirley Partridge):

"Shirley Partridge is not too far away from Shirley Jones as a person. I mean, I really found myself playing myself an awful lot. There wasn't a lot of acting that I had to do in that role. I was raising my own children at the time. I think Shirley Partridge probably came from a small town herself and had a good stable background as I did. I think the family values were pretty much what my own family values were. So, I think she is a good lady. I think she is a strong lady. I think her family is her nucleus, as is mine. I just think she was an all around good lady and a good person, and yet she was capable, she was one of these people who was able to pick herself up again and just keep going. And I like to think of myself that way, too.

"Shirley Partridge had come a long way from *The Donna Reed Show* and even *The Brady Bunch*. I mean Florence Henderson's role wasn't quite as liberated. Shirley Partridge was a real working person. Not just a working mother, yes, but a working person. She was an individual in her own right. That also was nice for me because, again, it was like who I am as a person too. I started working when I was eighteen. I never understood what women's lib was all about because I lived it from a very young age. When everybody was raving about women's rights, I thought, 'I don't understand it, I've always had women's rights.' Now, I've been lucky, but you know, I understand the reasons other people haven't been as fortunate as I've been, but it's always been there for me and I've always done it.

"In the pilot the narrator explained that Mr. Partridge had died and now I had to make it on my own. And that of course was the extent of it. We never heard about him again. Ever again! I mean, we lost Mr. Partridge and the dog very quickly! Simone went out the window, too. After the first season everyone asked, 'What happened to Simone?' Well, she went to doggie heaven. I think the producers really just wanted to get over Mr. Partridge. There was really no reason to do a story about him after that. Because they really wanted to progress with the show. They wanted me to have boyfriends, and they wanted to keep it going in that direction, rather than going back. Not to say that it wouldn't have been nice maybe to have some mention of him to find out who he was, but they didn't want to have a character or someone to refer to. They just wanted to get on with it.

"I had a few heavy dates, you know. But they didn't even want to touch on the fact that I might be having an affair with a man someplace. It was a little too early to get into that. It wasn't *Roseanne* time yet. So they just decided they didn't want to get too involved with that side of my life. You know, they only brought it in a few times. We made jokes about [Shirley's relationship with] Mr. Kincaid."

David Cassidy (Keith Partridge):
"She's the quintessential mother. She's just extremely maternal, and loving, nurturing, forgiving."

Susan Dey (Laurie Partridge):
"Shirley is all lady from top to toe, from beginning to end—and it's her quiet, feminine, almost regal 'ladylikeness' that keeps everything that occurs on the entire *Partridge Family* series at such a high level of 'niceness.' It's as though Shirley sets the pattern for our day-to-day life here. Because she is so fine, sweet, and considerate, we start to become that way. We catch her 'goodness' sort of by osmosis—and that's really nice and we're very grateful to Shirley for that." (in *16 Magazine*, July 1971)

Danny Bonaduce (Danny Partridge):
"She was a dominant mother into the tough-luck theory. She didn't let the kids get away with anything. She was always there for the kids, always doing the right thing. I would describe her as a great mother, maybe Mrs. Cleaver on steroids. If Mrs. Cleaver [on *Leave It to Beaver*] was to go into overdrive, you know. It's just that Mrs. Cleaver was oblivious to so much that was going on. Shirley was hip to everything that was happening around with the family."

Brian Forster (Chris Partridge):
"She was a very sweet, loving person with a lot of patience, but firm when she needed to be. She was just a very caring, loving mother. She had a traditional role. You know, I don't remember anything about her having a job and working all the time and coming home late, or any of that. She was always there cooking, cleaning, and taking care of the kids. In spite of the way it was set up, I don't know how nontraditional she was."

Jeremy Gelbwaks (Chris Partridge):

"I never knew Shirley Jones, I only knew Shirley Partridge. I remember her being very wholesome. There was that sense of optimism. She was very much a mother figure, and just sweet and pleasant and nice, and, I guess, Midwestern. Actually, I would say Shirley even had a touch of the naïf."

Suzanne Crough (Tracy Partridge):

"Very independent and very smart. Just a real classy lady, kind of like Shirley Jones herself."

Dave Madden (Mr. Kincaid):

"I would describe Shirley Partridge as perhaps a shade on the unbelievable side in terms of a mother. Of course, that's relative to my experience in life with mothers. I think anyone would say, 'Gee, I wish I had a mom like Shirley Partridge.' I have heard those words actually spoken by people, and I guess almost anybody would [want her for a mother] because it's a little hard to believe that a mother could be that wholesome and clean. A part of that was Shirley Jones and what she put into the mother, and then a very large part of it was how they wrote her part. *The Partridge Family* never dealt with really taboo subjects. The most taboo subject we ever dealt with in all 96 shows was the fact that Keith was flunking sex education in school. I mean, the fact that they said anything that involved the word sex was brazen for *The Partridge Family* in those day. In one show Danny was telling me about what they were doing in school, and I said, 'Well, gosh, Danny, I think that's really rotten.' The network came back and they told us to change the word 'rotten' to 'awful' because they felt that 'rotten' was a little strong. That gives you some idea of their concept of wholesome. You don't even want to say a discouraging word in a wholesome show.

"When you're talking about Shirley, you're talking about the show. Shirley represents the show. And she was clean and wholesome to the point of unbelievability. That was certainly Shirley's image and that was the image of the show.

"I would have believed Shirley's liberation to a greater extent if she had been married in the show. If she had done all the things that she did while married, I would have said, 'Yeah, there's a liberated woman.' But here's a woman that fell into being a part of the Partridge Family singing group. Her husband was dead, and she had to survive and take care of these kids and make a living. Well, I don't know if that necessarily qualifies as liberation. That qualifies as being a survivor, which is a little different concept. Liberation really kind of means, 'I'm going to go out there into a man's world, and I'm going to show them I'm just as good as they are.' It has more of a powerhouse feel to it, a driving, surging kind of thing, and I don't associate those words with Shirley Partridge."

Bernard Slade (Creator):

"She was the idealized mother. She was pretty and feminine in a classical old-fashioned sense and nurturing and could also carry a tune. So what could be better? She was like this real nice person with a sense of humor. That was a big thing. So she reacted. She didn't do funny things, but she would react to them."

Bob Claver (Executive Producer):

"She's Mother Theresa. She was a very patient woman. And also I think the funniest part was—we did two or three shows with men, Burt Convy, Dick Mulligan—and for the most part she led a rather virginal life. She was very liberated, but you had to do that if you wanted the show to be about anything. You couldn't have arguments about 'It's 9:30, you can't go out'; that just doesn't mean a thing. I mean, Shirley never looked like a fool, and that was one of the things we never allowed to happen. Maybe momentarily. We can all be fooled a little bit, but we never let Shirley come out of an episode looking foolish. I think that would have destroyed the show."

Paul Witt (Producer):

"Wholesome, loving, nurturing, caring, warm."

Keith

*"In this day and age, anything can happen.
Love does not ask to see your I.D."*
—*Keith Partridge*

Adorable Keith Partridge is an extremely talented and incredibly fallible sixteen-year-old, perpetually trapped in high school. He wears his blow-dried, shoulder-length hair in a shag. His baby-green eyes sparkle with wonder. He smiles coyly. Keith is extremely thin, and he wears clothes that hug his body: tight-fitting bell-bottom jeans, rib-tight shirts, leisure suits, pukka-shell necklaces, and a trademark ring on his right pinkie. The girls find him irresistibly cute, and he knows it.

Above all, Keith is an extremely talented songwriter, guitarist, and singer. He is the undisputed leader of the Partridge Family, writing the bulk of the group's songs, organizing band practice, and displaying a remarkable songwriting ability. While his success as a songwriter, performer, and teen idol sometimes goes to his

Keith's Girlfriends

♥ **Janet**—salesgirl at The Inner Place, a woman's undergarment shop [Episode 6]

♥ **Tina Newcomb**—feminist who convinces Keith and the Partridge Family to perform at a Power of Women rally [Episode 12]

♥ **Carol**—Keith sells his car to take her to the high school prom [Episode 21]

♥ **Dora Kelly**—gorgeous blond who can't sing a note on key [Episode 26]

♥ **Doris**—blond who discovers Keith at Muldune's Point with Gloria Neugast, a sixty-year-old Jewish mother who wins a week with the Partridge Family [Episode 27]

♥ **Bonnie**—mentioned [Episode 30]

♥ **Barbara**—mentioned [Episode 32]

♥ **Maureen**—romantic interest who tries to get Keith to say "I love you" over the phone in front of his siblings [Episode 40]

♥ **Lynn**—seen making out with Keith at Muldune's Point [Episode 41]

♥ **Vicky**—a college cheerleader whom he invites to his apartment [Episode 42]

♥ **Cynthia**—pen pal who addresses him as "bootsy" [Episode 47]

♥ **Naomi Ledbetter**—mentioned [Episode 52]

♥ **Princess Jennie**—foreign royalty who asks Keith to dress up as a bellboy, kidnap her from her hotel room, and take her to a drive-in movie, where they are photographed kissing each other [Episode 52]

♥ **Molly**—makes out with Keith in the park in the company of Danny and Gloria Hicky [Episode 55]

♥ **Mary Lou**—mentioned [Episode 56]

♥ **Cathy Lawrence**—daughter of attorney and congressional candidate Richard Lawrence [Episode 57]

♥ **Audrey Parson**—public relations person at King's Island Amusement Park; she is ten to twelve years older than Keith, guesses mother Shirley [Episode 66]

♥ **Bunny Hoffstedder**—mentioned [Episodes 67 and 74]

♥ **Laraine Price**—classmate who "knows nothing about sex," according to Laurie [Episode 69]

♥ **Eunice Ulbee**—mentioned [Episode 74]

♥ **Donna Stevens**—next-door neighbor, daughter of Doris Stevens, and sister of Ricky Stevens [Episode 75]

♥ **Dina Firmly**—a new girl in school with whom Laurie refuses to set him up on a date [Episode 76]

♥ **Rachel Weston**—romantic interest who encourages Keith to compose a classical concerto [Episode 77]

♥ **Sally Winkler**—Laurie's friend set to be Keith's date at a beach party until Keith pretends to have a cold to get out of the obligation [Episode 80]

♥ **Johanna Houser**—striking beauty invited to be Keith's date at a beach party while her boyfriend Spider is out of town [Episode 80]

♥ **Dory**—a married classmate with whom he teams up to work on a sociology project [Episode 83]

♥ **Belinda Payne**—one of Laurie's friends whom Keith would like to date [Episode 88]

♥ **Anonymous**—an unnamed girl in Rome whom Keith claims to know [Episode 92]

♥ **Nancy**—learns that her roommate Margaret is also dating Keith Partridge [Episode 93]

♥ **Margaret**—learns that her roommate Nancy is also dating Keith Partridge [Episode 93]

♥ **Patti**—Keith mentions that he plans to take her to a movie [Episode 95]

head, his siblings are always on hand to take him down a few notches.

As a teenager, Keith is simultaneously responsible and irresponsible. He stands on the brink of manhood, not quite ready to manage his own finances, not quite confident in his own self-esteem, but filled with integrity, honesty, and ambition.

Consequently, Keith is extremely vulnerable. He falls in and out of love with alarming frequency. He's always in debt to his younger brother and nemesis, Danny. And when tries to assume the male leadership role in the family, he is easily put in his place by his mother.

Keith is understanding, sensitive, and yet in need of constant nurturing. His priorities are music, his family, and girls. He tries desperately to impress girls, displaying all the typical teenage insecurities—much to the amusement of his younger teenage sister Laurie. He is overprotective of both his mother and his sister, often following them on dates and listening in on Laurie's private telephone calls. Danny constantly teases and insults him. Keith finds solace by closing the door to his bedroom and playing guitar.

Understandably, his songs are filled with the exuberance of adolescent yearning. In "I Think I Love You" he sings about his trepidation toward love and commitment. In "I Can Feel Your Heartbeat," he sings about his infatuation with infatuation. His songs are optimistic, adventurous, vivacious, and effervescent.

In school, Keith pursues girls over grades; he never pretends to have any serious academic ambitions. While he claims to be an expert in women, he still finds himself confronted with the usual teenage troubles. Keith has a reputation in school as a ladies' man because he starts the rumors himself. He expresses a desire to attend law school and claims to have seen every episode of *Perry Mason*, including all the reruns. He received a B minus in English composition, plays on the basketball team at San Pueblo High School, and dropped out of the Boy Scouts before reaching Tenderfoot when he realized that girls weren't allowed on the camping trips. The only other skills he displays are the ability to drive the family bus, fix the engine, and make corny jokes. The walls of his room are adorned with a Mondrian painting and a poster of Jimi Hendrix (his proclaimed musical idol). The wooden peace symbol in the shape of a teardrop hanging over his bed evidences his pacifism but belies his male chauvinism. With Gandhian calm, Keith refuses to get involved in any physical fights, yet he fiercely contests the slightest suggestion that women are on an equal footing with men. Not surprisingly, he boasts a collection of girlie magazines, and, like a typical teenage male, he is forever buying and selling cars and motorcycles.

Keith Partridge is an average teenager with above average talents, a trust fund, and an exceptionally supportive family. Frankly, he is the only member of the family who is truly multitalented. He composes songs, sings, has stage presence, and makes the girls swoon and scream. Keith Partridge is adorable, cute, and cuddly. Without him, there could be no Partridge Family.

How Would You Describe
Keith Partridge?

David Cassidy (Keith Partridge):

"He was an airhead. I don't know how else to describe him. It's hard for me to be objective about him, you know. You're asking me to be objective about me then. I think the character had no character when he was written. He had four lines in the pilot that were 'Hey Mom, can I borrow the keys to the car?' He had more than four lines, but you know what I mean. The most interesting aspect of his character was that he was an airhead. And the funniest aspect of him was that he was a fool. And for me as an actor, that became my task to try and find a way to make it interesting. And that was what I came up with, and the writers saw that I was willing to go for that, and it seemed to work. It played very well against Danny, Susan, and Dave in particular. And consequently, [that created] the conflict between the characters, which creates the comedy. But to describe his character, I'd just say he was an airhead."

Shirley Jones (Shirley Partridge):

"Keith was your typical teenage boy with all of the drives and new sensations that teenagers begin to have, you know, with the girls and all of that. He was also beginning to discover himself as a person, and, in doing so, would put his foot in it every now and then and find that he was tripping over himself—out of which came the humor of the show. Keith was always made out as the one who didn't get it, and Danny would have to explain things to him. You know, it was that kind of thing, which I don't think pleased David very much in some of those shows. He said, 'Why am I always the bumbling idiot in every episode?' But that was the character they established. Because Keith was the handsome one, Keith was the singer, and Keith was the teen idol. So

I think they didn't want to make him too slick. They wanted him to trip over himself every now and then. So they wrote episodes about that, which was fun. But I don't think David was too thrilled about them."

Danny Bonaduce (Danny Partridge):

"He's kind of the original male bimbo. You know, Keith was kind of an airhead, but he really always had people's best interests at heart. I mean, had it been today's television, with all those girls he was dating, he would have been a high risk for a sexually transmitted disease. In those days, they made it like he was always just going out on these dates. 'Uh-oh, I think they're going to be necking.' You know, in today's television, he would have been the biggest slut on TV. He would have made Kelly Bundy [on *Married with Children*] look like a good kid. I think that was part of the allure; none of us were [sluts]."

Brian Forster (Chris Partridge):

"In a way, I'd say Keith is vain, but not really. He was vain in a teenage kind of a way. You know, he really was soaking in that Keith Partridge [image], but yet retaining a sense of being normal and going to high school and all that kind of thing. Of course, he had that reputation; he was the ladies' man, and all the girls were falling all over him. But yet he also showed a soft, sensitive side about being a brother, like the show where he wanted to take care of the kids and try to take on a father role since Shirley was a single mother [Episode 32]. I think he often felt like he was the father of the family as the eldest son and had to take care of people."

Jeremy Gelbwaks (Chris Partridge):

"Keith was the prototypical big brother. He was cute, a little naive, tried hard, and was very talented. It was his voice that drove the show."

Suzanne Crough (Tracy Partridge):

"Very talented. Always looking over his shoulder watching for Danny. Kind of somewhat shy, I think."

Dave Madden (Mr. Kincaid):

"Keith Partridge is difficult to describe because Keith changed within the body of the four years. I don't mean just changed because he got older. I mean, the producers decided somewhere along the way in the third year that they wanted Keith to be funny. And so a self-deprecating Keith Partridge came into being who wasn't really there the first year. If you're going to have a Keith Partridge who is loved by the girls and who is supposed to be more or less the male hero of the show, I don't think you make him look like a fool as often as they did those last two years. Keith was not the one in the show that should have been the fool. They could make a fool out of me or Danny, but when you take the teenage idol and turn him into the fool, I'm not sure that was wise. Sure, you can make the guy fallible. I don't have a quarrel with that. But I think they made him Keith Partridge the idiot. How could girls possibly care anything about him? By the time we hit the third year, girls who loved David Cassidy were reaching an age—the ones who had grown up with him—where they had to reject this bubblegum rock and start making up reasons why they didn't like David Cassidy. Girls who had liked him all along would start saying, 'Oh, well, he's silly, he's egotistical, he's this, he's that.' They needed, psychologically, to find reasons to not like him so they could move on. While these girls were going away, I don't know how many girls were coming up behind them."

Bernard Slade (Creator):

"Keith was like a surrogate father having to go through adolescence. He was the most mature, but, as I recall, they made him flawed. He could do stupid things as well—which I think is the secret of all writing. You can't write these perfect people. You've got to have some sort of flaws. He was the one Shirley would talk to. It also gave us opportunities to have various girlfriends."

Bob Claver (Executive Producer):

"He was a perfect schmuck. David was and is very handsome. And we were all very careful to see that he lost a lot. He didn't get the girl a lot. He was always outsmarted by Laurie. And I think it made him much more likable. With those looks and being a singing star, if he was also the guy who got the girl and was star of the football team, he'd be somebody you hated. So I thought David was very funny, and he played this guy great. That was part of a plan. A lot of thought went into making Keith likable. Because boys don't like guys like that. And they did like Keith because he was very fallible."

Paul Witt (Producer):

"He was a normal kid who was sort of thriving in abnormal circumstances. He was a kid who was on the road and was the lead singer in a successful musical group who still was more of a teenager, a son, and a brother than he was a pop or rock star. So he had his priorities straight."

Laurie

"All you guys think we're interested in is being cheerleaders or homecoming queens. And then, if we're real lucky, we can all grow up to be Playboy bunnies."
—Laurie Partridge

Laurie is a fifteen-year-old activist with long brown hair, big green eyes, and a stick figure. Like her brother Keith, she too is perpetually in high school, but the comparisons stop there. Unlike Keith, Laurie is smart, although very sensitive about her appearance. She is often seen doing homework on the couch in the living room, sometimes with a towel wrapped around her wet hair. While quiet, she usually appears level-headed, stoic, and intelligent. In fact, she even considered becoming a translator for the United Nations, but gave up the idea when she discovered she had to learn a foreign language.

Laurie plays the piano and provides the harmonies in the group. She is extremely self-conscious, perhaps explaining why she never takes on a lead vocal. She shares a bedroom with Tracy, has a propensity for wearing turtlenecks all the time, and knits, though not very well. She enjoys playing

Laurie's Dates

💜 **Jerry**—boyfriend who asks her to go steady even though she has braces on her teeth [Episode 16]

💜 **Marc Baldwin**—old boyfriend who works himself through college at the Town House Quarter [Episode 19]

💜 **Lester Braddock**—"Don Juan with shoulder pads," says Keith; rumor has it the entire Girls Glee Club jumped out of his birthday cake [Episode 23]

💜 **Butch Murphy**—mentioned [Episode 28]

💜 **Harry "Snake" Murphy**—burly motorcyclist [Episode 28]

💜 **Paul Bruner**—19-year-old college student [Episode 29]

💜 **Freddy**—classmate [Episode 32]

💜 **Wendell**—awkward and insecure grocery boy [Episode 33]

💜 **Marvin**—editor of the high school newspaper [Episode 47]

💜 **Richard**—classmate [Episode 55]

💜 **Harvey Klemper**—mentioned [Episode 56]

💜 **Greg Houser**—a minister, once a childhood sweetheart with whom she took baths [Episode 59]

💜 **Sidney Kingman**—date at Muldune's Point [Episode 67]

💜 **Greely Winger**—classmate of Keith's who received an A in sex education class [Episode 69]

💜 **Tom Baker**—assistant to Byron Atwater at Bartlett's Department Store, he programs the store's computer [Episode 70]

💜 **Bobby Bather**—attractive classmate [Episode 72]

💜 **Jim**—mentioned [Episode 74]

💜 **Richard Whipple**—school treasurer who needs Laurie's help to balance the books [Episode 74]

💜 **Howard Krump**—imaginative liar who masquerades as Howard Wainwright III while aboard the T.S.S. *Fairsea* [Episode 81]

💜 **Mike**—a date Laurie cancels [Episode 84]

💜 **Jim Benson**—coerced by Keith into asking Laurie for a date, he cancels to go out with Patty Hall instead [Episode 84]

💜 **Andy and David Williams**—fourteen-year-old identical twin singers [Episode 88]

tennis, shopping for bargains, baking bread, and collecting recipes from the newspaper.

Laurie is also extremely principled. She is a pacifist willing to back any meaningful, relevant cause. As a feminist, she attends women's lib rallies and actually enters a homecoming queen pageant to use the podium as a venue to express her militant views. Not surprisingly, she has a subscription to *The Liberal Outlook*.

Laurie displays a deep loyalty to and trust in her friends. She refuses to compromise her ethical integrity even for the sake of the band. She discusses her problems openly with her mother, and, consequently, Shirley trusts her daughter implicitly, even seeking Laurie's advice when it comes to her own dating problems. Fortunately, Laurie often bones up on the subject by reading *Psychology and the Human Dilemma* by Rollo May.

As a former Girl Scout, Laurie knows the difference between right and wrong and never crosses that line, unlike Keith, who always finds himself in the gray areas—much to Laurie's amusement. She is constantly entertained by Keith's naiveté, fallibilities, egotism, and amorous entanglements, although, as a feminist, she finds herself equally appalled by his chauvinistic tendencies. She also seems to be far more worldly than her older brother—especially when it comes to dating, an area of expertise where she seems to get her fair share of the action. (It may interest some to know that Laurie got her first training bra at Hanran's Department Store at the age of twelve.)

Laurie Partridge is the ideal teenage girl: responsible, studious, giving, witty, and attractive—and just self-righteous enough to stay out of trouble.

How Would You Describe
Laurie Partridge?

Susan Dey (Laurie Partridge):

"She's a straight man. She's sweet. She's conniving. She's clever. She's enjoyable. Literally, she's an idiot and a fool. I'm not thrilled at all with Laurie's relationship with her mother. I think that's the biggest joke on earth. It's hysterical. Here are two people who are supposed to be so close in the sense that Laurie and her mom are always together, and yet we can never talk to each other. Half of the dilemma is that all of the shows I have with my mother are when I can't really talk to her. It's like crazy time. Laurie deals with women's lib like a kid who gets his first case of acne or like a girl who's going on her first date. I was furious. It got to the point where I was so upset I was losing sleep over it." (in *The National Insider*, April 7, 1974)

Shirley Jones (Shirley Partridge):

"Laurie was the real sort of feminine side of the family with good values and a good head on her shoulders. She was sort of the second mother, taking care of everybody and making sure everything was right. And yet she was certainly a beauty in her own right and very interested in the opposite sex, too. We had a few of those episodes, although I think there were more about David and the girls than Laurie and the guys. I think she was what I would call 'the old soul of the family'—ahead of her age and sort of the nucleus of the family, too, the second mother. She kept everybody together."

David Cassidy (Keith Partridge):

"Just a little too serious. In every way about life."

Danny Bonaduce (Danny Partridge):

"A militant, almost humorless, feminist. When I watch some of the episodes now, and maybe it's because everybody is so accepting of feminism as just part of everyday life, her overbearing [manner], the way she really thumps and thumps and thumps on feminist issues, makes her appear to be militant by today's standards."

Brian Forster (Chris Partridge):

"I think she was a very sweet girl, and she was really a younger reflection of Shirley Partridge. I mean, she sort of had a traditional female role, and was kind of in the background, somewhat quiet, didn't make a lot of waves, and was just kind of a teenage girl. But she had a witty, good sense of humor, which I always appreciated about the character. She was always coming up with good snappy answers to situations."

Jeremy Gelbwaks (Chris Partridge):

"Laurie was probably more brainy than she appeared on television and probably more shy than she seemed as well."

Suzanne Crough (Tracy Partridge):

"Very independent, very determined. I think she follows her heart sometimes; she wears her heart on her sleeve. She always had a moral that she was going after. She was very forthright."

Dave Madden (Mr. Kincaid):

"Laurie Partridge came along at the same time that women's lib came along. They made her a teenage girl, in the middle of this liberation thing, fighting for her rights as a woman even though she wasn't quite a woman yet. Male chauvinist pigs were everywhere, and she was a battler. I think she was cute enough that guys didn't care whether she thought they were male chauvinist pigs or not. They just thought she was cute. I thought her character in many ways might have been the best defined. You knew right where she was at. You could almost predict how she would react to any situation, even if she wasn't in the scene. When a subject that's never been raised before comes up and you think, 'Uh-oh, wait till Laurie hears about this!' and you end up being right, that's a well-defined character as far as I'm concerned."

Bernard Slade (Creator):

"Laurie's character developed. My daughter is about the same age, so Laurie was probably based on her, when you say the generic term 'teenager'. When it was written, I don't think I thought we'd get someone who looked like Susan, with that sort of great face. A lot of her contribution, too, at that point when she wasn't an experienced actress, was a visual one."

Bob Claver (Executive Producer):

"I think she was about perfect. And smart. Very, very bright, and witty. I thought she was a marvelous character. I remember doing a show where Laurie was the campaign manager for a girl running against Keith for class president [Episode 72]. We did a lot of women's lib things, and that was twenty years ago. Susan Dey was a junior model and never acted a day in her life. But she was bright and she could react. At the beginning she really had

nothing to do in the show. We always cut to her for reactions, but later we gave her more and more to do."

Paul Witt (Producer):

"There's kind of this emergence of a woman. We kind of got to watch her grow from a kind of very pretty but slightly cultish young woman into a truly beautiful woman in the years that the show was on. Sharing that experience with someone, watching them grow and become so graceful and skilled, was a pleasure for viewers. You know, it's a really meaningful experience to go through with someone, even though they're playing another character. So there was just a feeling of extraordinary normalcy and decency in that character."

Danny

Danny: *You can't blame me. I'm just a kid.*
Mr. Kincaid: *No you're not. You're a midget in a kid suit.*

Daniel Partridge is a clever, street-smart, business savvy, freckle-faced redhead with an impish grin. As the precocious Partridge, Danny schemes and conspires to make money and manipulate the others to get what he wants. He is a ten-year-old conservative, who reads the business section and the stock market report of the *San Pueblo Tattler* every day. According to mother Shirley, Danny is the next best thing to the *Wall Street Journal*. His older brother, Keith, is always in his debt, and only Danny has the audacity to charge interest. Not surprisingly, nine out of ten kids watched *The Partridge Family* for Danny.

Danny, a self-proclaimed tightwad, continually proposes unusual moneymaking schemes. He cleans up at poker, and he always wins at Monopoly and loves to put Keith out of the game. He keeps all his money in a combination safe in his room from the Jenkins County Bank, and he's always willing to listen to a good business proposition. Danny's favorite colors are 14-karat gold and money green. He subscribes to *U.S. Finances and Monetary Reports*, and the books in his private library include *So You Want to Be a Millionaire* and a couple of Keith's girlie magazines. Like Keith, Danny is also a male chauvinist pig.

Danny describes himself as "daring, debonair, and devilishly handsome." In reality, he has a small weight problem stemming from his love of candy bars and tacos with hot sauce and onions. He also eats peanut butter and tuna fish sandwiches (because the peanut butter keeps the tuna fish together). He does, however, dare to get into all kinds of trouble. When he was five years old, according to Shirley, he tried to jump off the roof in a homemade parachute. He is caught stealing, sneaking into the movie theater, and skipping school. In fact, his school record is filled with his exploits: he ran Carl Vendor's shorts up the flagpole; he put a king

Danny's Aliases

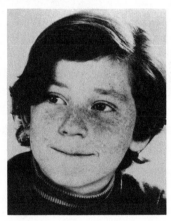

■ "Redheaded albatross"—Keith [Episode 21]
■ "Torture Incorporated"—Mr. Kincaid [Episode 45]
■ "Male chauvinist piglet"—Laurie [Episode 47]
■ "A liberated midget"—Keith [Episode 55]
■ "Herb Alpert and his Tijuana Knuckles"—Mr. Kincaid [Episode 58]
■ "Operation Big Mouth"—Mr. Kincaid [Episode 58]
■ "A walking *Wall Street Journal*"—Mr. Kincaid [Episode 62]
■ "Redheaded heather"—Keith [Episode 66]
■ "The Strike-Out Kid"—Coach Darby Willis [Episode 78]
■ "The Headache Kid"—Laurie [Episode 78]
■ "Meatball"—Keith [Episode 88]
■ "Mealy-mouthed munchkin"—Keith [Episode 93]
■ "Biscuit brain"—Keith [Episode 95]

snake in Herbie Twitchell's locker; he led a cafeteria strike to reinstate tacos; and he put a tape recorder in the girls' locker room. When he thinks that Keith is trying to steal his girlfriend Gloria Hicky, Danny puts molasses in his older brother's comb and corn flakes in his bed.

Danny was born two weeks early and 40 miles from San Pueblo in Napa County, weighing in at 8 lbs., 10 oz. In the band, Danny plays bass guitar and sings harmonies, considering himself more talented than fellow bass guitarist Paul McCartney. In his bedroom, shared with his brother Chris, he keeps a pet lizard in a glass tank. His prized possessions include a collection of *Spiderman* comic books and *Monster* magazines, a stamp collection, an adding machine, one share of AT&T stock, his catcher's mitt, and *The Sounds of Loneliness* by the San Quentin Glee Club. He enjoys croquet, riding his go-cart, taunting Keith, and insulting all the members of his family and Mr. Kincaid. Danny sometimes wears rings on the ring finger and pinkie of his left hand. His only dislikes are liver and when Laurie takes a long time in the bathroom. His best friend is Punky Lazaar, a transparent charmer who always seems to show up when Mrs. Partridge is baking cookies.

Above all, Danny is irrepressible. Only Mr. Kincaid appears truly to appreciate Danny's persistence and aspirations. In fact, only Danny can repeatedly deceive Mr. Kincaid, compelling the manager to come over to the house in the middle of the night or fly across the country to resolve a crisis that turns out to be nothing more than a minor domestic misunderstanding. While Shirley is constantly awed by Danny's astute insights, Danny's siblings reluctantly tolerate his conniving and find his sarcasm only remotely endearing. Still, Danny is unquestionably the brightest and most intriguing member of the Partridge Family, giving the group the very little edge they possess.

Danny's Crushes

💜 **Gloria Hicky**—neighbor and Girl Scout, Danny takes her to a sixth-grade dance [Episode 46], tries to lose weight to get her attention [Episodes 53], tries to act mature to impress her [Episode 55], and introduces her to Julie Lawrence [Episode 67]

💜 **Julie Lawrence**—daughter of attorney Richard Lawrence, Shirley's romantic interest [Episode 67]

💜 **Renee Stern**—daughter of Rabbi Stern of Temple Aaron [Episode 91]

Danny's Moneymaking Schemes

■ He wants to cash in on the ecology movement by hiring a whale as lead singer for the group [Episode 31].

■ He decides to raise hamsters as an investment and, unable to contain his homemade population explosion, proposes that the Partridge Family give away a free hamster with every purchase of a Partridge Family album at a local department store [Episode 34].

■ He recruits Chris to help him auction off Keith's belongings and locks of Keith's hair to the girls in school [Episode 36].

■ He finances Keith's movie [Episode 41].

■ When Keith moves next door into own apartment, Danny sells him food and laundry service [Episode 42].

■ He plans to have psychic Max Ledbetter predict the stock market [Episode 49].

■ He sets up a kissing booth, selling Keith's kisses for ten cents each. "When you have a shoddy product, you have to go for bulk," he says [Episode 49].

■ He sets up a cardboard cutout so fans can have their picture taken with Keith for 25 cents [Episode 60].

■ He offers tours of the Partridge Family's home in order to attract potential buyers [Episode 62].

■ He sells his ideas on how to win a woman's affections to Keith for one dollar each [Episode 93].

The Partridge Family

How Would You Describe Danny Partridge?

Danny Bonaduce (Danny Partridge):

"A decent kid, a little preoccupied with money. I think he really set the standard for a lot of television roles. I think Danny Partridge invented Alex Keaton [on *Family Ties*], not that I'm bitter. But he was a decent kid who loved his family, a little egotistical and overweight, with really bad hair. I think he and Mr. Kincaid tried to get together to run the family, but really kind of flubbed it up. I don't think he did a real good job. I tried to take care of the family, and it would turn out at the end of each episode that the family had to actually take care of me because of my misguided perceptions.

"The worst problems on *The Partridge Family* were caused by Danny Partridge. He was caught stealing in one show [Episode 71], he was caught sneaking into a movie in another [Episode 84], he was caught lying [Episode 84], he was caught cutting off Keith's hair and actually selling it for a profit [Episode 36]. So I think if there was any troublemaker on the show, it was Danny.

"Dave Madden once told me, 'Danny, you know how you and I got these parts?' I said, 'No.' I was only ten years old. He said, 'Because we're ugly.' And I said, 'What?!?' He said, 'Look at David, look at Shirley, look at Susan. They're beautiful. They had to balance it out so they hired us because we're ugly.' According to Dave Madden, that's why I got the part. You know, I think that would make a wonderful spin-off series: me and Reuben Kincaid."

Shirley Jones (Shirley Partridge):

"Danny was the devil, of course. A brilliant little devil, but a devil. He considered himself the manager. Actually I thought it was hysterical, now that I'm seeing some of the episodes again, but we all let him have that role. I mean, he was the manager of the family. You know, at first when we started doing that I remember thinking, 'This is a joke.' But it was for real. He did manage the family. He did negotiate, he did help Mr. Kincaid with all the contracts and all that kind of stuff, which is hysterical to me. Here's an eleven-year-old who's managing the family. But Danny Bonaduce was also very, very bright as a kid. He still is. He's got a mind that just never stops. And, of course, you can just imagine an eleven-year-old having that mind. That's why he was such a good actor. He was a wonderful, wonderful, very funny actor. I mean, his timing was that of an adult."

David Cassidy (Keith Partridge):

"I loved Danny's character. [He was] clever, opportunistic, resourceful, very funny."

Brian Forster (Chris Partridge):

"Charismatic, precocious, definitely a smart-ass. The whole interaction between him and Mr. Kincaid was always very funny, because here was Mr. Kincaid who said he hated kids, and Danny who, of course, was the perfect character to interact with, this precocious kid you just wanted to gag once in a while. So he definitely had a fun character. Very charismatic."

Jeremy Gelbwaks (Chris Partridge):

"Smart and a smart aleck. Probably the smartest person on the show. A driving force of the show."

Suzanne Crough (Tracy Partridge):

"Mischievous, funny, quick-witted, sometimes a terror. He put everything in upheaval in the sense of making people not know what was going on. He was always one step ahead."

Dave Madden (Mr. Kincaid):

"There was an awful lot of Danny Bonaduce in Danny Partridge, mostly the mischievous end of the character, not necessarily the financial brilliance of the character. I find it difficult today to separate Danny Partridge and Danny Bonaduce in my mind because I knew Danny very well and I knew that an awful lot of him went onto that screen as a kid. His precociousness, certainly. He played everything off the set almost the way he played it on the set. I guess the only thing that didn't really ring true to me was the idea that he could have taken over the family's financial planning. There were too many other aspects of his character that denied the brilliance he needed to guide a family financially through any kind of crisis. There were too many other things to say, 'Well, if he was so bright there, he's not going to be that stupid over here and make all these idiotic mistakes.' A bright, intelligent kid wouldn't make these mistakes. So there was an inconsistency of character, but it was a fun character."

Bernard Slade (Creator):

"Danny was really the comic in the show. I wrote him almost like an adult, essentially. He was like twelve going on forty. In an odd way, he was really a forerunner of the Michael J. Fox character [Alex Keaton on *Family Ties*] because he always had these schemes, and in the pilot he was the instigator in a lot of ways of putting that whole thing together. I just thought he had this great face and this great comic timing. All I know is that his performance was terrific, and when I tended to write scripts, I tended to do Danny stories because I knew it was gold. I think his contribution was very important.

"I did not visualize Danny being played by someone like Danny Bonaduce. It was written as a much more scholarly, sort of smart-ass kid that was sort of the parts Barry Gordon played as a kid. Danny Bonaduce was obviously gifted and funny, so the character changed slightly by having him play the part."

Bob Claver (Executive Producer):

"Danny was a comedy lead. I mean, that's what he was. He was very, very funny. I was once doing a pickup scene with him where he had a Harry Truman joke. And he does the joke, and everybody in the crew laughed. He said, 'I don't have any idea what I'm talking about.' But he said things funny. And he's still funny."

Paul Witt (Producer):

"Funny, rebellious, bright, quick, a gadfly, a catalyst, the straw that stirred the drink."

Chris

Laurie: *You know, it takes a warped mind to think of women as a hobby.*
Chris: *I'd rather collect stamps.*

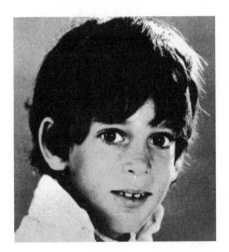 

Christopher Partridge is a typical, middle-class, seven-year-old who just happens to play drums in a successful family rock band. He would be just as happy playing baseball with the other kids in the neighborhood, going to the beach, or climbing a tree in the backyard. He shares a bedroom with his brother Danny, but, unlike his roommate, he is quiet and reserved. Chris enjoys painting, *Captain Thunder* comic books, the Los Angeles Dodgers, and collecting baseball cards. Despite his age, Chris and his younger sister Tracy are included in all the family discussions, but when asked for their opinions, they freely admit having no idea what the question means. Despite the family's rise to stardom, Chris and Tracy remain unaffected by their notoriety. They remain kids, more interested in playing outside than they are being members of a rock group.

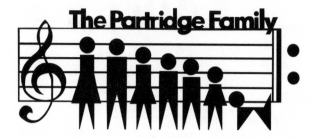

How Would You Describe Chris Partridge?

Brian Forster (Chris Partridge):

"Chris was just a little kid, basically, and very all-American and just very— I hate to say it—but just kind of a plain kid, you know. He just did what kids do. I don't think Chris was really old enough to really sort of establish a character of his own. I think he was just sort of a generic nine-year-old kid."

Jeremy Gelbwaks (Chris Partridge):

"The Chris I played was very naive, very much a child, practically a baby. Sort of a good younger brother who stayed out of the way and supplied the straight line when required, but very much a kid who was not going to get in trouble in later life and was going to stick to the straight and narrow."

Shirley Jones (Shirley Partridge):

"Well, you know the first year we had a different Chris than we had afterward. So I can describe both of them. The first season, Chris was a nice little actor. Brian [Forster], the next Chris, was very small for his age, but he was older so it helped a lot because he was very sensitive and sweet and a good actor. He really wasn't a big child actor. He wasn't somebody that had done everything, who had started when he was born, it wasn't that kind of thing. He was just a real nice little boy."

David Cassidy (Keith Partridge):

"It's funny. My recollection is a little vague. Was he dark-haired or was he blond? Oh no, I remember. He was both."

Danny Bonaduce (Danny Partridge):

"Chris was a good kid, played the drums, one time ran away, and if I had to think of the line that he said most often it would be 'Who?' He and Tracy would say it in unison. Shirley would say, 'Well, this band is nice, but they're no Tommy Dorsey,' and Chris and Tracy would both say, 'Who?'"

Suzanne Crough (Tracy Partridge):

"Just a nice cute kid. When it came to Chris and Tracy there wasn't a whole lot exposed, you know. We didn't really have characters, so to speak. They hadn't been developed. He was just a nice, cute kid."

Dave Madden (Mr. Kincaid):

"It's difficult to talk about Chris and Tracy separately because they weren't to that degree separate entities. They were 'the little kids.' They were kind of just there, you know. There was not much rebellion in them, except the one show where they ran away from home [Episode 40]. They didn't have a whole lot of input to decision making, and they didn't talk much. In terms

of lines, I think they just had a few more lines than Simone [the family sheepdog].

"It was kind of hysterical at the recording sessions where they pantomimed to the instruments. Now Chris didn't know how to play drums. He had all the natural rhythm of a whopping crane and so did Tracy. I mean, they were not musicians, that's all. I'm not putting them down for it. I'm sure at that age, I would have been exactly the same way. There would be a stepladder on each side of the camera, and there would be a woman on one and a guy on the other. The woman would be doing this [mimes woman playing triangle], and, of course, Tracy would be standing there with a triangle mimicking the woman, and then Chris would be imitating what the guy on the ladder was doing. I often watched that scene and thought, 'If the fans of this show could come in and watch this, it would all be over.' They would go out saying, 'They don't know anything about music!'"

Bernard Slade (Creator):

"Chris and Tracy were nice-looking, sweet kids, but not that brilliantly talented. So it was difficult to get performances from them, so they stayed away."

Bob Claver (Executive Producer):

"I'll tell you how unimportant Chris was. We had a kid named Jeremy Gelbwaks the first year. And I got a call from their lawyer, and he said, 'The family wants to move to Virginia. You don't think this show is going anywhere, do you?' And I said, 'Nahhhh.' You know, the show really caught on and got successful in reruns after the first year. So anyway, we replaced him with Brian Forster. And you know, we got one letter."

Paul Witt (Producer):

"Very bright, and precocious without being obnoxious. The decision that the Gelbwaks made in removing Jeremy from the series was a remarkable one and certainly, in their circumstances, the right one. It might not have been right for any of the other kids there, but given their sense of values, given what they wanted for their family, they did a difficult thing and absolutely the right thing by removing him from the series."

Tracy

Shirley: *Tracy, it's your turn to say grace.*
Tracy: *Dear Lord, thank you for our food, and please get Keith a date.*

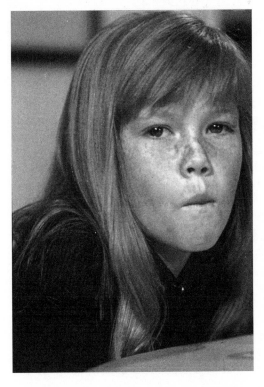

Tracy has dirty-blond hair and plays the tambourine. She shares a bedroom with her sister, Laurie. She has a turtle, a punching bag named Charlie, and her favorite meal is a peanut butter and jelly sandwich. We learn very little more about her.

As the youngest Partridge, Tracy is extremely quiet. In fact, Tracy is so quiet she seems almost comatose when performing onstage. She stands nearly motionless, gently shaking the tambourine, sometimes tapping it against her leg, sometimes against the palm of her other hand. She sings with the contagious enthusiasm of one of her pull-string dolls. In addition to the tambourine, Tracy also plays the triangle, the cowbell, and wood blocks, clearly showing her versatility as a musician.

Shunning the limelight, Tracy remains an essential member of the group. When the family faces a difficult problem, Tracy often proposes an overly simplistic yet completely appropriate solution that the awestruck adults immediately put into action, clearly demonstrating that her brilliant tambourine work isn't the only trait that makes her indispensable.

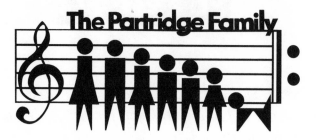

How Would You Describe
Tracy Partridge?

Suzanne Crough (Tracy Partridge):

"A nice, cute kid. She didn't really get in trouble, she didn't really have much to say, she was just kind of always in the background. I portrayed her pretty well. There wasn't a whole lot to it. The best way to put it is: Chris and Tracy were part of the family, but we didn't have developed characters. We were just these cute little kids in the background, you know, playing the part of the rest of the family. I mean, we grew up on the show, but we never had a chance to really have our characters developed. You only have a half hour of time and so many stars, and everyone's fighting for their meat of the show, and there's just not enough room for the two youngest, and that was okay."

Shirley Jones (Shirley Partridge):

"Suzanne had done some commercials, but she wasn't one of those kids whose family had been pushing her from the age of six months to work. It wasn't that kind of thing at all. And that really helped a lot. She came from a wonderful family, and they just adored her. They were real solid people, you know, salt-of-the-earth people, and therefore she was a very nice little girl. I don't think she was the best child actress that was ever put on the earth. But we didn't need that. She was pretty, and we just needed somebody to say 'yes' and 'no' once in a while and look wide-eyed and shake the tambourine."

David Cassidy (Keith Partridge):

"Who?"

Danny Bonaduce (Danny Partridge):

"Tracy is hard to describe because Chris and Tracy were just a drummer and tambourine player. They were good kids, but they did so little on the show, it's hard to imagine what they would have grown up to be."

Brian Forster (Chris Partridge):

"I think she was really the baby of the family in a lot of ways. I don't think of Chris as having a lot of responsibility, but I think he did take on the responsibility of his sister, you know, like taking care of Tracy and keeping her out of trouble. She was his sidekick. I mean, they were buddies. They were off doing things. I think he was sort of watching over her, making sure she was getting along okay."

Jeremy Gelbwaks (Chris Partridge):

"Tracy was probably shyer than Chris. But the two of them were really of the seen-and-not-heard school."

Dave Madden (Mr. Kincaid):

"Tracy played the triangle and the tam-bourine. Those were her two main instru-ments. And I don't know if you ever no-ticed, but if you really listen there isn't a tambourine or a triangle in the instrumen-tation anywhere. You're listening for it, and it's just not there. So she's playing an instrument that doesn't exist on the track."

Bernard Slade (Creator):

"Chris and Tracy were nice-looking, sweet kids, but not that brilliantly talented. So it was difficult to get performances from them, so they stayed away."

Bob Claver (Executive Producer):

"They were just there to round out the family. It was just one of those things. She was cute, and she looked good."

Paul Witt (Producer):

"Quiet, adorable. She was a little girl. Just this adorable little girl."

Mr. Kincaid

"Why couldn't I take a nice, safe job, like milking cobras?"
—Reuben Kincaid

Reuben Clarence Kincaid is a manager who claims to hate kids. He is a hands-on manager, overseeing all the arrangements for the Partridge Family's performances, recordings and photography sessions, and album promotions. Mr. Kincaid truly loves the family, and his affection for Shirley and her children is so deep that he would probably represent them even if they weren't successful. He had the chance to represent Reptilia the Snake Girl, and, during stressful moments, often wonders if he made the right decision by signing aboard with the Partridges instead.

Mr. Kincaid plays the role of surrogate husband and father, with Danny in tow as his protégé. In nearly every episode we see him at the kitchen table while Shirley pours him another cup of coffee. Mr. Kincaid is more than the group's business manager. He is also Shirley's closest friend, a substitute father to her children, and the man most likely to sweep her off her feet. Kincaid is a natural husband for Shirley; he loves the kids (though he refuses to admit it), considers himself a member of the family, and finds Shirley alluring and intelligent. Unfortunately, neither adult ever makes his or her feelings known.

Reuben does consider himself a ladies' man blessed with the "Kincaid charm." He lives in apartment 29 of a swinging singles complex with a pool. As a swinging bachelor, he drives a navy blue convertible with a white top, reads *Playpen* magazine, and frequents the racetrack. In bed, he wears pajamas imprinted with hearts (given to him as a gift) and an attractive black eyemask. His only steady date is stewardess Bonnie Kleinschmitt, a nice girl with marriage in mind, although her occupation helps keep her at a comfortable distance.

Also living a safe distance from Mr. Kincaid is his widowed mother, Clara. Her home is 1,500 miles from San Pueblo; roundtrip airfare amounts to $200, which helps keep the extraordi-nary cheapskate at bay. Reuben realizes how much he looks like his mother when he sees a picture of himself dressed as a good fairy. Kincaid also has an Aunt Rita, a cousin Dave (who ate too many fried foods and died while eating onion rings), and a teenage nephew, Alan Kincaid (implying that Reuben also has a married brother).

We learn very little else about his background. His childhood sweetheart was Rose Barker. He crashed the high school senior prom with his friend Bernard Tibley, played the role of the princess in his college drama department's production of *Rumpelstiltskin*, and dropped out of the pre-med program. He keeps a can opener in his car, smokes cigarettes, and is allergic to long-haired dogs. He was drafted in 1952 and served in Korea, where he learned to start fires with a flamethrower.

We never learn how or why Mr. Kincaid became a manager, but he is employed by a large management company based in another city. He works in San Pueblo out of his own one-man field office. He has also represented the Flying Zucchinis (who opened and closed in one day), psychic Max Ledbetter (who gave up show business to run a bakery), and Andy and David Williams (identical twin singers who record the hit "Say It Again").

As for his relationship with Danny, only Mr. Kincaid sees eye to eye with the precocious redhead, and this worries him. Perhaps Mr. Kincaid sees Danny as a genuine threat to his position as manager. After all, Danny continually questions Kincaid's expertise, forever tries to undermine his authority, and usually proposes some of the most ingenious plans to avert disaster. Danny's business savvy often exceeds that of Mr. Kincaid, much to the manager's chagrin. Maybe Mr. Kincaid subconsciously realizes that little Danny possesses sufficient know-how to unmask his entrepreneurial shortcomings and jeopardize his job as manager. Even so, Kincaid remains fond of the little rascal, admiring his spunk and keen wit.

Mr. Kincaid's Girlfriends

❤ **Cathleen Darcy**—a friend of Shirley's to whom he is engaged to be married until he learns she doesn't want children [Episode 20]
❤ **Bonnie Kleinschmitt**—stewardess whose brother has a club in the mountains; Reuben lures her with the line: "You don't want to go through your whole life with the name Kleinschmitt, do you?" He calls her sugarplum and introduces her to his mother [Episodes 11, 37, 40, 47, 57, 68, 79, and 80]
❤ **Candy**—mentioned [Episode 56]
❤ **Daisy**—mentioned [Episode 56]
❤ **Lola**—mentioned [Episode 58]
❤ **Penny Wentworth**—mentioned [Episode 69]
❤ **Greta**—mentioned [Episode 74]
❤ **Bubbles LaRue**—mentioned [Episode 79]

Mr. Kincaid's self-proclaimed disdain for children may only be a transparent veneer to hide his latent pedophilic tendencies toward the three younger Partridges. Or perhaps, like Beatles manager Brian Epstein and his client John Lennon, Mr. Kincaid decided to represent the Partridge Family because he had an unrequited homosexual interest in Keith. Then again, his interest in the group may have stemmed from a Lolita complex toward nubile Laurie Partridge. Since these relationships never materialize in any episode, we can safely assume Mr. Kincaid never felt these perverse needs. Either way, Reuben Kincaid is merely a frustrated man whose only gratification is the vicarious thrill of seeing the Partridge Family rise to the top.

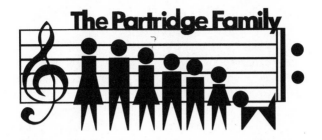

The Partridge Family

How Would You Describe Mr. Kincaid?

Dave Madden (Mr. Kincaid):

"Reuben Kincaid was a bungler. I mean, he was not a good manager. He screwed things up. After four years, the Partridge Family was still working toilets. That's not a good manager. They should have been at the top of the charts. But of course, the network didn't want them to get too big because they didn't want people to stop identifying with them. They wanted them to live in that same little middle-class house no matter what happened to their careers. So there was a strange dichotomy: they wanted the Partridge Family to be a successful rock group and yet they couldn't let them live like a successful rock group. They couldn't have them work where successful rock groups worked, because they couldn't shoot a concert.

"But all that reflected back on Reuben Kincaid within the reality of the show. Reuben Kincaid was a scatterbrain, you know, he was crazy. He would send them off to a fire station in a black ghetto one week, have them in Paris in a concert a few weeks later, and then have them back in some little dumb folk room. It didn't make any sense.

"There was a love-hate relationship with kids in general with Reuben Kincaid. Nobody was really quite sure a lot of the time whether he really did hate kids or whether that was a front. There were a couple of shows where it was rather obvious that it was a front. But the rest of the time I had to ride that tightrope between hating them and really liking them.

"I think Reuben was fascinated by kids in general and Danny in particular. He was a single man—as I was—who never had any children, hadn't really been around children much (except when he was a child), didn't really know how to deal with them, and just was not up to his potential when it came to children. He felt, I think, that Danny was always trying to make him look bad and was trying to point out to the rest of the family that this guy wasn't worth a damn as a manager. That was maybe the biggest threat of all, along with the fact that Danny destroyed any kind of relationship I could have had with Bonnie

Kleinschmitt, who was intermittently there as my stewardess girlfriend. Every time I got her on the couch and opened up the champagne bottle, the damn phone would ring, and that would go out the window.

"There are many people who, in retrospective confusion, think I was the kids' father. They watched the show when they were very young and somehow they didn't get the concept of a manager, and since I was always there, they assume I was the father. Some people told me, 'Shirley and Reuben should have gotten married.' I said, 'Well, if they had, I would have probably been involved with more of the plots because then I would have been their stepfather, but I just don't think that it would have worked because then this relationship between Danny and me would have been softened. Shirley Partridge wouldn't have tolerated that [constant antagonism]. So our relationship would have gone down the drain if I had become the stepfather. I'd also have been in a position of authority that I didn't necessarily have as a manager. A lot of the stuff that went down between me and the family would have been lost by a marriage. Plus, a marriage just didn't generally make a whole lot of sense between Shirley and me."

Shirley Jones (Shirley Partridge):

"Dave Madden was marvelous. I think he was just perfect for that role. Initially there was thought of having somebody that would be more of a leading-man type, but then they didn't really want you to believe that there was a relationship between Shirley Partridge and the manager. They didn't want that to happen. So they decided to go the other way with a comic type, which I thought was a much better idea and helped the show a lot.

"He was a very funny sort of buffoon who was always the last to know what was going to happen and was led by the nose by Danny. I mean, he thought he was our manager when in fact Danny, this little kid, this little redheaded snip, was the manager of the family and was always making all the decisions. And Mr. Kincaid would find himself in the soup half the time, not knowing what was going on. There's one episode with Arte Johnson where he broke out of prison [Episode 64]. He comes into the house. Well, I thought Dave Madden was hysterical in that show. I mean, he really was the bumbler. He did everything wrong, trying to escape from this heavy prisoner who was Arte Johnson. It was hysterical. He kept falling over himself and just doing all the wrong things. And that really was what his character was based on."

David Cassidy (Keith Partridge):

"Just smarmy enough to be Keith Partridge's manager and just honest enough to represent the Partridge Family. Considering the incredible success the Partridge Family had, I don't think they should have been playing Indian reservations and the lizard lounges that he booked us into."

Danny Bonaduce (Danny Partridge):

"My favorite character by far. Mr. Kincaid was disguised as a curmudgeon. He absolutely cared what happened to the family. He wanted to be around the kids, although he would pretend he didn't. He was just an all-around decent guy, possibly a bit befuddled. I think had the show gone another season there might have been a relationship between Mr. Kincaid and Shirley. I know there was talk about it."

Brian Forster (Chris Partridge):

"He was the bachelor, swinging single kind of guy. He was very much the epitome of what a male bachelor was thought of at that time as far as no responsibility and freewheeling and living in a bachelor apartment. He was obviously very much into show business and the whole pizzazz of it and promotion and all the energy that goes along with it. The Partridge Family was his main act, but I sort of get the idea that maybe he was working with other acts. So doing the Partridge Family was sort of his bread and butter, but it was a mixed feeling for him, like, 'Well, I sort of have to go hang out with all these kids.' But I think he secretly really wanted to be a dad, that he wanted to settle down and have some responsibility. I think that's why he sort of enjoyed hanging around with the kids, even though he complained about it."

Jeremy Gelbwaks (Chris Partridge):

"Mr. Kincaid was the same Dave Madden character from *Camp Runamuck* and *Laugh-In*. He's sort of a big, doofy, good-hearted, overwhelmed, undereffective kind of businessman."

Suzanne Crough (Tracy Partridge):

"Funny, talented, lots of humor. Short-fused. Couldn't handle Danny. He couldn't deal with kids. So we were definitely a challenge for him."

Bernard Slade (Creator):

"I just felt we needed somebody who could cut the saccharine a little bit. I wanted someone who was again a surrogate father figure but who was very human. He was written as much more dyspeptic. He was written in my mind as Oscar Levant or W. C. Fields. I wanted someone who didn't like kids and was really mean about it. It got softened. So I thought it was another opportunity to do comedy, and I think I was concerned that [the show] could make [the audience] get diabetes, so I wanted somebody that would give you some sort of acerbity. And as I say, Dave Madden, who was very good, was never as acerbic as I had imagined."

Bob Claver (Executive Producer):

"Dave Madden is marvelous. At the beginning, I didn't like Dave as much as everybody else did. But as time went on, he got better and better. He did a terrific job. And as I look at him now, he doesn't look like any manager or agent ever looked. He's a tall blond, and managers were always portrayed as, well, kind of Jewish really. And Dave can play frustration very well. And Danny drove him crazy, and we got a lot of mileage out of that. But I think David was a good choice. I was going for somebody who was a little bit more clichéd, and I'm glad I lost that argument."

Paul Witt (Producer):

"A manager in a difficult business with a very big heart. But the kind of manager that we liked to believe existed then, and might exist now, who really cared more about his clients than the dollar."

Simone

The Partridge Family often traveled with their dog, Simone (part-sheepdog), whose most memorable moment comes when she chases a skunk inside the Partridge Family bus. Understandably, Simone never accompanied the family on the road again and mysteriously disappeared from the series after the first season without any explanation. "That was a big joke on the set," recalls Brian Forster. "Every time we got on the bus, backed up, and hit a bump, we'd joke, 'Oops, there goes Simone.'"

Ricky Stevens

Cute little four-year-old Ricky Stevens, with his long black sheepdog bangs, moves into the house next door with his widowed mother, Doris, and his sister, Donna. Ricky hopes to one day be a singer, and the Partridges encourage him, letting him sing his original songs, accompanied by one or two family members on guitar or piano, to cheer up anyone in the house who just happens to be forlorn at that particular moment. When he's not singing one of his cloying tunes, he can usually be found playing outside with Chris and Tracy, where he should be relegated.

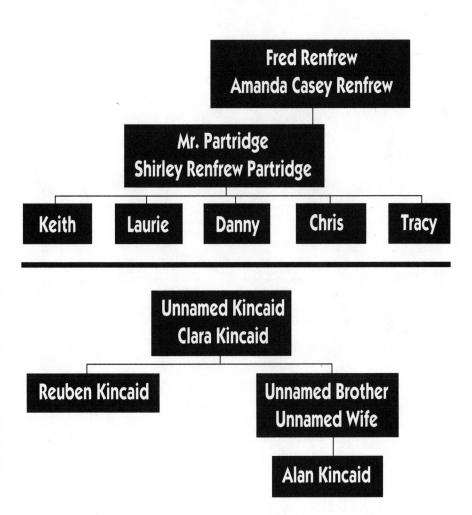

Partridge Family Tree

Fred Renfrew
Amanda Casey Renfrew

Mr. Partridge
Shirley Renfrew Partridge

Keith | Laurie | Danny | Chris | Tracy

Unnamed Kincaid
Clara Kincaid

Reuben Kincaid

Unnamed Brother
Unnamed Wife

Alan Kincaid

3

I Can Feel Your Feel Your Heartbeat

I Can Feel Your Heartbeat

I can feel your heartbeat and you didn't even say a word.
I can feel your heartbeat but you didn't even say a word.
Oh, I know pretty woman that your love can be heard.
You can feel my heartbeat too, I can see you're feelin' me.
You can feel my heartbeat too, I can see you're feelin' me.
Oh, I know pretty woman that your love can be heard.
Ooh, and we'll paint the night, let it shine in light of our love.
This is the night, yes, this is the night of our love.
I'll treat you like a woman, love you like a woman,
Lord, I'll prove it baby, I'm a man of my word.
Love love, can't you feel your heartbeat?
Love love, I can feel your heartbeat.
Love love, can't you feel your heartbeat?
Love.

And we'll paint the night, let it shine in light of our love.
This is the night, yes, this is the night of our love.
I'll treat you like a woman, love you like a woman,
Lord, I'll prove it baby, I'm a man of my word.
Love love, can't you feel your heartbeat?
Love love, I can feel your heartbeat.
Love love, can't you feel your heartbeat?
Love love, I can feel your heartbeat.
Love love, can't you feel your heartbeat?
Love love, I can feel your heartbeat.
Love love, can't you feel it?
Love love, I can feel it.
Love love, getting stronger.

he Partridge Family, like the Beatles and Rolling Stones before them, lived in the eye of the hurricane, sheltering themselves from frenzied fans with their own unique brand of humor. But unlike their predecessors, the Partridge Family was a television family trying their best to maintain a typical middle-class lifestyle in their suburban hometown of San Pueblo. Despite their success and popularity as performers, the family stayed in the same modest home, Shirley remained a homemaker, and her children were enrolled in public schools. The Partridge Family only digressed from the traditional nuclear family lifestyle by holding band rehearsals every afternoon in their garage. Of course, their life on the road also made them an atypical family, as did the fact that a quirky business manager visited their home with alarming frequency.

During their musical career, the Partridge Family met intriguing individuals from all walks of life, performed overly abundant acts of altruism, and shared their music with a variety of audiences at a wide range of night clubs, folk houses, and women's lib rallies. While the following list of concert appearances may seem sketchy and erratic (Mr. Kincaid provided the itinerary), the subsequent pages also list important landmarks in San Pueblo and the Partridges' neighbors, offer the floor plans to the Partridge Family house, give a brief history of the Partridge Family bus, and, most important, provide an invaluable dictionary so you can lace your vocabulary with groovy Partridge Family expressions.

Secrets of the Partridge Family House

The Partridge Family's home at 698 Sycamore Road is a modest two-story, wooden house, painted light yellow and surrounded by a white picket fence. The first floor contains a living room (carpeted in shag and furnished with a sofa, chairs, a television, and a piano), a dining room, and an eat-in kitchen (complete with all the modern appliances with the exception of a dishwasher). The stairs by the front door lead to the second floor where there are four bedrooms, a bathroom, and a master bedroom with a bathroom. The two-piece back door from the kitchen leads to the two-car garage behind the house

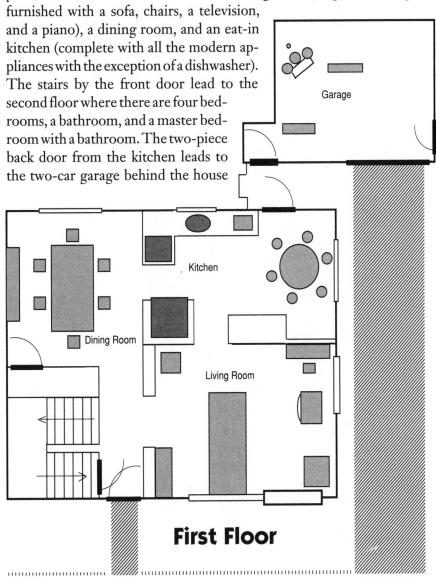

Garage

Kitchen

Dining Room

Living Room

First Floor

that the family uses exclusively for band rehearsals and storing their instruments. The house also has an attic and a basement.

Shirley sleeps in a brass bed in her own room; Keith's room is decorated with a Mondrian painting, a Jimi Hendrix poster, and a wooden teardrop peace symbol; Laurie shares a room with Tracy; and Danny shares a room with Chris, who later moves into the guest room. There is a tree house in the front yard. The Partridges park their restored school bus in the driveway next to the family station wagon.

In the fourth season, the Partridges redecorate and refurnish their home. The piano is against a different wall in the living room, the kitchen has new wallpaper and a new countertop, and the staircase has new carpeting.

The facade for the Partridge Family house can be found on the 40-acre back lot of the Warner Brothers Ranch at 3701 West Oak Street, Burbank, California.

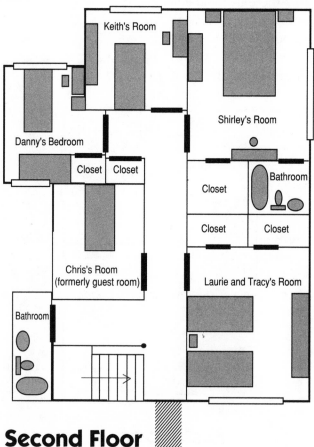

Keith's Room

Shirley's Room

Danny's Bedroom

Closet   Closet

Bathroom

Closet

Closet   Closet

Chris's Room
(formerly guest room)

Laurie and Tracy's Room

Bathroom

Second Floor

Back on the Bus

Immediately after signing a contract with Mr. Kincaid, the Partridges buy a used school bus at Al's Used Cars and paint it themselves before driving to Las Vegas to play their first gig at Caesars Palace. The school bus is painted in the geometric style of Dutch painter Piet Mondrian in keeping with the Beatles' *Magical Mystery Tour* bus, the Who's *Magic Bus*, and the psychedelic bus driven by Ken Kesey and his Merry Pranksters. The motto painted on the back of the Partridge Family's bus is "Caution Nervous Mother Driving" rather than "Further." Shirley and Keith share the driving, and Keith repairs the engine.

The bus itself was a used 1957 Chevrolet, purchased from the Orange County California School District. After *The Partridge Family* was canceled, the bus was sold several times; it was finally abandoned in the parking lot of Lucy's Tacos in East Los Angeles. The bus was junked in 1987. In 1993, when David Cassidy toured the country with the Partridge Family bus, he traveled aboard a new bus, painted to look exactly like the original. The second bus is on display at Universal Studios Florida.

The Most Interesting People the Partridge Family Ever Meets

As local celebrities, the Partridge Family are pillars of the community in San Pueblo. Shirley belongs to the PTA, Keith is a man about town, Laurie speaks out at women's lib rallies and other political events, Danny is the neighborhood terror, and Mr. Kincaid knows all the booking agents and local acts. Here are all their neighbors, friends, and associates:

Albert—professional protest organizer and friend of Laurie's, he helps her arrange a protest at Bartlett's Department Store [Episode 70]

Applebaum, Dr. Bernie—pediatrician who dates Shirley and treats Danny for a sore throat [Episodes 27 and 63]

Archie—one of Keith's classmates [Episode 23]

Argyle, Mrs.—[Episode 86]

Atwater, Byron—credit manager at Bartlett's Department Store [Episode 70]

Bailey, Karen—attractive blond who Keith tries to make jealous by having Laurie masquerade as his southern-belle date [Episode 93]

Baker, Tom—assistant to Byron Atwater at Bartlett's Department Store, he programs the store's computer, the 1984-Z, and dates Laurie [Episode 70]

Barfus, Sheila—"the girl with the tooth," recalls Keith. When the Partridges' house is burglarized, she tells people Keith is in traction and collects 28 cents to help him [Episode 64]

Barner, Sam—helps Mr. Kincaid install a burglar alarm in the Partridge Family's house [Episode 64]

Bartlett, Mr.—owner of Bartlett's Department Store [Episode 70]

Beeder, Dr.—school psychiatrist [Episode 55]

Benton, Wally—friend of Keith's in the Shakespeare Club with Sally Winkler [Episode 80]

Bernard, Lorenzo—eccentric painting instructor who considers Shirley Partridge his star pupil [Episode 87]

Betty—sat next to Keith for an entire year in history class in junior high school; she had a crush on him then and refuses to go out with him now [Episode 93]

Bishop, Jerry—first runner-up in the San Pueblo homecoming queen pageant [Episode 90]

Boone, Professor—Keith's sociology professor [Episode 83]

Brad—prosecuting attorney for the student court of San Pueblo High School, he prosecutes Laurie for allegedly stealing a test from Mr. Fletcher [Episode 65]

Brinn, Mrs.—Shirley's friend who loves to chat on the phone [Episode 84]

Brisler, Judy—third runner-up in the San Pueblo homecoming queen pageant [Episode 90]

Brown, Cindy—Laurie's friend and the principal's daughter, she steals a test from Mr. Fletcher [Episode 65]

Brown, Principal—principal of San Pueblo High School [Episode 65]

Bullock, Mrs.—Danny's English teacher who loses a diamond brooch [Episode 95]

Burgess, Wink—host of "The Wink Burgess Show" [Episode 16]

Burnes, Marty—booking agent who is convinced that Danny was adopted by the Partridges [Episode 24]

Burnett, Mr.—banker [Episode 61]

Burnhardt, John—ex-convict hired by the Partridge Family to drive their bus during a two-month tour [Episode 37]

Busby, Mr.—grocery store owner [Episode 33]

Buzby, Mrs.—mentioned [Episode 21]

Carol—one of Laurie's friends [Episode 65]

Carter, Clair—a former classmate of Keith's from high school, now pregnant [Episode 93]

Cinnard, Larry—booking agent who wants to book the Partridge Family to play a European tour including London, Brussels, and Amsterdam [Episode 92]

Cosell, Howard—ABC sportscaster who covers the Partridge Family's recording session at Marineland [Episode 31]

Damion, Mrs.—high school English teacher [Episode 43]

DiLelo, Ralph—venue operator who agrees to book the Partridge Family if Keith will date his daughter [Episode 84]

Farrenholtz, Cindy—one of Laurie's friends [Episode 65]

Feldman, Zack—spectator at Little League baseball game [Episode 78]

Fenster, Mr.—next-door neighbor to the right [Episode 41]

Fenway, Marcia—one of Laurie's classmates who dated Lester Braddock a week before he dated Charlotte Linamin [Episode 23]

Fiedermeyer, Dr.—Mr. Kincaid's doctor [Episode 79]

Fillmore, Marv—spectator at Little League baseball game [Episode 78]

Firmly, Dina—new girl in school whom Keith wants to date and whom Laurie wants to protect from Keith [Episode 76]

Fleming, Donna—second runner-up in the San Pueblo homecoming queen pageant [Episode 90]

Fletcher, Mr.—math teacher at San Pueblo High School [Episode 65]

Flicker, E. J.—property owner who alerted Marineland to get a beached whale out of his inlet, he demands 50 percent of the profits from a record the Partridge Family intends to make using the whale's song [Episode 31]

Fowler, Will—horse trainer [Episode 61]

Frankie—Laurie's friend who tries out for the varsity basketball team but is prohibited from joining because she is a woman [Episode 90]

George—handyman who has worked for the Partridges for over 13 years [Episode 70]

Gibson, Mrs.—seen at the Partridges' open house [Episode 62]

Goldberg, Phyllis—runs for class president of San Pueblo High School against Keith with Laurie as her campaign manager; she has also written for the school newspaper [Episode 72]

Gordley, Gus—talent scout for World International Pictures [Episode 60]

Gordy—Keith's friend who drives a car into the hidden stop sign on Oak Street [Episode 26]

Greasley, Sam—owner of the Royal Theater [Episode 41]

Grisbee, Mr.—Keith's sex education teacher at San Pueblo High School; he has identical twin nieces [Episode 69]

Gwen—a young girl who forces her parents to bring her to the Partridges' open house so she can admire Keith [Episode 62]

Jannis, Mr.—next door neighbor who rents Keith a room in his house in exchange for gardening duties [Episode 42]

Halstead, Miss—Danny's seventh-grade English teacher; Laurie becomes her student teacher [Episode 92]

Hendleman, Mrs.—mentioned [Episode 82]

Harriet—one of Laurie's friends [Episode 65]

Hensley, Mr.—curator of the Rothschild Museum of Art [Episode 44]

Hicky, Gloria—girlfriend of Danny's [Episode 53]

Hoffsteader, Mr. and Mrs.—seen at the Partridges' open house [Episode 62]

Hortense—woman who replaces Shirley at the bank [Episode 17]

Kelly, Stillman—owner of a San Pueblo radio station, father of the beautiful Dora Kelly, and former member of the rock group Golden Flash whose big hit record was "Stolen Kisses, Stolen Hubcaps" [Episode 26]

Kennedy, Miss—Danny's schoolteacher [Episode 55]

Kincaid, Alan—Mr. Kincaid's nephew from New York, who suffers from a lack of self-confidence and aspires to be a standup comedian [Episode 85]

Klein, Detective Harry—investigator hired by Danny to find his real parents [Episode 24]

Kleven, Mrs.—mentioned [Episode 87]

Koolic, Mr.—Laurie's history teacher [Episode 28]

Kornegge, Mrs.—neighbor who warns Keith about the evils of Hollywood, after reading *The Carpetbaggers* by Harold Robins [Episode 60]

Kramwater, Gloria—sexy girl who sits in front of Danny in assembly at school [Episode 5]

Larkin, Willie—motorist who tries to sue the Partridge Family for whiplash; they call him "Whiplash Willie" [Episode 2]

Laws, Harlan—collector for Simon Collection Agency [Episode 70]

Lazaar, Punky—Danny's best friend [Episodes 4, 30, 71, 89, 91, 92, and 95]

Ledbetter, Max—psychic once represented by Mr. Kincaid, he now owns a bakery [Episode 49]

Linamin, Charlotte—one of Laurie's classmates who dated Lester Braddock a week after he dated Marcia Fenway [Episode 23]

Lippencott, Myrna—a friend of Laurie's with a crush on Keith [Episode 49]

Lowenfeld, Leroy—the Partridge Family's insurance lawyer [Episode 2]

Mark—classmate of Keith and Laurie's who hangs out in Scooby's malt shop [Episode 76]

Mays, Logan—promoter who books the Partridge Family for a European tour [Episode 15]

Melinda—one of Laurie's friends, she agrees to testify on Laurie's behalf when she is accused of stealing a test [Episode 65]

Michaels, Dr. Ted—the Partridge Family's pediatrician [Episode 17]

Monahan, Mrs.—lives in the house on the corner and provides brownies when the Partridge kids run away from home; she also protests to the Partridge Family when Russian artist Nicholas Minski Pushkin paints a nude woman on their garage [Episodes 40 and 44]

Morality Watchdogs—a conservative watchdog group [Episode 12]

Mulvaney, Sam—police officer and friend of the family [Episode 75]

Murdeen, Marsha—Laurie's friend and "old megaphone mouth," according to Keith [Episode 65]

Murphy, Mr.—Keith threw a baseball through his window when he was a kid [Episode 65]

Neumeyer, Mr.—art museum curator [Episode 87]

Parkinson, George—Karen Bailey's date to Keith's party [Episode 93]

Pearson, Merl—television host of *Pearson to Person* [Episode 73]

Peck, Homer—stableboy [Episode 61]

Pepper, Max—promoter, owner of a Hawaiian hotel, and friend of Mr. Kincaid's, he assesses Danny's comedy routine [Episode 9]

Phelps, Mr.—neighbor who complains loudly when Russian artist Nicholas Minski Pushkin paints a nude woman on the Partridges' garage [Episode 44]

Pierson, Mrs.—advertises a $50 reward for her lost diamond brooch; she lives at 908 North Beverly Drive [Episode 95]

Power of Women—a feminist group working for equal rights [Episode 12]

Pushkin, Nicholas Minski—Russian artist who paints a nude woman on the Partridges' garage [Episode 88]

Radnitz, Skip—one of Keith's classmates [Episode 88]

Ralph—friend of Keith's [Episode 76]

Reinbolt, Mrs.—has lived next door to the Partridges for 15 years in the house to the right [Episode 24]

Rose, Sidney—reclusive millionaire and Melba toast baron worth $280 million [Episode 73]

Russell—Danny's friend [Episode 84]

Scotty—classmate of Keith and Laurie's who hangs out in Scooby's malt shop [Episode 76]

Sharp, George and Bea—couple who try to buy the Partridges' house [Episode 62]

Shnurr, Ziggy—comedy writer who sells Danny old jokes [Episode 9]

Skizzy—friend of Keith's [Episode 76]

Snake—biker who heads the Rogues, a motorcycle gang, he marries Penny Sweetweather in the Partridge Family's front yard; his real name is either Harry Murphy [Episode 28] or Hayman Timothy Goodrow [Episode 54]

Spindle, Mildred—San Pueblo's meter maid [Episode 47].

Steinman, Gloria—the Partridge Family's original lead singer who gets the mumps, prompting Shirley to join the group; her father is Rabbi Steinman [Episode 1]

Steinman, Rabbi—father of Gloria Steinman [Episode 1]

Stern, Rabbi and Mrs. Ben—neighbors who invite the Partridge Family to perform at Temple Aaron and to share a Shabbat dinner at their home [Episode 93]

Stevens, Donna—next-door neighbor and daughter of Doris Stevens [Episode 75]

Stevens, Doris—next-door neighbor and single mother who tries to prevent the Partridge Family from rehearsing in their garage [Episode 75]

Stevens, Ricky—next-door neighbor and four-year-old son of Doris Stevens; he occasionally sings with the Partridge Family [Episodes 75, 76, 77, 78, 79, 80, 82, 83, 84, and 86]

Stilman, Mr.—neighbor who complains about the Partridges' burglar alarm after it sounds continually [Episode 64]

Sweetweather, Penny—employee at Gilbo's Five & Dime who marries Snake [Episode 54]

Towbin, Mayor Robert—mayor of San Pueblo [Episode 94]

Tribble, Leonard—Danny's friend [Episode 55]

Tubbles, Claude—self-made millionaire who owns three or four hotels, a television station, a chain of restaurants, and several theaters; he never got beyond the sixth grade and holds an honorary Ph.D. he received after building a library on the campus of an unnamed college [Episode 89]

Twitchell, Herbie—one of Danny's classmates [Episode 89]

Vendor, Carl—one of Danny's classmates [Episode 89]

Weedback, Mike—one of Keith's classmates [Episode 88]

Weinstock, Mrs.—a candidate to be driver for Partridge Family bus, she drives over the curb [Episode 37]

Whelander, Dr.—Marineland curator who agrees to let the Partridge Family make a record with the song of the whale [Episode 31]

Williams, Andy and David—singing identical twins discovered by Mr. Kincaid [Episode 88]

Willis, Darby—Danny's Little League baseball coach and Mr. Kincaid's friend [Episode 78]

Wilsons—family with five kids: Billy, Margret, and six-month-old triplets [Episode 93]

Woodloe, Red—folksinger whom the Partridge Family helps overcome stage fright [Episode 14]

Yost, Walter—distinguished American composer who records on the same record label as the Partridge Family and who finds their music delightful [Episode 77]

Young, M.—the person Danny believes is his real father [Episode 24]

Bird Talk

As musicians and teenagers, the Partridges speak a lingo riddled with hip slang unique to the early seventies:

bag—*n* **1:** An appealing object **2:** An act one enjoys performing <That's not my *bag*—Keith Partridge>

bread—*n* **1:** money <It must have cost a lot of *bread*—Mr. Kincaid> **2:** what peanut butter and tuna fish, Danny's favorite, goes between best

bummer—*n* **1:** a bad experience <Wow, what a *bummer*—Danny Partridge>

cool—*adv* **1:** Extremely good <Now that's a *cool* song—Keith Partridge> **cool it**— *v* **1.** to allow passions to cool <All right everybody, *cool* it!—Shirley Partridge>

cop-out—*n* **1.** an excuse for backing out of a responsibility <That sounds like a *cop-out*—Laurie Partridge> **copping out**—*vi* **1:** to back out of a responsibility <I think your brother is *copping out*—Laurie Partridge>

drag —*n* **1:** a bad experience <What a *drag*!—Danny Partridge>

far out—*adj* **1:** exceptional <It's sort of *far out*, but it just might work—Keith Partridge>

groovy — *adj* **1:** terrific <She's really *groovy*—Keith Partridge>

gross—*adj* **1:** repulsive <Ewwww, *gross!*—Tracy Partridge>

heavy—*adj* **1:** intense <That was really *heavy*—Laurie Partridge>

out of sight—*adj* **1:** superlative, incredible <She's really *out of sight*—Keith Partridge>

put-on—*n* **1:** an instance of fooling someone through exaggeration or spoof <Is this a *put-on?*—Keith Partridge>

rap—*v* **1:** to engage in conversation <What do you want to *rap* about?—Danny Partridge>

right on—*adj* **1:** perfectly correct <That's *right on!*—Mr. Kincaid>

rip off—*v* **1:** to steal <Laurie couldn't possibly *rip off* a test—Keith Partridge>

split—*v* 1. to leave the immediate vicinity <I'd like to speak with Mom for a minute. Why don't you *split?*—Keith Partridge>

uptight—*adj* 1. stressed, tense <Don't be so *uptight*—Danny Partridge>

A Visitor's Guide to San Pueblo

The mythical town of San Pueblo, California, is located somewhere near the San Francisco Bay area, though we never learn exactly where. The town has three newspapers: the *San Pueblo Tattler*, which includes a magazine supplement on Sundays called *Today Magazine*, the *San Pueblo Daily*, and an underground newspaper called *Free Life*. Like any town in America, San Pueblo is filled with small businesses, restaurants, churches, and public facilities:

A & B Café—Mr. Kincaid's favorite restaurant [Episode 15]

Al's Used Cars—where the Partridge Family buys a used school bus [Episode 1]

Bank of San Pueblo—next door to the Crescent Bookshop and across the street from the Royal Theater [Episode 59]

Bartlett's Department Store—where Shirley has a charge account and where Byron Atwater is the credit manager with Tom Baker as his assistant in charge of the computer 1984-Z [Episode 70]

Barton's Drug Store—mentioned by Mr. Kincaid [Episode 83]

Big Herm's—an ice-cream stand where you can buy a Big Cherry Freeze [Episode 53]

Boathouse, The—a nightclub where Shirley's parents bring their dates to watch the Partridge Family perform [Episode 56]

Captain Chocolate's Ice Cream Emporium—ice-cream parlor [Episode 60]

Chez Pierre—French restaurant renowned for its chocolate mousse and where Dr. Bernie Applebaum takes Shirley on a date [Episode 63]

Church—where you'll find the Reverend Greg Houser and where the Partridges perform once [Episode 59]

Crescent Bookshop—next door to the Bank of San Pueblo and across the street from the Royal Theater [Episode 59]

Cronos Caverns—caves outside of San Pueblo [Episode 74]

Drive-In Theater—where Keith takes Princess Jennie [Episode 52]

Duncan Street—mentioned [Episode 45]

Elm Street—where psychic Max Ledbetter lives [Episode 49]

Feldman Armored Car Company—business down the block from Mr. Kincaid's favorite restaurant, the A & B Café [Episode 15]

Fleameyer's Garage—where Mr. Kincaid gets his car repaired [Episode 71]

Florist—next door to the Crescent Bookshop and across the street from the Royal Theater [Episode 59]

Hanran's Department Store—where Shirley bought Laurie's first training bra [Episode 47]

Hardware Store—not open on Sundays [Episode 44]

Hotel (unknown name)—where Princess Jennie stays [Episode 52]

KXIU—radio station in San Pueblo [Episode 61]

Lorenzo Bernard School of Art—where Shirley Partridge takes painting lessons [Episode 87]

Maple Street—mentioned by Mr. Kincaid [Episode 24]

Moo Ducks Restaurant—Chinese restaurant from which Mr. Kincaid orders meals delivered for himself and Bonnie Kleinschmitt [Episode 80]

Muldune's Point—town Lover's Lane [Episodes 23, 41, 59, 67, 74, 96]

Murphy's Department Store—where Laurie buys a pocketbook for $6.95 and where Princess Jennie buys one for $5.95 [Episode 52]

Oak Street—where Keith's friend Gordy drives into a hidden stop sign [Episode 26]

Oro Lake—mentioned by Danny [Episode 83]

Phelps' Drugstore—drugstore run by Mr. Phelps, where Danny and Punky Lazaar each shoplift a yo-yo [Episode 71]

Pinaco Peak—where Shirley and Laurie go wilderness camping and where Keith, Danny, and Mr. Kincaid get lost [Episode 45]

Point Loomis Air Force Base—where the Partridge Family performs a concert and backs up Dora Kelly [Episode 26]

Police Station, Third District—where Danny turns himself in to Sergeant Donakovsky and asks to have himself locked up for shoplifting [Episode 71]

Race Track—where racehorse F. Scott Fitzgerald wins a race during the San Pueblo County Fair [Episode 61]

Recording Studio—where the Partridge Family records their first album [Episode 4], "Echo Valley 2-6809" [Episode 27], and "Twenty-Four Hours a Day" [Episode 34], and where Andy and David Williams record their first single, "Say It Again" [Episode 88]

Reuben Kincaid's Office—unknown location [Episodes 15 and 89]

Rothschild Museum of Art—where curator Mr. Hensley and a piece of artwork by Nicholas Minksi Pushkin can be found [Episode 44]

Royal Theater—movie theater run by Sam Greasley; the Partridge Family's movie premieres here as a short before *Gone with the Wind* [Episode 41]; also playing here is *The Billion Dollar Racoon* [Episode 59]

Saffany's Jewelry Store—where Danny buys a $12 brooch for Shirley [Episode 95]

San Pueblo Airport—[Episode 52]

San Pueblo Children's Home—the Partridge Family's favorite charity and where they perform a benefit concert [Episode 74]

San Pueblo College—where Shirley takes a psychology course and where Keith attends college [Episodes 29, 77, and 83]

San Pueblo High School—where Keith and Laurie attend school

San Pueblo Hospital—where Dr. Bernie Applebaum practices pediatrics and where Shirley Partridge gave birth to all five of her children [Episode 63]

Scooby's—malt shop where Keith meets Dina Firmly and his sister Laurie [Episode 76]

Simon Collection Agency—collection agency for Bartlett's Department Store, which repossesses the Partridge Family's furniture [Episode 70]

Student Union Cafeteria—cafeteria on San Pueblo College campus where Keith graciously treats Shirley and Mr. Kincaid to lunch [Episode 77]

Taco Stand—where the kids congregate after school [Episodes 33, 60, 65, 80, 88, 89, and 91]

Temple Aaron—local synagogue led by Rabbi Stern [Episode 93]

Uncle Erwin's Country Chicken— fast-food restaurant chain [Episode 68]

Partridge Family Gigs

The Partridge Family performs concerts at innumerable venues and for events in a variety of cities and locations:

- Caesars Palace in Las Vegas, Nevada [Episode 1]
- An unnamed venue in an unnamed town [Episode 3]
- An unnamed hotel in an unnamed town [Episode 5]
- An unnamed hotel owned by Harry Harrington in Las Vegas, Nevada [Episode 7]
- St. Mark's Hospital, from the operating room, in an unknown city [Episode 8]
- An unnamed venue in an unnamed town [Episode 9]
- Another unnamed venue in an unnamed town [Episode 9]
- An unnamed penitentiary in an unnamed city [Episode 10]
- An unnamed venue in an unnamed town [Episode 11]
- At a Power of Women rally at the band shell in the park in San Pueblo [Episode 12]
- An unnamed venue in an unnamed town [Episode 13]
- An unnamed venue in an unnamed town [Episode 14]
- In a church where folksinger Red Woodloe performs regularly, a two-hour drive from San Pueblo [Episode 14]
- An unnamed venue in Paris, France [Episode 15]
- The Engine House, a nightclub in Detroit, Michigan [Episode 18]
- Town House Quarter in an unnamed town [Episode 19]
- An unnamed venue in Seattle, Washington [Episode 20]
- The Redwood Lodge in Redwood City, California [Episode 23]
- A hotel in a Canadian forest [Episode 24]
- At the Carriage House Hotel in Denver [Episode 25]
- At Loomis Air Force Base [Episode 26]
- An unnamed venue in an unnamed town (most likely San Pueblo) [Episode 32]
- An unnamed venue in an unnamed town (most likely San Pueblo) [Episode 35]
- An unnamed venue in an unnamed town [Episode 39]
- An unnamed venue in an unnamed town [Episode 40]

- Royal Theater in San Pueblo [Episode 41]
- An unnamed venue in an unnamed city [Episode 42]
- An unnamed venue filled with male conventioneers in San Pueblo [Episode 43]
- Yet another unnamed venue in another unnamed town [Episode 44]
- At a Girl Scout pack meeting in the auditorium of the elementary school at San Pueblo [Episode 46]
- An unnamed venue in San Pueblo [Episode 47]
- An unnamed venue in Los Vegas run by a Mr. Manoogie [Episode 48]
- The Papago Indian Fair on the Papago Indian Reservation (approximately forty miles west of Piedmont) [Episode 48]
- An unnamed venue in an unnamed town with psychic Max Ledbetter for an opening act [Episode 49]
- At the bandstand in the park for San Pueblo's 103rd Anniversary Festival [Episode 50]
- At a banquet dinner in Shirley's honor as "Mother of the Year" chosen by *Woman's Journal* magazine [Episode 51]
- An unnamed venue in an unnamed town (most likely San Pueblo) [Episode 53]
- At Snake's wedding in the Partridge Family's front yard [Episode 54]
- An unnamed venue in an unnamed town (most likely San Pueblo) [Episode 55]
- The Boathouse, a nightclub in San Pueblo [Episode 56]
- At a campaign rally for congressional candidate Richard Lawrence at the band shell in the park in San Pueblo [Episode 57]
- A ski lodge in Lake Tahoe [Episode 58]
- A church in San Pueblo [Episode 59]
- An unnamed venue in an unnamed town [Episode 60]
- At the San Pueblo County Fairgrounds [Episode 61]
- An unnamed venue in San Pueblo [Episode 62]
- An unnamed venue in San Pueblo [Episode 63]
- King's Island Amusement Park in Cincinnati, Ohio [Episode 66]
- In front of a swimming pool at an unknown venue in an unnamed town [Episode 67]
- At a convention of Uncle Erwin's Country Chicken franchisees in San Pueblo [Episode 68]
- At an unnamed venue in San Pueblo [Episode 69]
- At an unnamed venue in San Pueblo [Episode 70]
- At an unnamed auditorium to receive the "San Pueblo Citizen of the Year Award" [Episode 71]

- At a school dance at San Pueblo High School [Episode 72]
- At Rose Mansion, home of reclusive and eccentric millionaire Sidney Rose [Episode 73]
- At several unnamed venues in several unnamed towns [Episode 73]
- At a benefit concert for the San Pueblo Children's Home [Episode 74]
- At a public park in San Pueblo [Episode 75]
- An unnamed venue in San Pueblo [Episode 76]
- An unnamed venue in San Pueblo [Episode 77]
- At the Dodgers banquet dinner [Episode 78]
- An unnamed venue in San Pueblo [Episode 79]
- Aboard the T. S. S. *Fairsea*, a cruise ship sailing to Mazatlán, Mexico [Episode 81]
- An unnamed venue in an unnamed town [Episode 84]
- The Westwinds Hotel in an unnamed town [Episode 85]
- An unnamed venue in San Pueblo [Episode 86]
- An unnamed venue in an unnamed town [Episode 89]
- Temple Aaron in San Pueblo [Episode 91]
- At an unnamed venue in another unnamed town [Episode 93]
- At an energy conservation rally in an unnamed auditorium in San Pueblo [Episode 94]
- An unnamed venue in San Pueblo [Episode 96]

Spread a Little Lovin'

True to the lyrics of their theme song, the idealistic Partridge Family do a good deed wherever they go:

■ Danny convinces mobster Harry Harrington to marry LaVon LaVern [Episode 7].
■ The Partridge Family plays a benefit concert at St. Mark's children's hospital, despite the fact that they all smell of skunk [Episode 8].
■ They play a benefit concert at a high security prison [Episode 10].
■ They discover the songwriting talents of a prison inmate and prevent his songs from being stolen by a fellow prisoner [Episode 10].
■ They play a benefit concert at a rally for Power of Women, a feminist group [Episode 12].
■ They help folksinger Red Woodloe overcome stage fright [Episode 14]
■ They organize and perform a benefit concert at a block party in a Detroit ghetto to raise funds for a community nightclub [Episode 18].
■ They help negotiate a settlement between a nightclub owner and his striking college employees [Episode 19].
■ Keith sells his car to take his girlfriend Carol to the high school prom [Episode 21].
■ The Partridge Family takes a runaway teenage girl into their custody and drive her to Albuquerque to reunite her with her father [Episode 22].
■ They discover the talents of songwriter Bobby Conway and drive him to Denver, Colorado, to match him up with lyricist Lionel Poindexter [Episode 25].
■ They make a record featuring the song of a whale and donate the profits to the New York Zoological Society to save the whales [Episode 31].
■ They return $1 million to a hippie girl, despite the fact that she gave it to them of her own free will [Episode 39].
■ When a museum purchases the mural of a naked woman painted on the Partridges' garage, Shirley gives the huge sum of money to the artist, Russian immigrant Nicholas Minski Pushkin ("I've never seen so many zeroes," claims Danny) [Episode 44].
■ The Partridge Family performs a benefit concert for the Papago Indians at the Papago Indian Fair [Episode 48].

■ They invite psychic Max Ledbetter to perform as their opening act so he can earn enough money to make the mortgage payment on his bakery [Episode 49].

■ Shirley intervenes to convince Penny Sweetweather to marry biker Snake, and the Partridge Family hosts the wedding in their front yard with Chris as the ring bearer, Tracy as the flower girl, Danny as best man, and Laurie playing "Here Comes the Bride" on the electric organ [Episode 54].

■ The Partridge Family performs for free at a campaign rally for congressional candidate Richard Lawrence at the band shell in the park in San Pueblo [Episode 57].

■ They convince escaped convict Morris Dinkler to turn himself in to the police, and then they promise to serve as character witnesses at his trial [Episode 64].

■ Laurie organizes a protest against Bartlett's Department Store for putting computers before people [Episode 70].

■ Danny returns a yo-yo he shoplifted from Phelps' Drugstore and apologizes to Mr. Phelps [Episode 71].

■ Keith endorses his opponent, Phyllis Goldberg, as the better candidate in the election for student class president of San Pueblo High School [Episode 72].

■ The Partridge Family teaches reclusive millionaire Sidney Rose to face the world [Episode 73].

■ They try to hide from mystery writer Michelangelo Rezo for twenty-four hours in order to win $25,000 for their favorite charity, the San Pueblo Children's Home, where they play a benefit concert [Episode 74].

■ They try to make peace with their new next-door neighbor, Doris Stevens, by inviting her four-year-old son, Ricky, to perform with them [Episode 75].

■ They throw a surprise birthday party for Mr. Kincaid [Episode 79].

■ They encourage Mr. Kincaid's nephew, Alan Kincaid, to perform as a standup comedian as their warm-up act, launching his career as a comic [Episode 85].

■ They let Mr. Kincaid's new act, singing identical twins Andy and David Williams, stay at their home until the brothers finish their first recording session [Episode 88].

■ They spread love and understanding by performing at a synagogue and then have Shabbat dinner with the rabbi and his family [Episode 91].

■ They volunteer to serve as a model family by cutting down their electricity consumption by ten percent and performing at an energy conservation rally [Episode 94].

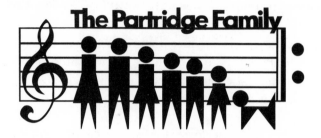

How Did the Partridge Family Influence Your Music?

"I was more into *The Monkees*, and when *The Partridge Family* was on, I thought to be in a group with your mother would be a nightmare. The reason I still watched *The Partridge Family* was because I did have a minor crush on Susan Dey. But I never thought the show compared to *The Monkees* which was much hipper."

—Stephen Bishop

"I just couldn't understand how I was a product of my parents because they weren't artistic like I was. I liked music and they didn't. Subconsciously maybe I thought I was adopted—ever since that episode of *The Partridge Family* when Danny thought he was adopted [Episode 11]. I really related to that."

—Kurt Cobain of Nirvana
in *Come As You Are* by Michael Azerrad

"It scared me to death when the Partridge Family got that new kid to be their drummer. It made me practice the accordion especially hard, because I suddenly realized . . . I could be *replaced*."

—"Weird Al" Yankovic

"Phil is sorry he's unable to help you as the Partridge Family didn't do anything to influence him!"

—Annie Callingham
production assistant to Phil Collins

"Chrissie Hynde never saw *The Partridge Family* TV series and therefore felt unable to contribute to a book about them."

—Norma Bishop
Gailforce Management Limited

FINE FETID FRIENDS DEPT.

Every now and then, a TV Situation Comedy Series comes along that captures the hearts and imagination of the country by depicting contemporary American life as it really is! Like the comedy series about a bus . . . and the wonderfully real and believable people who depend upon it for a living. Naturally, we're talking about "The Honeymooners." However, if you want a show about a bus . . . and some unbelievably unreal kids singing off-key, try watching:

The Putrid Family

> Will somebody take over the wheel? I'm **exhausted!**

> I'd **like** to help out, Mom, but I'm **too young** to drive!

> And **I'm too** young to drive!

> And **I'm too** young to drive!

> And **I'm too** young to drive!

> And I'm **too** pretty to drive!

ARTIST: ANGELO TORRES   WRITER: ARNIE KOGEN

> Teeth Putrid! Are you inferring that you're prettier than I am?

> Not only is he **prettier!** He's **richer!**

> I'm not vain, Mom! It's just that we have a **concert** to do, and if I drive, the wind will blow my **hair** in the **wrong direction!**

> How about in the direction of **over your face?!** That would be an **improvement!**

> **Watch** that **smart stuff,** Subby! The way we replaced **last year's kid,** we can get someone to replace **you!**

> That's how we open each show, folks!

> We'd better dazzle 'em with **SOMETHING,** considering there's never any **plot!** What's our little crisis going to be **tonight,** anyway?

> We **dazzle** 'em with our **banter!**

> Don't sweat it! Something is **bound** to turn up!

4

I Woke Up in Love This Morning

I Woke Up in Love This Morning

*Last night, I turned out the lights, laid down,
and thought about you.
I thought about the way that it could be.
Two o'clock, wondering what I'm doing here
alone without you.
So I closed my eyes and dreamed you here with me.
I woke up in love this morning.
I woke up in love this morning.
Went to sleep with you on my mind.*

*Hello girl, yes, it's five o'clock I know, but you just listen.
There's something that I've got to let you know.
This is you, this pillow that I'm hugging and I'm kissing.
And one more thing before I let you go.
I woke up in love this morning.
I woke up in love this morning.
Went to sleep with you on my mind.*

*Do dreams come true?
Well, if they do I'll have you.
Not just for a night but for my whole life through.
I woke up in love this morning.
I woke up in love this morning.
Went to sleep with you on my mind.*

Irwin Levine-L. Russell Brown • ©1971 Screen Gems-EMI Music Inc.

Rock musicians are generally an expressive lot both musically and philosophically. The Partridge Family left an indelible mark on America's collective consciousness not simply because their music forever altered the face of rock 'n' roll, but because each member of that remarkable family shared his or her own unique perspective and provocative insights with millions of Americans.

Each episode of that innovative television series offers a twenty-three-minute glimpse into the minds of the Partridges themselves. Their candid wit and wisdom remains unmatched. The deep thoughts expressed by Shirley, Keith, Laurie, Danny, Chris, Tracy, and Mr. Kincaid that follow have been categorized so future generations can study and cherish the penetrating witticisms that helped make the Partridge Family an unparalleled phenomenon.

Partridge Family Values

Adventure

Mr. Kincaid: Danny, if you'd like to go the beach with me, I'll let you swim in the riptide.
Danny: Riptides are dangerous.
Mr. Kincaid: Aw, who told you that?

Age

Danny: I've been a kid, and I've been an adult. And believe me, adultery isn't what it's cracked up to be.

Assistance

Danny: I need help.
Keith: We know that. But Mom won't let us have you committed.

Autobiographies

Mr. Kincaid: You can read about it when I write my memoirs, *The Thrilling Adventures of Reuben Kincaid.*
Laurie: It will be a thin book.

Bachelor Life

Shirley: Reuben, why is it you always manage to drop in when I bake an apple pie?
Tracy: He gives me a dime to tell him.

Mr. Kincaid: I hate to not-eat-and-run, but I have to go.

Bad Seed

Danny: I guess every family has to have a black sheep. I always thought ours was Keith.

Birthdays

Keith: Has anybody got any ideas about what they're going to do for Mom's birthday?

Laurie: I thought about offering to do all the cooking for a month. How about you?

Keith: I'll buy the family a stomach pump.

Campus Radicals

Danny: I wonder if your going to college is such a good idea.

Shirley: I don't think a little psychology course is going to take up that much time.

Danny: Well, campuses are a hotbed of radicals. I'm afraid you're going to get mixed up in some kind of protest march.

Laurie: I though you had to be over 30 to be that establishment.

Keith: Maybe it's inches instead of years.

Censorship

Keith: Nobody—*nobody*—censors our material. Censorship is not the path to equal rights.

Childhood

Danny: It's not normal for kids to be quiet. I might end up maladjusted.

Companionship

Shirley: Whatever gave you the idea you could operate your own Lonely Hearts Club?

Danny: I didn't think I was doing anything wrong. What you said is "Reuben needs a wife."

Mr. Kincaid: I need a what?!?

Tracy: I told them to get you a goldfish, but they wouldn't listen.

Courtesy

Laurie: Keith, don't you ever knock before coming into a person's room?
Keith: You're not a person, you're my sister.

Creativity

Keith: Look, I just want to play music the best way I know how. Now is that wrong?

Critics

Shirley: I keep seeing the headline in *Variety*: "Partridges Lay an Egg."

Crushes

Shirley: Kids your age tend to fall in love very easily, sometimes even give up other relationships for what they think is love. Now I know you think you're in love with Laurie, but love at your age can pass just as quickly as it came, and your relationship as brothers is too much to give up for what could be a passing crush. What I'm trying to say is: What you think now will last forever, probably won't, and what you're sacrificing will. You have no idea what I'm trying to say, do you?

Daredevils

Keith: You know, I wish you'd read the story of Evel Knievel.
Danny: Why's that?
Keith: Well, then maybe you might go take a flying leap.

Dating

Shirley: There's no sense in waiting up. Laurie's in good hands.
Danny: That's what I'm afraid of.

Keith: I wouldn't worry about him. He's an archeologist. He can always dig up a girl.

Keith: This date is an opportunity.
Danny: I thought you considered every date an opportunity.

Deception

Danny: (to Keith) That's the meanest, rottenest, dirtiest trick anyone can play on his sister. No wonder you're my idol.

Democracy

Tracy: It's not fair. I yelled dibbies on the bed.

Laurie: Tracy has a point, Mom. Seems to me that we should all get a chance to vote. After all, this is a democracy.

Shirley: Well, I certainly don't want to be undemocratic. So, I vote for the bed, and since you two are too young to vote, I win.

Encouragement

Mr. Kincaid: Danny, if you're ever thinking of running away from home, do it.

Fame

Laurie: When you're well known, it's an opportunity to set a good example.

Shirley: In fact, it's an obligation.

Fault

Keith: This whole thing is your fault! You and your dumb ideas!

Danny: Anyone can come up with a dumb idea, but it takes a real numbskull to listen to it.

First Amendment

Mr. Kincaid: Free speech is great, until it's someone else speaking.

Friends

Laurie: Are you saying my friends are ding-a-lings?
Keith: Not all of them. Only the ones I've met.

Fringe Benefits

Shirley: Well, kids, how do you like performing in an amusement park?
Danny: Great! But it would be even perfect if cotton candy was deductible.

Games

Chris: C'mon, let's play a game, Mr. Kincaid.
Tracy: Yeah, let's play a game.
Mr. Kincaid: Okay, okay. Let's play a game called "Lost."
Danny: How do you play?
Mr. Kincaid: Well, I'll hide my eyes and you three kids run away from home—far and fast—and keep running until you're lost.
Tracy: Then what?
Mr. Kincaid: In three weeks, I'll come look for you. If I find you, I lose.
Tracy: What if you don't find us?
Mr. Kincaid: Well, then I win.

Good Fortune

Keith: I think we're lucky. I mean, we do work hard, but let's face it, there are worse ways of making money.

Harmony

Danny: In case you haven't heard, there are two words that are never used in the Partridge Family vocabulary: brotherly love.
Laurie: However, there are two words more commonly used.
Danny: Yes?
Keith: Get even.

Heights

Keith: If man was supposed to sing in high places, he would have been born a soprano.

Housework

Shirley: I think it's wonderful the way this whole family pitches in to help.
Keith: You know, Mom, if you weren't always busy cleaning the house, you wouldn't be so tired.

Independence

Shirley: Honey, I'm curious about something. It's purely hypothetical, of course. But suppose a boy were very interested in you when you weren't interested in him. How do you . . .

Laurie: Get rid of Bernie?

Shirley: Well, it has been a while since I've done that kind of thing.

Laurie: Well, you could start off by mentioning that you two have absolutely nothing in common.

Shirley: That's right. We don't.

Laurie: Then you can tell him that you're a very independent woman. You know, a loner.

Shirley: A loner? With five kids?

Laurie: Those are my two best ones, Mom.

Insults

Mr. Kincaid: Shirley, trust me.
Danny: That's asking too much.

Laurie: I have got the greatest news!
Keith: You're taking your own apartment?

Danny: You know, we think a lot alike.
Mr. Kincaid: I know. And sometimes it scares me.

Tracy: I like you, Mr. Kincaid.
Mr. Kincaid: Thanks.
Danny: She hasn't developed a lot of taste yet.

Mr. Kincaid: Good day.
Danny: It was until now.

Mr. Kincaid: You know, Shirley, I was thinking . . .
Danny: In Mr. Kincaid's case, that can be dangerous.

I Woke Up in Love This Morning 131

International Law

Mr. Kincaid: If you are big enough to get away with it, it's right. That's international law.

Keith Partridge

Danny: That's our Keith. Talented, handsome, and wishy-washy.

Lawyers

Danny: So as an attorney, what do you think of Perry Mason?

Loneliness

Shirley: Let me explain something to you. I'm your mother, and in that way I'll always belong to all of you. But I'm also a woman. And even with five children whom I love very, very much, and who I know love me, there are times when I still feel lonely.

Love

Danny: All's fair in love and Parcheesi.

Laurie: Well, to me love is total. It's a direct communication between two people. The key word is honesty.
Keith: Right. When you love someone you know you can trust them. That's another big part of it. Trust.
Laurie: Yes, but you have to earn that. You just can't take it.
Keith: Sure you can. Haven't you ever heard of stolen kisses?

Male Chauvinist Pigs

Laurie: (To Keith) If men like you had their own country, Hugh Hefner would be king.

Marriage

Laurie: Every daughter wants her mother to marry a doctor.

Maturity

Mr. Kincaid: How old is Danny?
Tracy: Ten. Why?
Mr. Kincaid: I keep getting this funny feeling that I'm dealing with a 40-year-old midget.

Memory

Danny: A Partridge never forgets.

Danny: I have a photographic mind.
Laurie: Sure you do, except you always forget to put the film in.

Military Intelligence

Mr. Kincaid: The army hasn't admitted making a mistake since 1952.
Danny: What happened in 1952?
Mr. Kincaid: They drafted me.

Modesty

Danny: Don't you think one genius in the family is enough?
Keith: Who might that be?
Danny: Modesty prevents me from stating the obvious.
Shirley: Danny . . .
Danny: Well, at least I know my limitations. All I want to be is Howard Hughes.
Keith: Then why don't you disappear?
Danny: I refuse to get into a battle of wits with an unarmed man.

Money

Shirley: Danny wanted an advance on his allowance.
Mr. Kincaid: What's so strange about that?
Shirley: A six-year advance?

Navigation

Chris: Here's my compass. It doesn't work though. It always points in the same direction.

New Math

Tracy: If six ducks are on a pond and three more ducks land on the pond, what would you have?

Danny: Several hundred duck hunters.

Nonviolence

Keith: I'm not going to fight you, Goose. I'll fight you for something I believe in, but I'm not going to fight you just because your ego's hurt. It's just not a good enough reason.

Optimism

Mr. Kincaid: You know, we'll laugh about this in five or ten years—whenever we get out of prison.

Parenthood

Keith: I'm beginning to realize that responsibilities are something you have to assume gradually.

Shirley: Well, you are a little young to be raising four kids.

Keith: I'm old enough to handle them all right. It's just that it doesn't leave enough time to do my homework.

Privacy

Laurie: When are you going to learn to respect Keith's privacy?

Danny: As soon as he gets a window shade.

Psychology

Laurie: You know, there's one good thing about being paranoid: You're always the center of attention.

Rejection

Danny: Look, Keith, you've got to help me.

Keith: No, I don't.

Danny: All I need is a little advice.

Keith: About what?

Danny: About how to get rid of a woman that's crazy about you.

Keith: All right. You might start by revealing some of your bad points, which shouldn't be too difficult. Discourage her.

Danny: It wouldn't work. She'd know I was lying.

Keith: One thing's for sure: she's not hooked on your humility.

Responsibility

Shirley: I appreciate your volunteering to take the kids to the beach, but it just doesn't sound like you.

Keith: I've been thinking, since I am the eldest male, I have a lot of influence on them. Besides I'm old enough to accept my responsibilities and give them the kind of leadership they need.

Mr. Kincaid: Keith, have you been talking to a Marine recruiter?

Risk

Danny: Keith, we can't gamble with our family. They're worth a lot more than $156. Even Tracy.

Rules

Mr. Kincaid: Tell me, did your mother ever tell you not to play in traffic?

Danny: Of course.

Mr. Kincaid: Too bad.

Self-improvement

Keith: I think the whole thing taught me a lesson.

Shirley: What's that?

Keith: I don't know yet. But there must be a lesson in there somewhere for all this suffering.

Sex

Mr. Kincaid: Danny, if there's anything you want to know about handling women, you want to get it from a real pro. You know who to ask.

Danny: Yeah, but I already asked Keith. He was no help.

Mr. Kincaid: I was talking about myself.

Danny: Mr. Kincaid, I know you're trying to make me feel better by making me laugh. Bless you.

Sex Education

Mr. Kincaid: I just can't believe it! Keith Partridge flunking sex education! Well, he and I finally share something in common.

Shirley: Reuben, they didn't teach sex education when you went to high school.

Mr. Kincaid: Yeah, I know. But I flunked it anyway.

Show Business

Mr. Kincaid: Kincaid's Law: A dry client equals a broke manager.

Success

Keith: Look, you don't want to be mother to a bunch of illiterate bums, do you?

Danny: He's right, Mom. Do you want Chris to pump gas all his life and Tracy to wait on tables in some sleazy strip joint while I work as a garbage collector just because you were chicken?

Tonsillectomies

Mr. Kincaid: There is a good side to Danny getting his tonsils taken out.

Shirley: Oh?

Mr. Kincaid: He may not be able to talk for days.

Trouble

Laurie: Mom, if I get into any trouble I can always run for help. I don't need Keith to do it for me.

Trust

Mr. Kincaid: You have my word as a gentleman.

Danny: Thanks, but I'd rather have someone watching you.

Vanity

Shirley: Danny, there's more to life than taking bows.

Danny: Not when you're an egomaniac with grease paint in your blood.

Voyeurism

Danny: I've spied on Keith on lots of dates. Don't bother.

Wealth

Keith: Now that you've got a million dollars, what's the first thing you're going to do?

Danny: Gloat.

Keith: Besides that.

Danny: Invest it.

Keith: I think the first thing I'm going to do is charter a boat and sail to the Caribbean.

Danny: Great. I'll rent it to you.

Chris: Why don't you buy a boat, Keith?

Danny: Because I bought it first.

Keith: What are you going to do, Chris?

Chris: Buy a catcher's mitt.

Keith: No wonder you're so short. You think small.

Chris: But then I'm going to buy the Los Angeles Dodgers.

Danny: I'm not selling.

Wisdom

Danny: (to Chris and Tracy) You'll understand when you're my age, although I'm my age and I don't understand.

Work Ethic

Laurie: I guess when you get something for nothing, you just don't appreciate it as much as when you have to work for it yourself.

The Shirley Partridge Philosophy

"'Tis better to have loved and lost than never to have loved at all."
—Alfred Lord Tennyson

"Sometime or another, everyone has to face losing. I know it's hard, but it isn't the end of the world. I mean, after all, if people didn't lose sometime, I guess winning wouldn't mean very much."
—Shirley Partridge

"We are apt to shut our eyes against a painful truth, and listen to the song of that siren till she transforms us into beasts."
—Patrick Henry

"You shouldn't be afraid to tell me the truth, even if it does hurt a little."
—Shirley Partridge

"It is a consolation to the wretched to have companions in misery."
—Pubilius Syrus

"Too bad it took an energy crisis for us to realize how much fun it is just to sit around together."
—Shirley Partridge

"Knowledge is power."
—Francis Bacon

"You won't learn anything unless you do your own homework."
—Shirley Partridge

"If you're not part of the solution, you're part of the problem."
—H. Rap Brown

"Instead of sitting here complaining about the way things are, why don't you do something about it?"
—Shirley Partridge

"Those who cannot remember the past are condemned to repeat it."
—George Santayana

"Saying you're sorry doesn't always erase the thing you do."
—Shirley Partridge

"A truth that's told with bad intent / Beats all the lies you can invent."
—William Blake

"Sometimes the truth can be misused. The important thing is that you care about people."
—Shirley Partridge

"Gossip is mischievous, light and easy to raise, but grievous to bear and hard to dismiss."
—Hesiod

"You can't believe rumors."
—Shirley Partridge

"If one advances confidently in the direction of his dreams, and endeavors to live the life which he has imagined, he will meet with a success unexpected in common hours."
—Henry David Thoreau

"Most things in life that people want aren't just handed to them. If you really want something, you have to keep trying."
—Shirley Partridge

"Pains of love be sweeter far than all other pleasures are."
—John Dryden

"As you get older, you'll find out that most of the time, love doesn't work out the way you want it to, and it does hurt."
—Shirley Partridge

"Man is a prisoner who has no right to open the door of his prison and run away."
—Plato

"I can't imagine what it's like to be a convict, but I think in some real way, we're all prisoners."
—Shirley Partridge

"A man of genius makes no mistakes. His errors are volitional and are the portals of discovery."

—James Joyce

"You can't give up just because you've made mistakes. You can do anything you want to do as long as you're willing to keep trying and not afraid of making more mistakes. Almost everything we know is learned by trial and error."

—Shirley Partridge

"I see the cure is not worth the pain."

—Plutarch

"Sometimes when you try not to hurt someone, you end up hurting yourself more."

—Shirley Partridge

"It is not the strength but the duration of great sentiments that makes great men."

—Friedrich Nietzsche

"You can't put a price on sentiment."

—Shirley Partridge

"Unthread the rude eye of rebellion,
And welcome home again discarded faith."

—William Shakespeare

"If you force a child to stay at home, it's only going to make him want to run away more."

—Shirley Partridge

"If you are lucky enough to have lived in Paris as a young man, then wherever you go for the rest of your life, it stays with you, for Paris is a moveable feast."

—Ernest Hemingway

"[Paris is] kind of a Disneyland for grownups."

—Shirley Partridge

"Justice is my being allowed to do whatever I like. Injustice is whatever prevents my doing so."

—Samuel Johnson

"It's never too late for justice."

—Shirley Partridge

"Laws are like cobwebs, which may catch small flies, but let wasps and hornets break through."
—Jonathan Swift

"There's no sense in calling the police or running away. That never solves anything."
—Shirley Partridge

"We find it as difficult to forgive a person for displaying his feeling in all its nakedness as we do to forgive a man for being penniless."
—Honoré de Balzac

"You can forgive anyone who acts out of love."
—Shirley Partridge

"Nonviolence is the first article of my faith. It is also the last article of my creed."
—Mahatma Gandhi

"Maybe threats are your solution to a problem, but they're not mine. I haven't decided what I'm going to do yet, but I will not allow you to intimidate my family. Is that clear?"
—Shirley Partridge

"It's a kind of spiritual snobbery that makes people think they can be happy without money."
—Albert Camus

"There's nothing wrong with money, if you work for it. It's a symbol for your labor so you can respect it and appreciate it. But if it's given to you, it isn't the same. It isn't really yours."
—Shirley Partridge

"If anything is sacred the human body is sacred."
—Walt Whitman

"The human body is beautiful. There's nothing wrong with it . . . but it doesn't belong on a garage."
—Shirley Partridge

"If youth is a defect, it is one that we outgrow too soon."
—Robert Lowell

"It may sound corny, but some people think that being a kid is the best time of your life. Most kids never realize that."
—Shirley Partridge

The Partridge Family

5

Point Me in the Direction of Albuquerque

Point Me in the Direction of Albuquerque

Window walkin' downtown, feelin' mighty good,
And I noticed from the corner how all alone she stood,
Underneath a lamplight, an angel in disguise,
Lonely little runaway with tear drops in her eyes.
Crazy little rag doll, her hair was wild and tossed,
I put my arm around her 'cause I knew that she was lost.
She didn't seem to notice that anyone was near.
'Til suddenly she turned to me and whispered in my ear:
Point me in the direction of Albuquerque.
I want to go home, and help me get home.
Point me in the direction of Albuquerque.
I need to get home, need to get home.

Showed me a ticket for a Greyhound bus.
Her head was lost in time.
She didn't know who or where she was.
And anyone that helps me is a real good friend of mine.
Point me in the direction of Albuquerque.
And help me get home, help me get home.

Walked her to the station and kissed away the tears,
Knowing I'd remember through all the coming years,
Rag doll on the Greyhound who waved with all her might,
And weeped against the window as the bus drove out of sight.
Point me in the direction of Albuquerque.
I want to go home, and help me get home.
Point me in the direction of Albuquerque.
I need to get home, need to get home.

The Shows

FIRST SEASON

Aside from their psychedelic bus, the Partridge Family also has a blue station wagon. The opening theme song to the series is "When We're Singing," music by Wes Farrell, lyrics by Dianne Hilderbrand.

KEY

Out of sight
Right on
Groovy
Bummer

1: What? And Get Out of Show Business?

After recently widowed Shirley Partridge joins her kids' rock band to record a song in the garage, ten-year-old Danny compels manager Reuben Kincaid to listen to the recording by slipping a tape deck under a restroom stall. After Shirley agrees to sign the contract in order to put the kids through college, the family buys a used school bus, paints it in psychedelic colors, gets matching maroon crushed-velvet costumes, and drives to Caesars Palace in Las Vegas for their first gig, where the kids all get stage fright.

Writer: Bernard Slade
Director: Jerry Paris
Cast: William Wintersole as Club Manager, Debra Pearce as Gloria Steinman, Gordon Jump as Man, Gail Cabot as Woman, Hal Taggert as Desk Clerk, Felton Perry as Airport Clerk

SONGS:
- "Let the Good Times In," music and lyrics by Carole Bayer and Neil Sedaka
- "Together," music by Shorty Rogers, lyrics by Kelly Gordon

NOTES:
- Commented *Daily Variety* of September 28, 1970: "'It's all so phony and commercial,' bleats Susan Dey as the Partridge Family's kaleidoscope-colored school bus rolls through Hollywood in the first scene of the opening seg[ment]. It will do for a capsule description of the whole show."
- Commented *Variety* of September 30, 1970: "Miss Jones does what she can to generate the proper flippant approach of a struggling mother thrown into the rock music world, and young Bonaduce reads his grown-up lines like a young pro, but beyond that, credulity is strained. Madden overplays unmercifully, only Miss Jones and David Cassidy look like they're singing their own roles, the songs were nondescript bubblegum tunes with no believable hit potential, and there are just too many loopholes. Even the teenage girls who buy records will see through the flimsy premise that the Partridge kids could make it in today's record market. Show's chances look slim."
- The lip-syncing in this episode is noticeably off cue.
- The layout of the Partridge Family house is completely backward compared with subsequent episodes.
- Director Jerry Paris is best known as Jerry Helper on *The Dick Van Dyke Show*. He also played Artie on *Those Whiting Girls*, Major "Willie" Williston on *Steve Canyon*, Agent Martin Flaherty on *The Untouchables*, and Tim Rourke on *Michael Shayne*. He appeared on *The Millionaire*, *The Bob Cummings Show*, *77 Sunset Strip*, *The Lloyd Bridges Show*, *Death Valley Days*, and *Love, American Style*. He also directed episodes of *The Dick Van Dyke Show*, *The Mary Tyler Moore Show*, *Happy Days*, and *Mork & Mindy* and the television movies *But I Don't Want to Get Married!* (1970), *The Feminist and the Fuzz* (1970), *What's a Nice Girl Like You . . . ?* (1971), *Two on a Bench* (1971), *The Couple Takes a Wife* (1972), and *Every Man Needs One* (1972).
- William Wintersole played George Bailey on the television western *Sara*. He played Dr. Kessler in Episode 16 of *The Partridge Family*.
- Gordon Jump starred as Mr. Carlson on *WKRP in Cincinnati* and plays the Maytag repairman in television commercials. He has appeared on *Get Smart*, *Mannix*, *The Brady Bunch*, *Love, American Style*, *The Mary Tyler Moore Show*, *That's My Mama*, *Harry-O*, *The Streets of San Francisco*, *Alice*, *Good Times*, *The Love Boat*, *Growing Pains*, *The Golden Girls*, *Simon & Simon*, and *Murder, She Wrote*. He played Albertson in Episode 34, a policeman in

Episode 47, a minister in Episode 56, a father in Episode 62, Zack Feldman in Episode 78, and Man #2 on Episode 87 of *The Partridge Family*.
■ Felton Perry played Jimmy on *Matt Lincoln*.

2: The Sound of Money

When Shirley accidentally bumps into motorist Willie Larkin while driving in the Partridge Family bus, Larkin tries to sue for whiplash—until the Partridges move into his home to nurse him back to health.
Writer: Martin Ragaway
Director: Peter Baldwin
Cast: Harry Morgan as Willie Larkin, Farrah Fawcett as Pretty Girl, Kelly Britt as Doris, Ivan Bonar as Leroy Lowenfeld
SONG:
■ "I'll Leave Myself a Little Time," music and lyrics by Steve Dossick (on *Up to Date*)

NOTES:

■ Harry Morgan is best known as Colonel Sherman Potter on *M*A*S*H*, Detective Bill Gannon on *Dragnet*, and Pete Porter on *December Bride* and *Pete and Gladys*. He appeared in dozens of films, most notably *To the Shores of Tripoli* (1942), *The Ox-Bow Incident* (1943), *From This Day Forward* (1946), *The Big Clock* (1948), *Madame Bovary* (1949), *Dark City* (1950), *High Noon* (1952), *The Glenn Miller Story* (1954), *Inherit the Wind* (1960), *How the West Was Won* (1962), *Frankie and Johnny* (1966), *The Barefoot Executive* (1971), *Snowball Express* (1972), *The Apple Dumpling Gang* (1975), *The Apple Dumpling Gang Rides Again* (1979), and *Dragnet* (1987). On television, he made guest appearances on *Alfred Hitchcock Presents*, *The Untouchables*, *Have Gun, Will Travel*, *The Virginian*, *The Wackiest Ship in the Army*, *Dr. Kildare*, *Love, American Style*, *Gunsmoke*, *Night Gallery*, *The Love Boat*, and *Murder, She Wrote*. He appeared as Cal Courtney in Episode 48 of *The Partridge Family*.

■ Farrah Fawcett played Jill Munroe for one season on *Charlie's Angels* and was a sex symbol of the 1970s. Her motion pictures include *Love Is a Funny Thing* (1969), *Myra Breckinridge* (1970), *Logan's Run* (1976), *Somebody Killed Her Husband* (1978), *Sunburn* (1979), and *Saturn 3* (1979). On television, she has appeared on *I Dream of Jeannie*, *The Flying Nun*, *The Girl with Something Extra*, *McCloud*, *Marcus Welby, M.D.*, *Harry-O*, and *The Arsenio Hall Show*. Her television movies include *The Feminist and the Fuzz* (1971), *The Great American Beauty Contest* (1973), *The Girl Who Came Gift-Wrapped* (1974), *Murder on Flight 502* (1975), *Murder in Texas* (1981), *Between Two Women* (1986), *Poor Little Rich Girl* (1987), *Margaret Bourke-White* (1989), and *Small Sacrifices* (1989).

3: Whatever Happened to the Old Songs?

Shirley's father decides to leave her mother and join the Partridge Family as a mandolin player.

Writer: Bernard Slade
Director: Jerry Bernstein
Cast: Ray Bolger as Grandpa Fred Renfrew, Rosemary DeCamp as Grandma Amanda Renfrew

SONGS:

■ "Baby I Love Love I Love You," music and lyrics by Derek Lawrence, Tony Wilson, and Errol Brown

- "Together," music by Shorty Rogers, lyrics by Kelly Gordon
- "Bye Bye Blackbird," music and lyrics by R. Hendersen and M. Dixon, vocal by Grandpa Fred Renfrew

NOTES:

- Ray Bolger is best remembered as the Scarecrow in *The Wizard of Oz* (1939). He started in vaudeville as a dancing partner in "Sanford and Bolger, a Pair of Nifties," then appeared on Broadway in *George White's Scandals*, *Life Begins at 8:40*, and *On Your Toes*. His movies included *The Great Ziegfeld* (1936), *Rosalie* (1937), *Sweethearts* (1938), *Sunny* (1941), *Four Jacks and a Jill* (1941), *Stage Door Canteen* (1943), *The Harvey Girls* (1946), *Make Mine Laughs* (1949), *Look for the Silver Lining* (1949), *Where's Charley?* (1952), *April in Paris* (1953), *Babes in Toyland* (1961), *The Daydreamer* (1966), and *The Runner Stumbles* (1979). On television, Bolger starred as Raymond Wallace on *The Ray Bolger Show (Where's Raymond?)* and appeared on dozens of shows, including *The Perry Como Show*, *Christophers*, *The Dinah Shore Chevy Show*, *I've Got a Secret*, *Pontiac Star Parade*, *G.E. Theatre*, *The Bell Telephone Hour*, *What's My Line?*, *Walt Disney's Wonderful World of Color*, *The Red Skelton Hour*, *Perry Como's Kraft Music Hall*, *The Judy Garland Show*, *Password*, *Nanny and the Professor*, *The Mike Douglas Show*, *Little House on the Prairie*, *The Love Boat*, *Diff'rent Strokes*, and the television movie *The Entertainer* (1976). He also appeared as Grandpa in Episodes 35 and 56 of *The Partridge Family*.
- Rosemary DeCamp starred as Peg Riley on *The Life of Riley*, Margaret MacDonald on *The Bob Cummings Show*, and Helen Marie on *That Girl*. Her films include *Yankee Doodle Dandy* (1942), *This Is the Army* (1943), *Rhapsody in Blue* (1945), *Pride of the Marines (1945)*, *From This Day Forward*

(1946), *Look for the Silver Lining* (1949), *On Moonlight Bay* (1951), *By the Light of the Silvery Moon* (1953), and *Many Rivers to Cross* (1955). She also made guest appearances on *Ford Theatre, Calvalcade Theatre, TV Reader's Digest, Studio One, G.E. Theatre, The Red Skelton Show, 87th Precinct, Follow the Sun, Rawhide, Hazel, Ensign O'Toole, The Beverly Hillbillies, Dr. Kildare, Amos Burke, Secret Agent, Death Valley Days, Love, American Style, Mannix, Night Gallery, Longstreet, Marcus Welby, M.D., The Rockford Files, B.J. and the Bear, Quincy,* and *St. Elsewhere.* She also appeared as Grandma in Episodes 35, 56, and 86 of *The Partridge Family.*

4: See Here, Private Partridge 🐦🐦🐦🐦

While the Partridge Family records their first album, Danny receives an army draft notice, and when Shirley fails to get the army to correct the matter, Danny fails the examination—because he doesn't meet the height requirement.

Writers: Lloyd Turner and Gordon Mitchell
Director: Claudio Guzman
Cast: Jonathan Daly as Officer Moody, Laurence Haddon as Sgt. Sizemore, Jack Riley as Corporal Wrzesinkski, Jared Martin as Recording Engineer, Ted Scott as Eye Doctor

SONG:

■ "I'm on the Road," music and lyrics by Barry Mann and Cynthia Weil (on *Family Album*)

NOTES:

■ The Partridge Family's first album, according to this episode, has an illustration of a partridge on the back cover.

■ Jonathan Daly played Peter Howard on *The Jimmy Stewart Show* and Lt. Whipple on *C.P.O. Sharkey*, starring Don Rickles. He played Tommy Phillips in Episode 16 of *The Partridge Family.*

■ Laurence Haddon played the Foreign Editor on *Lou Grant*. He played Coach Dawson in Episode 32 of *The Partridge Family.*

■ Jack Riley played Elliot Carlin on *The Bob Newhart Show*. He was also a regular on *Occasional Wife, The Tim Conway Show*, and *Roxie*. He made guest appearances on *Gomer Pyle, U.S.M.C., Rowan & Martin's Laugh-In, Hogan's Heroes, The Mary Tyler Moore Show, M*A*S*H, Columbo, Happy Days, Barnaby Jones, Barney Miller, Alice, The Rockford Files, Diff'rent Strokes, Family Ties, One Day at a Time, Night Court,* and *The Love Boat*. He is a major voice-over talent for commercials.

■ Jared Martin starred as Varian on *Fantastic Journey* and played Dusty

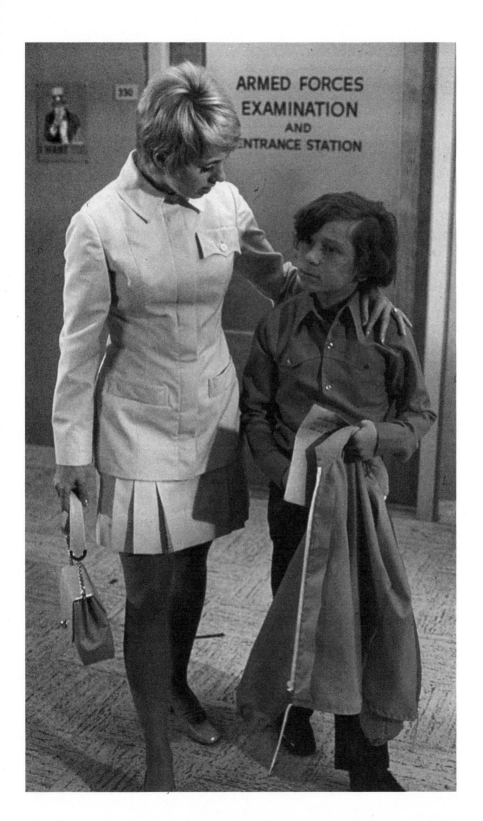

Farlow on *Dallas*. He also appeared on *The Bold Ones, The Rookies, Columbo, Shaft, Switch, CHiPs, The Love Boat, Knight Rider, Murder, She Wrote, Scarecrow and Mrs. King, Hotel, Hunter,* and *The New Mike Hammer*.

5: When Mother Gets Married

When Shirley dates an old flame, engineer Larry Metcalf, her children discover Metcalf buying a diamond ring for a young woman.
Writer: Bernard Slade
Director: Ralph Senensky
Cast: John McMartin as Larry Metcalf, Jaclyn Smith as Tina, Pitt Herbert as Clerk
SONG:
■ "I Really Want to Know You," music by Barry Mann, lyrics by Cynthia Weil (on *Family Album*)
NOTES:
■ Chris Partridge's drums are painted with the words "The Partridge Family" rather than the familiar Partridge Family logo.
■ John McMartin starred in *Higher and Higher* with Sally Kellerman. He also guest-starred on numerous television shows, most notably as a priest on *The Bob Newhart Show*.
■ Jaclyn Smith starred as Kelly Garrett on *Charlie's Angels* and Christine Cromwell on *Christine Cromwell*. She made guest appearances on *McCloud, The Rookies, Switch, The Love Boat, Dinah!, Donny and Marie, The Toni Tennille Show,* and *The Pat Sajak Show*. Her television movies include *Jacqueline Bouvier Kennedy* (1981), *Rage of Angels* (1983), *The Night They Saved Christmas* (1984), *Florence Nightingale* (1985), *Rage of Angels: The Story Continues* (1986), *Windmills of the Gods* (1988), *The Bourne Identity* (1988), and *Settle the Score* (1989).

6: Love at First Slight 🐦🐦

In the wake of the Partridge Family's first album, Keith, constantly pursued by a flock of girls, falls in love with a girl named Janet who has no interest in him while spurning a girl named Cathy who has a crush on him. He tries to resolve the situation by inviting both to dinner.
Writer: Steve Pritzker
Director: Bob Claver
Cast: Lane Bradbury as Janet, Claire Wilcox as Cathy, Denice Stadling as

Sandy, Elaine Fielding as Registrar, Sheri Cowart as Debbie, Lisa Jill as Suzy

SONG:

■ "Somebody Wants to Love You," music and lyrics by Mike Appel, Jim Cretecos, and Wes Farrell (on *Family Album*)

NOTES:

■ Claire Wilcox played Deedee Harris on the short-lived situation comedy *Harris Against the World*. She played Cindy in Episode 60 of *The Partridge Family*.

7: Danny and the Mob 🐦🐦🐦🐦

When Danny gives the sexy LaVon LaVern financial advice, LaVon's mobster boyfriend, Harry Harrington, sends his two thugs, Rocco and Skee, to "lean on" Danny.

Writer: Ron Friedman

Director: Jerry Bernstein

Cast: Pat Harrington, Jr., as Harry Harrington, Barbara Rhoades as LaVon LaVern, Dick Bakalyan as Skee, Vic Tayback as Rocco, Jack Collins as Investor, Julio Medina as Chavez, Henry Hunter as Minister

SONG:

■ "That'll Be the Day," music and lyrics by Tony Romeo (on *Up to Date*)

NOTES:

■ Pat Harrington, Jr., played Guido Panzini on *The Steve Allen Show*, Pat Hannigan on *The Danny Thomas Show*, Tony Lawrence on *Mr. Deeds Goes to Town*, and won an Emmy Award as handyman Dwayne Schneider on *One Day at a Time*. He has appeared on dozens of television shows including *Alfred Hitchcock Presents*, *The Spike Jones Show*, *Grindl*, *The Munsters*, *The Man from U.N.C.L.E.*, *The Lucy Show*, *The Flying Nun*, *The Courtship of Eddie's Father*, *Columbo*, *McMillan and Wife*, *The Love Boat*, and *Murder, She Wrote*. He played Roger Harper in Episode 82 of *The Partridge Family*.

■ Barbara Rhoades played Melody Feebeck on *Busting Loose*.

■ Dick Bakalyan was a regular on *The Bobby Darin Show* and *Dean Martin Presents*.

■ Vic Tayback starred as Mel, owner of Mel's Cafe, on *Alice* from 1976 to 1985 and in the film *Alice Doesn't Live Here Anymore* (1975). He has appeared in dozens of television shows, and his other films include *Bullitt* (1968), *With Six You Get Egg Roll* (1968), and *Thunderbolt and Lightfoot* (1974). He played Ingram in Episode 37 and Harlan Laws in Episode 70 of *The Partridge Family*.

■ Jack Collins was a regular on *The Milton Berle Show* and played Max Brahms on *Occasional Wife*. He played the Emcee in Episode 71 of *The Partridge Family*.

8: But the Memory Lingers On

After a skunk stows away aboard the Partridge Family's bus, Mr. Kincaid forces everyone to bathe in tomato juice and then charm hotel guests into lending them their clothes so the Partridge Family can play a benefit concert for children at St. Mark's Hospital.

Writer: Bernard Slade
Director: E. W. Swackhamer
Cast: Gino Conforti as First Bell Boy, Howard Morton as Jerome Donkin, Joseph Perry as Sergeant, Bob Gibbon as Clerk, George Spell as Boy, Dick Balduzzi as Elevator Boy, JoAnne Meredith as Matron, Bill Luckino as Sweeney, A'Leshia Lee as Cigarette Girl
SONGS:
■ "I Think I Love You," music and lyrics by Tony Romeo (on *Family Album*)
■ "Brand New Me," music by Wes Farrell, lyrics by Eddie Singleton (on *Family Album*)
NOTES:
■ String and brass sections can be heard when the Partridge Family played "Brand New Me," although no one is seen playing either a violin or horns.
■ Gino Conforti plays Logan Mays in Episode 15 and the Maître d' in Episode 85.

9: Did You Hear the One About Danny Partridge?

Danny tries to become a comedian by buying old jokes from comedy writer Ziggy Shnurr.

Writer: Ron Friedman
Director: Paul Junger Witt
Cast: Morey Amsterdam as Ziggy Shnurr, Jackie Coogan as Max Pepper, Warren Miller as First Musician, Kip King as Second Musician
SONGS:
■ "Somebody Wants to Love You," music and lyrics by Wes Farrell, Jim Cretecos, and Mike Appel (on *Family Album*)

Which Episode Is Your Favorite?

Shirley Jones *(Shirley Partridge):*

"That's hard, because there were several that I love a lot. I love the Christmas show [Episode 38], and we have the album that came out as a result. Dean Jagger was in it. He was one of my favorite character actors. He played this old miner who lived in a ghost town, and it was a lovely Christmas episode. We had these wonderful episodes where we had these great guest stars who went on to become big heavyweight actors and stars in their own right. And some of the shows were the first time they were on television, I think. You know, Jodie Foster [Episode 67]. And in particular the show I loved was the one with Richard Pryor and Lou Gossett, Jr. [Episode 18]. That was a fun show. I loved that show. So you know, there were several. And the skunk show was fun [Episode 8]. The pilot I thought was a great show. You know, how it all came to be [Episode 1]."

David Cassidy *(Keith Partridge):*

"The Christmas show [Episode 38]. I just enjoyed it more than any other episode, and I've seen it once or twice since then and I think it's funny It's the ultimate kind of fantasy. We didn't do a lot of fantasy, and we took some liberties in that show, and I think they worked. I also got to be sillier than I ever got to be."

Danny Bonaduce *(Danny Partridge):*

"I have a couple of favorite episodes. Of course, the one we shot at King's Island Amusement Park, Ohio, was one of my favorites, the one at the amusement park [Episode 66]. And the other one was when gangsters mistakenly thought I was dating the boss's wife and sent gangsters out after me [Episode 7]. I thought that was pretty fun. I really liked the cast of those episodes, the gangsters chasing me around; I got to drive a go-cart in it. You know, just normal kid stuff."

Brian Forster (Chris Partridge):

"Probably one of my favorite episodes was the Christmas show [Episode 38]. I mean, they really spent a lot of time on that, painting up the sets, and I think the script was really good, and it was a lot of fun to do, you know, dressing up in period costumes. Some of the shows really tended to focus on one character or the other, but that one really kind of involved all of us."

Jeremy Gelbwaks (Chris Partridge):

"I guess there would have to be two shows. One is the Ray Bolger show [Episode 3] because I had the most lines in that show of any that I did, and I thought I did a pretty good job. And because I liked working with Ray. The other one was the Dinah Shore reference in the very first show [Episode 1]. My response was, 'Who?' in what became my prototypical Chris-look with those giant eyes and sort of glazed look. People remember the face I made on that show, that wide-eyed, round mouth 'Who?' In fact, my wife still teases me mercilessly about that high-pitched voice."

Suzanne Crough (Tracy Partridge):

"Some stand out in my memory more so, but I don't know that I have a favorite episode, by any means. There are so many different ones where we had special guest stars or something that, you know, has special memories. But I don't really have a special episode."

Dave Madden (Mr. Kincaid):

"The Christmas show where we went off into a dream sequence and we all got to go back into the days of the old west [Episode 38]. After a certain amount of time sitting around the dining room and the garage discussing things, it was kind of fun to go out and get on a horse. That would certainly be one of my favorites. The prison show was fun for me [Episode 10]. I ended up living in a cell next to some convict. There was a show about Indians that I thought was kind of interesting [Episode 48]. Obviously, shows in which you are featured are fun, too. I mean, I'm not putting that down. An actor wants to work, he wants to act. He wants to be involved in the plot. There were a lot of times when I wasn't involved in the plot. I was in the opening sequence and in the tag. I'd say, 'Well, you guys have a good time. I have to go off to Washington.' I'd see that in the script, and I'd say, 'See you guys in the tag.'"

Bernard Slade (Creator):

"I thought the pilot was pretty good [Episode 1]. That's maybe because we took more time with it. In those days the script would go to a reading, and they would shoot three and a half days, and once they started shooting, the script never changed. It's not like today's television. Scripts were not changed at all."

Bob Claver *(Executive Producer)*:

"I enjoyed the one where Danny falls in love with the Jewish girl [Episode 91]. I liked the whole idea, it was very different. I liked that kind of thing because that was something you didn't see on every sitcom. And it's a problem that never seems to go away."

Paul Witt *(Producer)*:

"My favorite episode was one that I directed with Richard Pryor and Lou Gossett in which there was a screwup in bookings and theTemptations got sent to some city and the Partridge Family got sent to a club in Detroit [Episode 18]. It was not a typical episode in that we weren't on the road the whole time. It was just fun. Musically, it was fun to work with Louis, who's a good friend, and Richie. It was a good episode."

■ "All of the Things," music and lyrics by Richard Klein
NOTES:
■ When the Partridge Family performs "All of the Things," the organ solo is as powerful as anything by the Doors.
■ Morey Amsterdam starred as Buddy Sorrell on *The Dick Van Dyke Show*. He was a regular on *Stop Me If You've Heard This One, The Morey Amsterdam Show, Broadway Open House, Can You Top This?, Battle of the Ages, Who Said That?, Make Me Laugh, Keep Talking, Honeymoon Suite*, and *The Young and the Restless*. He made guest appearances on *The Tonight Show, The Jackie Gleason Show, The Danny Thomas Show, How to Marry a Millionaire, Gunsmoke, The Ed Sullivan Show, The Phil Silvers Show, Have Gun, Will Travel, The Garry Moore Show, The Match Game, Daktari, The Merv Griffin Show, Love, American Style*, and *Alice*.
■ Jackie Coogan is best remembered as Uncle Fester on *The Addams Family*. The former child actor starred with Charlie Chaplin in *The Kid* (1921). His many motion pictures include *Oliver Twist* (1922), *Tom Sawyer* (1930), *Huckleberry Finn* (1931), *The Buster Keaton Story* (1957), *High School Confidential* (1958), *The Beat Generation* (1959), and *The Shakiest Gun in the West* (1968). On television, he was a regular on *Pantomime Quiz, Cowboy G-Men*, and *McKeever and the Colonel*. He made guest appearances on *Playhouse 90, Studio One, The Red Skelton Show, Peter Gunn, Perry Mason, The Andy Griffith Show, The Joey Bishop Show, Family Affair, I Dream of Jeannie, The Name of the Game, Love, American Style, The Brady Bunch, Marcus Welby, M.D., McMillan and Wife, Hawaii Five-O, Ironside*, and *Gunsmoke*. He played Grandpa Walter Renfrew in Episode 86 of *The Partridge Family*.

10: Go Directly to Jail 🐦🐦

When the Partridges perform at a penitentiary, a prisoner arranges for a quarantine, forcing the family to stay overnight to hear his songs—which he just so happened to steal from another prisoner.
Writer: Dale McRaven
Director: Claudio Guzman
Cast: Stuart Margolin as Hank, Ron Feinberg as Max, Ken Swofford as Monty, Lindsay Workman as Warden, Ben Frank as Convict, Ron Pinkhard as Guard, Frank Baron as Joe
SONGS:
■ "Singing My Song," music by Wes Farrell, lyrics by Diane Hilderbrand (on *Family Album*)

■ "Only a Moment Ago," music by Terry Cashman, lyrics by Tommy West (on *Family Album*)

NOTES:

■ When the Partridges perform "Singing My Song" and "Only a Moment Ago" before a group of convicts, violin strings can clearly be heard despite the fact that no one in the family appears to be playing a violin.

■ Stuart Margolin was a regular on *Love, American Style*, played Mitch on *Nichols*, and starred as Angel Martin on *The Rockford Files*. He also made guest appearances on *The Monkees*, *M*A*S*H*, *Gunsmoke*, *The Mary Tyler Moore Show*, *Rhoda*, *Magnum, P.I.*, and *Hill Street Blues*. He played Snake in Episode 54 of *The Partridge Family*.

■ Ken Swofford played Lt. Griffin on *Switch*, Al Barber on *Rich Man, Poor Man—Book II*, and J. J. Devlin on *The Eddie Capra Mysteries*. He also played Coach in Episode 90 of *The Partridge Family*.

■ Ron Pinkhard played Dr. Morton on *Emergency*.

11: This Is My Song

While Keith struggles to overcome a creative dry spell, Danny tries to become a songwriter and comes up with an original melody that just happens to be Keith's new composition.

Writer: Richard DeRoy
Director: Jerry Paris
SONG:

■ "To Be Lovers," music and lyrics by Mark Charron (on *Family Album*)

■ The references to *Oklahoma!* and composers Rodgers and Hammerstein are inside jokes on Shirley Jones, who was discovered by the composer team and cast in their film *Oklahoma!*

■ See Episode 1 for notes on director Jerry Paris.

12: My Son, the Feminist

After Keith's new girlfriend, Tina Newcomb, convinces the Partridge Family to perform at a Power of Women rally (against the protests of the Morality Watchdogs), she tries to censor the group's lyrics.

Writer: Richard DeRoy
Director: Peter Baldwin
Cast: Jane Actman as Tina Newcomb, Leonard Stone as Clauson, Fran Ryan as First Wife, Sari Price as Second Wife, Dort Clark as First Husband

SONG:
■ "I Think I Love You," music and lyrics by Tony Romeo (on *Family Album*)

NOTES:
■ Jane Actman played Barbara Simms on *The Paul Lynde Show*.
■ Leonard Stone played Doc Joslyn on *Camp Runamuck* and Morton on *The Jean Arthur Show*.

13: Star Quality

When syndicated columnist Sheila Faber writes a review lauding Danny as the star of the Partridge Family, Danny decides to leave the group and pursue a solo career.

Writer: Bernard Slade
Director: Harry Falk
Cast: Dick Clark as himself, Mitzi Hoag as Sheila Faber, Judy March as Mother, Gerald Michenaud as Norman Farrell

SONG:

■ "Singing My Song," music by Wes Farrell, lyrics by Diane Hilderbrand (on *Family Album*)

NOTES:

■ When the Partridge Family performs "Singing My Song," Tracy displays her versatility as a musician by playing the cowbell.

■ Dick Clark has hosted *American Bandstand, The Dick Clark Saturday Night Beechnut Show, Dick Clark's World of Talent, The Object Is, Missing Links, Dick Clark Presents the Rock and Roll Years, Dick Clark's Live Wednesday, The $25,000 Pyramid, The Krypton Factor, Inside America, TV's Bloopers & Practical Jokes, Dick Clark's Nighttime*, and *The Challengers*. He has appeared on *The Steve Allen Show, Pantomime Quiz, This Is Your Life, Talent Scouts, Burke's Law, Honey West, Batman, The Odd Couple, The Merv Griffin Show, Dinah!, Sha Na Na*, and *The Pat Sajak Show*.

■ Mitzi Hoag played Essie Gillis

on *Here Come the Brides* and Liz Platt on *We'll Get By*. She played Mrs. Fergusson in Episode 43, Mrs. Maifussi in Episode 51, and Miss Farrow in Episode 89 of *The Partridge Family*.

14: The Red Woodloe Story

When the Partridge Family invites folksinger Red Woodloe to stay with them, Red teaches Tracy to overcome her fear of the dark, and, in return, Tracy teaches Red to overcome his stage fright.

Writer: Coslough Johnson
Director: Peter Baldwin
Cast: William Schallert as Red Woodloe
SONGS:
■ "I Can Feel Your Heartbeat," music and lyrics by Wes Farrell, Mike Appel, and Jim Cretecos (on *Family Album*)
■ "Find Peace in Your Soul," music and lyrics by Bill Dorsey, performed by Red Woodloe
NOTE:
■ William Schallert has appeared in over 80 motion pictures, including *The Red Badge of Courage* (1951), *Lonely Are the Brave* (1962), *In the Heat of the Night* (1967), *Charley Varrick* (1973), *Twilight Zone—The Movie* (1983), *Teachers* (1987), and *Innerspace* (1987). On television, he starred as an understanding father with a teenaged daughter on four television series

(*The Patty Duke Show*, *The Nancy Drew Mysteries*, *Little Women*, and *The New Gidget*). He also played English teacher Leander Pomfritt on *The Many Loves of Dobie Gillis* and the Admiral on *Get Smart*, and starred in the *Hardy Boys Mysteries*, *Ike*, and *The Torkelsons*. He has appeared on over 650 television episodes, including guest appearances on *Leave It to Beaver*, *Perry Mason*, *Gunsmoke*, *The Andy Griffith Show*, *The Lucy Show*, *The Virginian*, *Mission: Impossible*, *The Wild Wild West*, *Ironside*, *Hawaii Five-O*, *Star Trek* (in the classic "The Trouble with Tribbles" episode), *The F.B.I.*, *Love, American Style*, *Little House on the Prairie*, *The Waltons*, *Lou Grant*, *St. Elsewhere*, *Quantum Leap*, *Murphy Brown*, and *In the Heat of the Night*. His television movies include *The North and the South* and *War and Remembrance*, and *The Incident*. He has also done thousands of voice-over commercials for countless products and companies, including, for many years, the voice of Milton the Toaster for Kellogg's Pop-Tarts. He served as President of the Screen Actors Guild.

15: Mom Drops Out 🐦

When Shirley, cajoled by promoter Logan Mays, drops out of the group so the family can tour Europe, the kids conspire to make her reconsider.

Writer: Peter Meyerson

Director: Harry Falk

Cast: Gino Conforti as Logan Mays, Joel Warfield as Emcee, Renee Tetro as Young Girl

SONGS:

■ "Baby I Love Love I Love You," music and lyrics by Derek Lawrence, Tony Wilson, and Errol Brown

■ "I Can Feel Your Heartbeat," music and lyrics by Wes Farrell, Mike Appel, and Jim Cretecos (on *Family Album*)

NOTE:

■ Gino Conforti played the First Bell Boy in Episode 8 and the Maître d' in Episode 85.

16: Old Scrapmouth

When Laurie gets braces on her teeth, she refuses to perform with the family on *The Wink Burgess Show* or go steady with her boyfriend Jerry.

Writer: James Henerson
Director: Herb Kenwith
Cast: Alan Oppenheimer as Wink Burgess, Jonathan Daly as Tommy Phillips, Mark Hamill as Jerry, William Wintersole as Dr. Kessler
SONG:
■ "The Love Song," music and lyrics by Steve Dossick
NOTES:
■ Alan Oppenheimer played Dr. Rudy Wells on *The Six Million Dollar Man*, provided the voice of Mighty Mouse in the Ralph Bakshi cartoon series, and played Gene Kinsella on *Murphy Brown*. He played Byron Atwater on Episode 70 and Lorenzo Bernard on Episode 87 of *The Partridge Family*.
■ Jonathan Daly played Peter Howard on *The Jimmy Stewart Show* and Lt. Whipple on *C.P.O. Sharkey*, starring Don Rickles. He played Officer Moody in Episode 4 of *The Partridge Family*.
■ Mark Hamill starred as Luke Skywalker in *Star Wars* (1977), *The Empire Strikes Back* (1980), and *Return of the Jedi* (1983). He has also appeared on *Room 222*, *The Streets of San Francisco*, *Medical Center*, *One Day at a Time*, *Amazing Stories*, and *Hooperman*.
■ William Wintersole played George Bailey on the television western *Sara*. He played the Club Manager in Episode 1 of *The Partridge Family*.

17: Why Did the Music Stop?

The kids quit the group so Shirley can date the handsome obstetrician who delivered Tracy, but the only question Dr. Jim Lucas pops is "Will you look at the songs I've written?"

Writer: Bernard Slade
Director: Alan Rafkin
Cast: Richard Mulligan as Dr. Jim Lucas, Reva Rose as Mabel
SONGS:
■ "I'm Here, You're Here," music by Wes Farrell, lyrics by Gerry Goffin (on *Up to Date*)
■ "I Can Feel Your Heartbeat," music and lyrics by Wes Farrell, Mike Appel, and Jim Cretecos (on *Family Album*)
NOTES:
■ Richard Mulligan starred as Sam Garret on *The Hero*, played Burt Campbell on *Soap*, and stars as Dr. Harry Weston on *Empty Nest*. He has also appeared on *Gunsmoke*, *I Dream of Jeannie*, *Love, American Style*, *Medical Center*, *Little House on the Prairie*, *The Love Boat*, *Highway to Heaven*, *The Twilight Zone*, and *The Golden Girls*. He played Ambassador Howard Lipton in Episode 82 of *The Partridge Family*.
■ Reva Rose played Marcy on *That Girl* and Nurse Mildred MacInerny on *Temperatures Rising*.

18: Soul Club 🐦🐦

When the Partridges and the Temptations get their bookings crossed, the Simon brothers, owners of a Detroit nightclub called the Engine House, may have to go out of business to a loneshark—until the Partridges organize a block party and Danny rallies the support of the Afro-American Cultural Society.
Writers: Harry Winkler and Harry Dolan
Director: Paul Junger Witt
Cast: Richard Pryor as A.E. Simon, Lou Gossett, Jr., as Sam Simon, Charles Lampkin as Heavy, Herbert Jefferson, Jr., as Black Leader, Morris Buchanan as Baker, Ben Frank as Policeman
SONG:
■ "Bandala," music by Wes Farrell, lyrics by Eddie Singleton (on *Family Album*)
NOTES:
■ String and brass sections can be heard when the Partridge Family plays "Bandala," yet while Danny recruits a violin section, no one is seen playing a horn.
■ Comedian Richard Pryor has starred in numerous motion pictures, most notably *The Green Berets* (1968), *Wild in the Streets* (1969), *Lady Sings the Blues* (1972), *Uptown Saturday Night* (1974), *Silver Streak* (1976), *Car Wash*

(1976), *Which Way Is Up?* (1977), *Greased Lightning* (1977), *California Suite* (1978), *The Wiz* (1978), *The Muppet Movie* (1979), *Stir Crazy* (1980), *Bustin' Loose* (1981), *Some Kind of Hero* (1982), *The Toy* (1982), *Superman III* (1983), *Brewster's Millions* (1985), *Harlem Nights* (1989), *See No Evil, Hear No Evil* (1989), *Look Who's Talking* (1990), and several live concert films. He also cowrote *Blazing Saddles* (1974). On television, he starred on the short-lived variety show *The Richard Pryor Show* and has made guest appearances on *On Broadway Tonight, The Wild Wild West, The Ed Sullivan Show, The Tonight Show Starring Johnny Carson, The Mod Squad, The New Bill Cosby Show, Lily, Saturday Night Live, Dinah!,* and *Sammy and Company.*

■ Lou Gossett, Jr., won an Academy Award as Best Supporting Actor for *An Officer and a Gentleman* with Richard Gere (1982). He also starred in *Jaws 3-D* (1983), *Iron Eagle* (1986), *Firewalker* (1986), *The Principal* (1987), *Iron Eagle II* (1988), and *Iron Eagle III* (1992). On television, Gossett was a regular on *The Young Rebels, The Lazarus Syndrome, The Powers of Matthew Star,* and *Gideon Oliver.* He has made guest appearances on *The Mod Squad, Daktari, The Bill Cosby Show, Bonanza, The Rookies, Love, American Style, Good Times, McCloud, Little House on the Prairie, The Rockford Files,* and *Saturday Night Live.*

■ Charles Lampkin played Tiger the Bartender on *Frank's Place,* and made guest appearances on *Please Don't Eat the Daisies, Daktari, The F.B.I., Marcus Welby, M.D., The Odd Couple, The Streets of San Francisco, Barnaby Jones, Night Court,* and *Webster.*

■ Herbert Jefferson, Jr., played Lt. Boomer on *Battlestar Galactica* and Ray Dwyer on *Rich Man, Poor Man—Book I.*

19: To Play or Not to Play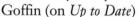

When Laurie refuses to cross a picket line and play with the Partridges at a club where the college workers are on strike, Danny locks the two disagreeing parties into a room and acts as a binding arbitrator.
Writers: Stan Cutler and Martin Donovan
Director: Ralph Senensky
Cast: Harvey Lembeck as Marino, Michael Lembeck as Marc
SONGS:
■ "There's No Doubt in My Mind," music by Wes Farrell, lyrics by Gerry Goffin (on *Up to Date*)

■ "Umbrella Man," music and lyrics by Wes Farrell, Jim Cretecos, and Mike Appel (on *Up to Date*)
NOTES:
■ Throughout this episode, David Cassidy has a small, unexplained laceration on his left cheek.
■ Harvey Lembeck played Rocco Barbella on *The Phil Silvers Show* and Seaman Gabby Di Julio on *Ensign O'Toole*.
■ Michael Lembeck, son of Harvey Lembeck, was a regular on *The Funny Side*, played Max Horvath on *One Day at a Time*, and was a regular on *Foley Square*. He has made guest appearances on *Room 222*, *Love, American Style*, *Happy Days*, *Barney Miller*, *The Love Boat*, and *Murder, She Wrote*.

20: They Shoot Managers, Don't They?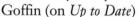

When Shirley plays matchmaker for Mr. Kincaid and her friend Cathleen Darcy, Reuben decides to marry Cathleen and work for her company, leaving the Partridge Family without a manager—until he learns that his bride to be doesn't want to have children.

Writers: Lloyd Turner and Gordon Mitchell
Director: Peter Baldwin
Cast: Nancy Malone as Cathleen Darcy
SONG:
■ "She'd Rather Have the Rain," music by Terry Cashman, lyrics by Tommy West (on *Up to Date*)
NOTES:
■ Violin strings and a triangle can be heard when the Partridge Family plays "She'd Rather Have the Rain," yet no one can be seen playing the violin or the triangle.
■ Nancy Malone played Libby on *Naked City* and Clara Varner on *The Long, Hot Summer*.

21: Partridge Up a Pair Tree

After giving Danny the right of attorney to manage his money, Keith works as a plumber's assistant, a vegetable-slicer salesman, and a newsboy to raise money to repair his car and take his girlfriend Carol to the prom —only to wind up selling his car.

Writers: Lloyd Turner and Gordon Mitchell
Director: Ralph Senensky
Cast: Annette O'Toole as Carol, Carl Ballantine as Pitchman, Joseph Perry as Mr. Jenkins
SONGS:
■ "You Are Always on My Mind," music and lyrics by Tony Romeo (on *Up to Date*)
NOTES:
■ Carl Ballantine is a comedian and magician best remembered as Lester Gruber on *McHale's Navy*. He played Becker on *The Queen and I* and was a regular on *One in a Million*. He has made guest appearances on *The Garry Moore Show*, *The Jackie Gleason Show*, *The Steve Allen Show*, *Car 54, Where Are You?*, *That Girl*, *The Monkees*, *I Dream of Jeannie*, *Mayberry R.F.D.*, *Love, American Style*, *Alice*, *Night Court*, and *The Cosby Show*.
■ Joseph Perry played Police Sergeant Donakovsky in Episode 71 and the Policeman in Episode 84.

22: Road Song 🐦🐦

When a runaway girl headed for Albuquerque hitches a ride with the Partridge Family aboard the bus, Shirley convinces the police to allow her to reunite the girl with her father.

Writer: Dale McRaven
Director: Alan Rafkin
Cast: Laurie Prange as Maggie Newton, Sandy Kenyon as Father, Ian Wolfe as Grandfather, Harry Hickox as Sheriff, Stuart Nisbet as Patrolman, Dick Wilson as Cowboy

SONG:

■ "Point Me in the Direction of Albuquerque," music and lyrics by Tony Romeo (on *Family Album*)

NOTES:

■ A brass section can be heard when the Partridge Family plays "Point Me in the Direction of Albuquerque," yet no one is seen playing horns.

■ Sandy Kenyon played Shep Baggott on *The Travels of Jamie McPheeters* and Jim Lucas on *Love on a Rooftop*.

■ Harry Hickox played Sgt. King on *No Time For Sergeants*.

■ Dick Wilson is best known as Mr. Whipple on television commercials for Charmin toilet paper (exclaiming "Ladies, please don't squeeze the Charmin!"). He frequently played drunks on television shows, most notably *Bewitched*. His daughter Melanie Wilson played Jennifer on *Perfect Strangers*.

23: Not with My Sister, You Don't 🐦🐦🐦🐦

When Laurie gets a date with Lester Braddock, a young man with a reputation, Keith and Danny follow the couple to Muldune's Point.

Writer: Dale McRaven
Director: Mel Swope
Cast: Michael Ontkean as Lester Braddock, Mike Rupert as Bob, Jeremy Burke as Archie, Cindy Crosby as Doris

SONG:

■ "I'll Meet You Halfway," music by Wes Farrell, lyrics by Gerry Goffin (on *Up to Date*)

NOTES:

■ When the Partridge Family performs "I'll Meet You Halfway," a string section can be heard although no one can be seen playing the violin.

■ Michael Ontkean starred as Officer Willie Gillis on *The Rookies* and Sheriff Harry S. Truman on *Twin Peaks*.

24: A Partridge by Any Other Name

When the Partridges can't locate Danny's birth certificate, Danny is convinced he was adopted and searches San Pueblo for his real parents.

Writer: Ron Friedman

Director: Harry Falk

Cast: Bernard Fox as Marty Burnes, Art Metrano as Mike Young, Ned Glass as Detective Harry Klein, Jim Connell as Orderly, Renie Riano as Mrs. Reinbolt, Sid McCoy as M. Young, Jeff Burton as Workman

SONGS:

■ "Doesn't Somebody Want to Be Wanted," music and lyrics by Wes Farrell, Jim Cretecos, and Mike Appel (on *Up to Date*)

■ "I Can Feel Your Heartbeat," music and lyrics by Wes Farrell, Jim Cretecos, and Mike Appel (on *Family Album*)

NOTES:

■ Mr. Kincaid insists that the Partridges obtain passports to travel to Canada, despite the fact that American citizens do not need passports to cross that border. Although Shirley cannot locate Danny's birth certificate, she waved a copy under the noses of several army induction officers when Danny received a draft notice in Episode 4.

■ Bernard Fox starred as Dr. Bombay on *Bewitched*, Malcolm Meriwether on *The Andy Griffith Show*, and Colonel Crittenden on *Hogan's Heroes*. He guest starred on *The Danny Thomas Show*, *The Andy Griffith Show*, *The Dick Van Dyke Show*, *McHale's Navy*, *Twelve O'Clock High*, *The Farmer's Daughter*, *Perry Mason*, *F-Troop*, *I Spy*, *The Man from U.N.C.L.E.*, *The Monkees*, *The Wild Wild West*, *Love, American Style*, *M*A*S*H*, *Lou Grant*, *Simon & Simon*, and *Murder, She Wrote*. He also appeared in the television movies *The Hound of the Baskervilles* (1972) and *Gauguin the Savage* (1980).

■ Art Metrano was a regular on *The Tim Conway Comedy Hour* and played

Nick Marr on *The Chicago Teddy Bears*, Detective Rod Pena on *Amy Prentiss*, Benjy on *Movin' On*, and Tom on *Loves Me, Loves Me Not*.

■ Ned Glass starred as landlord Sol Cooper on *Julia* and as Uncle Moe on *Bridget Loves Bernie*. He has appeared on hundreds of television shows, including *Medic, Studio One, Have Gun, Will Travel, Gunsmoke, Peter Gunn, The Danny Thomas Show, Slattery's People, The Dick Van Dyke Show, Bewitched, The Monkees, Mr. Terrific, Love on a Rooftop, The Man from U.N.C.L.E., Love, American Style, The Mary Tyler Moore Show, Kojak*, and *Barney Miller*.

■ Jim Connell played Junior on *Run Buddy Run* and was a regular on *Donny and Marie*. He also played Gus Gorney in Episode 60 of *The Partridge Family*.

■ Sid McCoy played Mr. Langford on *The Bill Cosby Show*.

25: A Knight in Shining Armor 🐦🐦🐦🐦🐦

When the Partridges find songwriter Bobby Conway living in their garage, they help him find a lyricist, eccentric Lionel Poindexter, who lives in Denver.

Writer: Bernard Slade

Director: Earl Bellamy

Cast: Bobby Sherman as Bobby Conway, Wes Stern as Lionel Poindexter

SONGS:

■ "Stephanie," music by Richard Klein, lyrics by Richard Klein, John Henning, and David Price

NOTES:

■ This episode was the preview for the short-lived spin-off *Getting Together*, starring recording star Bobby Sherman as songwriter Bobby Conway and Wes Stern as offbeat lyricist Lionel Poindexter.

■ Commented television reviewer Sue Cameron in *The Hollywood Reporter* of March 22, 1971: "As a segment of *The Partridge Family* it was warm and entertaining. To see Bobby Sherman each week as a song-writer in Hollywood trying to make it is a different story . . . . Standout of the show is the performance by Wes Stern. He is charming."

■ Teen idol Bobby Sherman starred as Jeremy Bolt on *Here Come the Brides* and as Bobby Conway on *Getting Together*. He made guest appearances on *Honey West, The Monkees, The F.B.I., The Don Knotts Show, The Mod Squad, Emergency!, Three's Company, The Love Boat, Murder, She Wrote*, and *Blacke's Magic*.

■ Wes Stern starred as Lionel Poindexter on *Getting Together*.

The lyrics to the opening theme song were rewritten by lyricist Danny Janssen, and the title was changed to "Come On Get Happy." Brian Forster replaced Jeremy Gelbwaks as Chris Partridge, and Keith now sports a shag haircut.

26: Dora, Dora, Dora

When Mr. Kincaid books the Partridge Family to play the Point Loomis Air Force Base and back up gorgeous Dora Kelly, who can't sing a note on key, the servicemen drown out her singing with their cheers and applause.
Writers: Lloyd Turner and Gordon Mitchell
Director: Ralph Senensky
Cast: Robyn Millan as Dora, Jack Burns as Stillman Kelly
SONG:
■ "I Woke Up in Love This Morning," music and lyrics by Irwin Levine and L. Russell Brown (on *Sound Magazine*)
NOTES:
■ Robyn Millan played Vicky Lucas on *Where the Heart Is.*
■ Jack Burns played Deputy Warren Ferguson on *The Andy Griffith Show*, was a regular on *Our Place*, played Officer Rudy Colcheck on *Getting Together* starring Bobby Sherman and Wes Stern, and co-hosted *The Burns*

and Schreiber Comedy Hour with Avery Schreiber. He made guest appearances on *The Jack Paar Program*, *The Glen Campbell Goodtime Hour*, *Love, American Style*, *Nanny and the Professor*, *The Dean Martin Show*, and *Saturday Night Live*. He was also a writer for *The Muppet Show* and *Fridays*.

27: In 25 Words or Less 🐦🐦🐦🐦🐦

When Mr. Kincaid stages a contest in *Bopper Beat* magazine in which the winner will spend a week with the Partridge Family, the winner is Gloria Neugast, a 60-year-old Jewish mother.

Writer: Martin Ragaway
Director: Richard Kinon
Cast: Kay Medford as Gloria, Gerald Hiken as Bernie Applebaum, Monie Ellis as Doris, Martin Speer as Engineer, Dennis Lee Smith as Voice #1, Scott McCartor as Voice #2

SONG:
■ "Echo Valley 2-6809," music and lyrics by Kathy Cooper and Rupert Holmes (on *Sound Magazine*)

NOTES:
■ Dr. Bernie Applebaum, again played by Gerald Hicken, returns to date Shirley in Episode 63.
■ Kay Medford played Aunt Harriet Endicott on *To Rome with Love* and was a regular on *The Dean Martin Show*.
■ Martin Speer played the Engineer in Episodes 31 and 34, and Lazaar Hannibal in Episode 74.
■ Dennis Lee Smith played the First Guy in Episode 41 and the Waiter in Episode 67.

28: A Man Called Snake 🐦🐦🐦

When a burly character named Snake roars into Laurie's life on a motorcycle, Laurie, finding him sensitive, invites him to the school prom.

Writers: Chuck Shyer and Alan Mandel
Director: Richard Kinon
Cast: Rob Reiner as Snake, Bryan O'Byrne as Mr. Koolic, Michael Gregory as Quinton, Henry Olek as Geek, Sandi Schrader as Fran, Mark Malmborg as Adonis #1, Bobby Griffin as Adonis #2

SONG:
■ "Listen to the Sound," music and lyrics by John Michael Hill

NOTES:

■ Laurie claims she got braces on her teeth when she was eight years old, yet when she gets braces in Episode 16, she acts as if it's the first time. Obviously, Laurie required a second set of braces because her first orthodontist was a quack, explaining why she repressed all memory of the first experience.

■ Rob Reiner starred as Michael (Meathead) Stivic on *All in the Family*. He directed *This Is Spinal Tap* (1984), *Stand By Me* (1986), *When Harry Met Sally* (1989), and *A Few Good Men* (1992). He is the son of Carl Reiner.

■ Bryan O'Byrne played Hodgkins on *Get Smart*. He played Snake's Father in Episode 54 of *The Partridge Family*.

■ Henry Olek played Gorgo in Episode 54 and Skip Radnitz in Episode 88.

■ Sandi Schrader played the Third Girl in Episode 33 and the Cute Girl in Episode 83.

■ Snake returns to visit the Partridge Family again in Episode 54.

29: The Undergraduate

When Shirley takes a college psychology course, a nineteen-year-old student named Paul Bruner falls in love with her, prompting his parents to drop in on the Partridge home while Shirley is trying on a new hot-pants outfit, compelling Shirley to invite Paul to dinner to meet her kids.

Writer: Susan Silver

Director: Ralph Senensky

Cast: Michael Burns as Paul Bruner, Norman Fell as Mr. Bruner, Ann Morgan Guilbert as Mrs. Bruner, Carol O'Leary as Margo

SONGS:

■ "Brown Eyes," music and lyrics by Wes Farrell and Danny Janssen (on *Sound Magazine*)

■ Michael Burns played Barnaby West on *Wagon Train* and Howie Macauley on *It's a Man's World*.

■ Norman Fell is best known as Stanley Roper on *Three's Company* and its spin-off *The Ropers*. He also played Detective Meyer Meyer on *87th Precinct*, Smitty on *Rich Man, Poor Man - Book I*, Sgt. Charles Wilentz on *Dan August*, and Nathan Davidson on *Needles and Pins*. He has guest- starred on hundreds of television shows, including *The Untouchables, Ben Casey, Dr. Kildare, Bewitched, The Man from U.N.C.L.E., The Wild Wild West, The F.B.I., Love, American Style, Marcus Welby, M.D., McMillan and Wife, Rhoda, The Streets of San Francisco, The Love Boat, Murder, She Wrote,* and *Magnum, P.I.*

■ Ann Morgan Guilbert played Laura Petrie's best friend, Millie Helper, on *The Dick Van Dyke Show* and Nora on *The New Andy Griffith Show*.

30: Anatomy of a Tonsil 🐦🐦

When Danny has to have his tonsils removed, his best friend, Punky Lazaar, convinces him the operation may kill him. Danny advertises in the newspaper to find his own replacement and wills all his prized possessions to his siblings; but when he survives the operation, Danny insists he can no longer sing and refuses to leave his bed—until the Partridges convince him that Mr. Kincaid has found the perfect redheaded replacement.

Writer: Coslough Johnson
Director: Lou Antonio
Cast: Marshall Thompson as Dr. Milstead, Gary Dubin as Punky Lazaar
SONG:
■ "Love Is All That I Ever Needed," music and lyrics by David Cassidy and Wes Farrell (on *Sound Magazine*)
NOTES:
■ "Love Is All That I Ever Needed" sounds suspiciously like "The Letter" by the Box Tops.

■ Marshall Thompson starred as John Smith on *Angel* and Dr. Marsh Tracy on *Daktari*. He also appeared on *Science Fiction Theater, Perry Mason, Wagon Train, The Streets of San Francisco, Ironside,* and *Lou Grant*.

■ Gary Dubin played Mark Grant on *Bracken's World*. He also played Punky Lazaar in Episodes 71, 89, 91, 92, and 95 of *The Partridge Family*.

31: Whatever Happened to Moby Dick? 🐦🐦🐦🐦

When the Partridge Family decides to make a record at Marineland featuring the song of a whale and to donate the profits to the New York Zoological Society, E. J. Flicker, the man who alerted Marineland to get the whale out of his inlet, demands 50 percent.

Writer: Peggy Chandler Dick

Director: E. W. Swackhamer

Cast: Howard Cosell as Himself, Bert Convy as Dr. Whelander, Dub Taylor as Flicker, George O'Hanlon as Bear Man, Martin Speer as Engineer, Mat Reitz as Man's Voice

> **Jobs Offered**
> ### WANTED
> One singing whale. Must have talent. Others need not apply. Contact Danny Partridge.

SONG:

■ "The Whale Song," music and lyrics by Dan Pevton and Marty Kaniger

NOTES:

■ Sportcaster Howard Cosell hosted *Sports Focus*, *Monday Night Football*, *Saturday Night Live with Howard Cosell*, *Monday Night Baseball*, and *Speaking of Everything*. He has appeared on *Nanny and the Professor*, *The Odd Couple*, *The Sonny and Cher Comedy Hour*, *Saturday Night Live*, and *The Tonight Show Starring Johnny Carson*.

■ Bert Convy is best known as the host of such game shows as *Tattletales*, *Password*, *People Do the Craziest Things*, and *Win, Lose or Draw*. He also appeared on *77 Sunset Strip*, *Perry Mason*, *Hawaiian Eye*, *The Defenders*, *Bewitched*, *The Mary Tyler Moore Show*, *Love, American Style*, *McMillan and Wife*, *Match Game '75*, *Charlie's Angels*, *The Love Boat*, *Hotel*, *Murder, She Wrote*, and *It's Gary Shandling's Show*. He played congressional candidate Richard Lawrence in Episodes 57 and 67 of *The Partridge Family*.

■ Dub Taylor played Ed Hewley on *Please Don't Eat the Daisies*.

■ George O'Hanlon played Calvin Dudley on *The Life of Riley*, was a regular on *Pantomime Quiz*, provided the voice of George Jetson on *The Jetsons*, and played Artie Burns on *The Reporter*. He made guest appearances on *I Love Lucy*, *Maverick*, *How to Marry a Millionaire*, *The Red Skelton Show*, *The Ann Sothern Show*, *Love, American Style*, and *The Odd Couple*.

■ Martin Speer played the Engineer in Episodes 27 and 34 and Lazaar Hannibal in Episode 74.

32: Dr Jekyll and Mr. Partridge 🐦🐦🐦

When Keith decides to take on more responsibility as the eldest male, bringing Danny, Chris, and Tracy to a classical concert and a modern art museum and then ruining a date for Laurie, Danny schemes with the others to make Keith realize he is in way over his head.

Writer: William S. Bickley
Director: Mel Swope
Cast: Lawrence Haddon as Coach Dawson, Bruce Kimmel as Freddy
SONG:
■ "Summer Days," music and lyrics by Tony Romeo (on *Sound Magazine*)
NOTES:
■ The song "Summer Days" starts out sounding suspiciously like the Rolling Stones' "Paint It Black." Also, when the Partridge perform the song in a nightclub, a horn section can be clearly heard, although no one onstage is playing a brass instrument.
■ Laurence Haddon played the Foreign Editor on *Lou Grant*. He played Sgt. Sizemore in Episode 4 of *The Partridge Family*.
■ Bruce Kimmel was a regular on *Dinah and Her New Best Friends*. He played Laurie's boyfriend Marvin in Episode 47, her boyfriend Richard in Episode 55, her boyfriend Richard Whipple in Episode 74, and her boyfriend Howard Krump in Episode 81 on *The Partridge Family*.

33: Days of Acne and Roses 🐦🐦🐦

An awkward sixteen-year-old named Wendell has a crush on Laurie, but once she goes out with him, he decides he wants to date other girls.
Writer: Dale McRaven
Director: Richard Kinon
Cast: Jay Ripley as Wendell, Robert B. Williams as Mr. Busby, Eileen Ramsey as Waitress, Mark Malmborg as First Guy, Scott McCartor as Second Guy, Susan Foster as First Girl, Ann Jilliann as Second Girl, Bill Ewing as Third Guy, Sandi Schrader as Third Girl
SONG:
■ "I'm on My Way Back Home," music by Jack Keller, lyrics by Bobby Hart (on *Sound Magazine*)
NOTE:
■ Sandi Schrader also played Fran in Episode 28 and the Cute Girl in Episode 83.

34: Tale of Two Hamsters 🐦🐦🐦🐦

When Danny decides to raise hamsters, Mother Nature gives him an overwhelming return on his investment.

Writer: Lloyd Turner and Gordon Mitchell
Director: Roger Duchowny
Cast: Martin Speer as Engineer, Lindsay Workman as Hotel Manager, Dick Yarmy as Patterson, Gordon Jump as Albertson, Brian Touchi as Young Boy, Karen Lee Bowman as Karen

SONGS:
- "Twenty-Four Hours a Day," music and lyrics by Wes Farrell and Danny Janssen (on *Sound Magazine*)
- "I Woke Up in Love This Morning," music and lyrics by Irwin Levine and L. Russell Brown (on *Sound Magazine*)

NOTES:
- When the Partridge Family records "Twenty-Four Hours a Day" in the studio, a horn section can be heard, although no one can be seen playing a brass instrument.
- Martin Speer played the Engineer in Episodes 27 and 31, and Lazaar Hannibal in Episode 74.
- Actor/director Dick Yarmy was comedian Don Adams's younger brother, best known for his George and Marge television commercials for Union Oil. He appeared with the road company of *The Odd Couple* and made many television guest appearances, most notably on *That Girl*, *Get Smart*, *Laverne & Shirley*, and *Mork & Mindy*.
- See Episode 1 for notes on Gordon Jump.

35: The Forty-Year Itch 🐦🐦

When Shirley's parents are on the verge of breaking up because her father is dressing young and insisting on hitchhiking to Big Sur, Shirley drags them both to a Partridge Family club date where she sings them a sentimental song, forcing them to reconcile their differences.

Writer: Steve Pritzker
Director: Ralph Senensky
Cast: Ray Bolger as Grandpa, Rosemary DeCamp as Grandma

SONGS:
- "Together," music by Shorty Rogers, lyrics by Kelly Gordon
- "My Best Girl," music and lyrics by Jerry Herman

NOTE:
■ See Episode 3 for notes on Ray Bolger and Rosemary DeCamp.

36: I Can Get It for You Retail

Determined to buy a mink coat for his mother, Danny recruits Chris to help him auction off Keith's belongings and locks of Keith's hair to the girls in school.

Writer: Bernard Slade
Director: Russ Mayberry
Cast: Darcy Klega as First Girl, Amber Smale as Second Girl, Donna Lynn as ten-year-old Girl, Sari Price as Saleswoman

SONG:
■ "Every Little Bit o' You," music and lyrics by Irwin Levine and L. Russell Brown (on *Shopping Bag*)

NOTES:
■ Sari Price also played the Mother in Episode 62 and the Woman in Episode 73.

37: Guess Who's Coming to Drive

When the Partridge Family hires a driver who turns out to be on parole for armed robbery, Danny's suspicions cause Mr. Kincaid to wind up in jail.

Writer: Bob Rodgers
Director: Ralph Senensky
Cast: Milt Kamen as John Burnhardt, Vic

Tayback as Ingram, Yvonne Wilder as Waitress, Naomi Stevens as Mrs. Weinstock, John Lawrence as Desk Sergeant

SONGS:
■ "Rainmaker," music and lyrics by Wes Farrell, Jim Cretecos, and Mike Appel (on *Sound Magazine*)

NOTES:

■ Milt Kamen was a regular on *Pantomime Quiz*, *The Sid Caesar Show*, and *Perry Como's Kraft Music Hall*, and played Murray Bronson on *Love Thy Neighbor*. He also appeared on *The Arlene Francis Show*, *The Garry Moore Show*, *The Jack Paar Show*, *Naked City*, *The Merv Griffin Show*, *The Match Game*, *The Mike Douglas Show*, *The Tonight Show Starring Johnny Carson*, *The Dean Martin Show*, *The F.B.I.*, *Love, American Style*, *Mannix*, *The Streets of San Francisco*, and *Switch*.

■ See Episode 7 for notes on Vic Tayback.

■ Yvonne Wilder played Major Edna Howard on *Operation Petticoat*. She played Sheila in Episode 51 of *The Partridge Family*.

■ Naomi Stevens played Juanita on *The Doris Day Show*, Rose Montefusco on *The Montefuscos*, and Sgt. Bella Archer on *Vegas*.

38: Don't Bring Your Guns to Town, Santa

When the Partridge Family bus breaks down in a ghost town on Christmas Eve, an old prospector named Charlie entertains the Partridges with a story about the town in which

Keith is singing Sheriff Swell, Laurie is the schoolmarm, Shirley is saloon mistress Belle, Mr. Kincaid is Mean Sidney, and Danny is Little the Kid.

Writer: Bernard Slade
Director: Richard Kinon
Cast: Dean Jagger as Charlie, Britt Leach as Jess
SONG:
■ "Have Yourself a Merry Little Christmas," music and lyrics by Hugh Martin and Ralph Blane (on *Christmas Card*)
NOTES:
■ Dean Jagger starred as Albert Vane on *Mr. Novak* and won an Academy Award as Best Supporting Actor for *Twelve O'Clock High* (1950). Among his many motion pictures are *Betrayed* (1944), *Dark City* (1950), *Rawhide*

(1951), *Executive Suite* (1954), *White Christmas* (1954), *Bad Day at Black Rock* (1955), *King Creole* (1958), *Elmer Gantry* with Shirley Jones (1960), and *Vanishing Point* (1971). On television, he appeared on *Playhouse 90, The Twilight Zone, The F.B.I., The Fugitive, The Name of the Game, Bonanza, Columbo, Medical Center, Harry-O,* and *This Is the Life*. His television movies include *The Lonely Profession* (1969), Truman Capote's *The Glass House* (1972), and *Gideon's Trumpet* (1980).
■ Britt Leach played Mickey Wiggins on *Spencer's Pilots*.

39: Where Do Mermaids Go?

When the Partridges give a hippie girl a lift on their bus and put her up for the night, she deposits a million dollars in Shirley's bank account, causing the Partridges to be inundated with salesmen and plagued by ungrateful friends, compelling them to return the money.

Writer: Peggy Chandler Dick
Director: Lou Antonio

Cast: Meredith Baxter Birney as Jenny, Herb Rudley as L. J. Belson, Richard X. Slattery as Policeman, Val Bisoglio as Palmer, Donald Phelps as Sir Guy, Mel Gallagher as Telephone Man, Carroll Roebke as Model #1, Sue Linden as Model #2

SONG:

■ "It's Time That I Knew You Better," music and lyrics by Terry Cashman and Tommy West

NOTES:

■ Oddly, Mr. Kincaid makes no attempt to convince the family to keep the money or, at the very least, donate it to charity.

■ Meredith Baxter Birney starred as Bridget Fitzgerald Steinberg on the controversial comedy *Bridget Loves Bernie*, Nancy Lawrence Maitland on *Family*, and Elyse Keaton on *Family Ties*. She has also made guest appearances on *The Interns*, *The Young Lawyers*, *The Doris Day Show*, *Owen Marshall, Counselor at Law*, *Barnaby Jones*, *Young Love*, *Medical Center*, *The Streets of San Francisco*, *McMillan and Wife*, *City of Angels*, *Police Woman*, *The Love Boat*, *What Really Happened to the Class of '65?*, and *The Pat Sajak Show*. Her television movies include *The Cat Creature* (1973), *The Stranger Who Looks Like Me* (1974), *Target Risk* (1975), *The Imposter* (1975), *The Night That Panicked America* (1975), *Little Women* (1978), *Beulah Land* (1980), *Take Your Best Shot* (1982), *Family Ties Vacation* (1985), *Kate's Secret* (1986), *The Long Journey Home* (1987), and *She Knows Too Much* (1989). While best known as a blond, she appears as a brunette is this episode.

■ Herb Rudley played Sam Brennan on *The Californians*, Will Gentry on *Michael Shayne*, General Crone on *Mona McCluskey*, and Herb Hubbard on *The Mothers-in-Law*.

■ Richard X. Slattery played Sgt. John McKenna on *The Gallant Men*, Captain John Morton on *Mr. Roberts*, Lt. Modeer on *Switch*, and Captain "Buck" Buckner on *C.P.O. Sharkey*.

■ Val Bisoglio played Captain Rocco Calvelli on *Roll Out*, Lt. Paul Marsh on *Police Woman*, and Danny Tóvo on *Quincy, M.E.*

40: Home Is Where the Heart Was

When Shirley punishes Chris and Tracy for not cleaning up a mess, they run away from home and don't get any further than Mr. Kincaid's apartment.

Writers: Richard Bensfield and Perry Grant
Director: Jerry London
Cast: Elaine Giftos as Bonnie Kleinschmitt

SONGS:

- "Summer Days," music and lyrics by Tony Romeo (on *Sound Magazine*)
- "I Would Have Loved You Anyway," music and lyrics by Tony Romeo (on *Sound Magazine*)

NOTES:

- The song "Summer Days" was also performed in Episode 32 with the exact same footage seen in this episode. As previously noted, "Summer Days" starts out sounding suspiciously like the Rolling Stones' "Paint It Black." When the Partridges perform this song in a nightclub, a horn section can be clearly heard, although no one onstage is playing a brass instrument.
- Elaine Giftos played Bobbe Marsh on *The Interns*. She also played Bonnie Kleinschmitt in Episodes 68, 79, and 80 of *The Partridge Family*.

41: Fellini, Bergman, and Partridge

After seeing an avant-garde film, Keith makes a short movie starring the members of his family, and when Danny shows it at Muldune's Point, Sam Greasley, owner of the Royal Theater, offers Keith $100 for the rights to show it as a short before *Gone with the Wind*— much to the family's dismay. The home movie features Laurie posing as Cleopatra, Chris painting at an easel, Tracy in a bubble bath, Keith dancing under a sprinkler, Shirley clipping the hedges, Danny making faces, and Mr. Kincaid prancing about as a good fairy.

Writer: Martin Cohan
Director: Jerome Courtland
Cast: Tony Ballen as Sam Greasley, Dick Stahl as Mr. Fenster, Gaye Nelson as Lynn, Judson Pratt as Cab Driver, Dennis Lee Smith as First Guy, Rick Metzler as Second Guy

SONGS:
- "Together," music by Shorty Rogers, lyrics by Kelly Gordon
- "Hello, Hello," music and lyrics by Wes Farrell and Tony Romeo (on *Shopping Bag*)

NOTES:
- The Partridges now own a yellow station wagon with wood-paneled sides.
- The song "Hello, Hello" sounds suspiciously like portions of "Harmony" by Elton John and Bernie Taupin, and is reminiscent of the Beatles' "Hello Goodbye," and the Doors' "Hello, I Love You."
- Dick Stahl was a regular on *The Jim Stafford Show*. He made guest appearances on *All in the Family*, *Barney Miller*, *The Bob Newhart Show*, *The Mary Tyler Moore Show*, *The Dick Van Dyke Show*, *House Calls*, *Laverne & Shirley*, *Love, American Style*, *The Odd Couple*, and *WKRP in Cincinnati*. He played Michelangelo Rezo in Episode 74 of *The Partridge Family*.
- Dennis Lee Smith also played Voice #1 in Episode 27 and the Waiter in Episode 67.

42: Waiting for Bolero 🐦🐦🐦

When Keith gets his own apartment next door in exchange for some light gardening work, he finds bachelor life more than he bargained for.
Writer: Martin Cohan
Director: Jerry London
Cast: Pam Peters as Vicky, Leigh Webb as Archie, Ric Carrott as Bernie

SONGS:
- "Every Song Is You," music and lyrics by Terry Cashman and Tommy West (on *Shopping Bag*)

NOTES:
- When the Partridge Family performs "Every Song Is You," horns and violins can be heard, although no one in the family can be seen playing brass instruments or strings.

43: I Am Curious Partridge 🐦🐦🐦🐦

When Danny sells two stories to the *San Pueblo Tattler Sunday Magazine* (the first claiming that Keith has a rose tattoo on his behind and a crush on his English teacher and the second claiming that Shirley once ran a school for exotic dancers and is helplessly attracted to men in trench coats and

men with beards), the Partridges retaliate by selling their own story to the paper (claiming that Danny loves giving his money to charity).

Writer: Bob Rodgers

Director: Lou Antonio

Cast: Carl Byrd as Reporter, Maxine Stuart as Mrs. Damion, Bobby Baum as Milkman, Mitzi Hoag as Mrs. Fergusson

SONG:

■ "If You Ever Go," music and lyrics by Wes Farrell and Tony Romeo (on *Shopping Bag*)

NOTES:

■ Maxine Stuart played Ruth on *Room for One More*, B. J. Clawson on *Slattery's People*, Scotty on *Doctors' Hospital*, and Marge Newberry on *Executive Suite*. She played Gloria Hoffsteader in Episode 62 and Miss Halstead in Episode 92 of *The Partridge Family*.

■ Mitzi Hoag played Essie Gillis on *Here Come the Brides* and Liz Platt on *We'll Get By*. She played Sheila Faber in Episode 13, Mrs. Maifussi in Episode 51, and Miss Farrow in Episode 89 of *The Partridge Family*.

44: My Heart Belongs to a Two-Car Garage 🐦🐦🐦🐦

When a grateful Russian immigrant paints a mural of a naked woman on the Partridges' garage, the neighbors decide to paint it over themselves—until a museum curator declares the nude a masterpiece.

Writer: William S. Bickley

Director: Jerry London

Cast: Arte Johnson as Nicholas Minksi Pushkin, Dave Ketchum as Mr. Phelps, Jeff Donnell as Mrs. Monahan, Ivor Barry as Mr. Hensley, John Qualen as the Old Man, Frank Welker as Sioux

SONG:

■ "Last Night," music and lyrics by Tony Romeo

NOTES:

■ Arte Johnson is best known for his regular appearances on *Rowan & Martin's Laugh-In* as the German soldier who proclaimed the catchphrase "Very Interesting!" and as dirty old man Tyrone F. Horneye. He played Bascomb Bleacher, Jr., on *Sally*, Corporal Lefkowitz on *Don't Call Me Charlie*, and was a regular on *The Gong Show, Knockout, Games People Play*,

and *Glitter*. He has guest starred on *The Twilight Zone, Peter Loves Mary, Bringing Up Buddy, Alfred Hitchcock Presents, The Andy Griffith Show, General Electric True, McHale's Navy, No Time for Sergeants, Bob Hope Presents the Chrysler Theatre, The Dick Van Dyke Show, The Donna Reed Show, Hollywood Squares, I Dream of Jeannie, Love, American Style, The Glen Campbell Goodtime Hour, Sesame Street, Here's Lucy, Kojak, The Love Boat, The A-Team, The New Mike Hammer*, and *Murder, She Wrote*. He played Morris Dinkler on Episode 64 of *The Partridge Family*.

■ Dave Ketchum starred as Mel Warshaw on *I'm Dickens—He's Fenster*, played Spiffy on *Camp Runamuck*, and played Agent 13 on *Get Smart*. He has also appeared on *The Real McCoys, The Munsters, The Joey Bishop Show, Hey Landlord, Green Acres, Petticoat Junction, That Girl, Gomer Pyle, U.S.M.C., The Mod Squad, The Courtship of Eddie's Father, Love, American Style, The Mary Tyler Moore Show, The Odd Couple, Happy Days, Laverne & Shirley, Mork & Mindy*, and *Perfect Strangers*. His film appearances include *The Interns* (1962), *Good Neighbor Sam* (1964), *Love at First Bite* (1979), and *Main Event* (1979).

■ Jeff Donnell appeared on *The U.S. Steel Hour*, starred as Alice on *The George Gobel Show*, and played Ethel on *Matt Helm* and Stella Fields on *General Hospital*. She made hundreds of guest appearances on television, including spots on *Studio 57, Playhouse 90, The Adventures of Ellery Queen*,

Perry Mason, *Gidget*, *Julia*, *Chico and the Man*, and *The Bob Newhart Show*.
■ The reference to a boy named Sioux refers to the hit single "A Boy Named Sue" by Johnny Cash.

45: Hel-l-l-l-p 🐦🐦

When Shirley and Laurie decide to go wilderness camping at Pinaco Peak, Keith, Danny, and Mr. Kincaid secretly follow after them, neglect to bring along food and blankets, and get lost—all fifty yards from a Girl Rangers Lodge.
Writer: Dale McRaven
Director: Paton Price
Cast: Cindy Henderson as Girl Scout
SONG:
■ "I'm on My Way Back Home," music by Jack Keller, lyrics by Bobby Hart (on *Sound Magazine*)

46: Promise Her Anything but Give Her a Punch 🐦🐦🐦🐦

Danny has a crush on Gloria Hicky and wants to ask her to the sixth grade dance, but Gloria has a crush on Keith.
Writer: Dale McRaven
Director: Bob Claver
Cast: Patti Cohoon as Gloria Hicky
SONG:
■ "I Would Have Loved You Anyway," music and lyrics by Tony Romeo (on *Sound Magazine*)
NOTES:
■ Patti Cohoon played Cathy Apple on *Apple's Way*. She also played Gloria Hicky on Episode 55 of *The Partridge Family*.

47: The Partridge Papers 🐦🐦

When Danny accidently gives Laurie's diary to Marvin, the editor of the high school newspaper, Keith, Laurie, and Danny break into the newspaper office to steal it back.

Writer: William S. Bickley
Director: Jerry London
Cast: Gordon Jump as Policeman, Bruce Kimmel as Marvin
SONG:

■ "It's One of Those Nights (Yes Love)," music and lyrics by Tony Romeo (on *Shopping Bag*)

NOTES:

■ See Episode 1 for notes on Gordon Jump.

■ Bruce Kimmel was a regular on *Dinah and Her New Best Friends*. He played Laurie's boyfriend Freddy in Episode 32, her boyfriend Richard in Episode 55, her boyfriend Richard Whipple in Episode 74, and her boyfriend Howard Krump in Episode 81.

■ When the Partridges perform "It's One of Those Nights," horns and violin strings can be clearly heard, despite the fact that no one in the family is playing a brass instrument or a violin.

48: All's War in Love and Fairs 𝕎𝕎𝕎

When the Partridge Family's bus breaks down in the middle of the desert (forty miles from Piedmont) on the way between Las Vegas and Holiday Mountain Resort, mechanic Cal Courtney and his wife, Amanda, stall the repairs and send Mr. Kincaid on a wild goose chase in order to persuade the family to perform a benefit concert at the Papago Indian Fair.

Writer: John Wilder
Director: Mel Swope
Cast: Harry Morgan as Cal Courtney, Josephine Hutchinson as Amanda

May Courtney, Ivan Naranjo as Paul, Sandra Ego as Ruth, Lee Casey as Tommy

SONG:

■ "Come On Love," music and lyrics by Terry Cashman and Tommy West (on *Crossword Puzzle*)

NOTES:

■ Although the Papago Indians are a fictitious tribe, this episode is a thinly veiled public service announcement to educate the public about the low standard of living on Native American reservations.

■ See Episode 2 for notes on Harry Morgan.

■ Josephine Hutchinson starred in dozens of films, most notably *The Melody Lingers On* (1935), *The Story of Louis Pasteur* (1936), *Son of Frankenstein* (1939), *North by Northwest* (1959), and *Baby, the Rain Must Fall* (1965). On television she made guest appearances on *Perry Mason*, *Wagon Train*, *The Rifleman*, *The Real McCoys*, *Rawhide*, *The Twilight Zone*, *Burke's Law*, *Dr. Kildare*, *Gunsmoke*, *The Name of the Game*, *The F.B.I.*, *The Mod Squad*, *Mannix*, and *Little House on the Prairie*.

■ Sandra Ego played Joannie Little Bird on *Cade's County*.

49: Who Is Max Ledbetter and Why Is He Saying All Those Terrible Things? 𝄢𝄢

When psychic Maximilian Ledbetter learns that the bank is about to foreclose on his bakery, he convinces Keith and Danny that a disaster will befall the Partridge Family unless they give him $156.

Writer: Bernie Kahn

Director: Christopher Morgan

Cast: John Banner as Max Ledbetter, Joseph D. Reda as Coach, Greg Vigan as Peterson, and Richard Bull as Thompson

SONG:

■ "You Don't Have to Tell Me," music and lyrics by Tony Romeo (on *Sound Magazine*)

NOTES:

■ John Banner is best remembered as the buffoonish Sgt. Schultz on *Hogan's Heroes*. He also starred as Uncle Latzi on the short-lived situation comedy *The Chicago Teddy Bears* with Dean Jones in 1971. He appeared in the motion pictures *Once Upon a Honeymoon* (1942), *The Moon Is Down* (1943), *The Fallen Sparrow* (1943), *My Girl Tisa* (1948), *Guilty of Treason* (1949), *The Juggler* (1953), *The Rains of Ranchipur* (1955), *The Beast of*

Budapest (1958), *The Blue Angel* (1959), *The Story of Ruth* (1960), *Operation Eichmann* with Werner Klemperer (1961), *Hitler* (1962), *The Interns* (1962), *The Yellow Canary* (1963), *36 Hours* (1965), and *The Wicked Dreams of Paula Schultz* with Bob Crane, Werner Klemperer, and Leon Askin (1968). On television, he appeared on *Member of the Jury, Father Knows Best, Cimarron City, The Roaring Twenties, My Sister Eileen, Michael Shayne, Dante, 77 Sunset Strip, The Du Pont Show with June Allyson, The Untouchables, The Many Loves of Dobie Gillis, The Virginian, My Three Sons, The Man from U.N.C.L.E., The Donna Reed Show, Hazel, The Lucy Show,* and *The Doris Day Show.* He died in 1973. His last television appearance was this episode of *The Partridge Family* in 1972.

■ Richard Bull played Nels Oleson on *Little House on the Prairie* and the Doctor on *Voyage to the Bottom of the Sea.*

THIRD SEASON

50: This Male Chauvinist Piggy Went to Market 🐦🐦🐦🐦🐦

After Keith loses a competition against Laurie to determine whether men or women are more skilled, Laurie tells everyone in school, prompting Goose, the head of a motorcycle gang, to pick a fight with Keith.

Writer: Dale McRaven

Director: Richard Kinon

Cast: James C. Gordon as Goose Waller, David Jolliffe as First Biker, Tim Patrick as Guy, Cindy Cassell as Girl

SONG:

■ "God Bless You, Girl," music and lyrics by Irwin Levine and L. Russell Brown

NOTES:

■ Commented *Variety* of September 20, 1972: "For its genre (wholesome sitcom descended from *Father Knows Best*), *Partridge* is probably as good as anything around, with a resident cast that seems to have entrenched itself . . . The season's opener held right to the formula—a bit of heart, a bit of comedy, a bit of insight, and a bit of song . . . Nice and simple, easy to take, familiar. Go beat it."

■ Mr. Kincaid is seen hanging out at the Partridges' house for absolutely no reason other than a social visit.

■ David Jolliffe played Bernie on *Room 222.* He does extensive work as a commercial voice-over talent.

■ Cindy Cassell played Kitty in Episode 60 and Sally Winkler in Episode 80.

51: M Is for the Many Things

When Shirley is chosen "Mother of the Year" by *Woman's Journal* magazine and invited to a banquet dinner in her honor in Sacramento, she decides to drive the family up in the bus, neglects to bring along any money, gets a speeding ticket in Crater City, and runs out of gas.

Writer: William S. Bickley

Director: Lou Antonio

Cast: Edgar Buchanan as Judge McElwreath, Rick Hurst as Deputy Haynie, Yvonne Wilder as Sheila, Mitzi Hoag as Mrs. Maifussi, Jack Lukes as Driver

SONG:

■ "As Long as There's You," music and lyrics by Tony Romeo (on *Crossword Puzzle*)

NOTES:

■ Edgar Buchanan is best remembered as Uncle Joe Carson on *Petticoat Junction*. He also played Red Connors on *Hopalong Cassidy* and J. J. Jackson on *Cade's County*. He appeared in nearly 100 films, primarily Westerns, most notably *Penny Serenade* (1941), *Rawhide* (1951), *Shane* (1953), and *The Lonesome Trail* (1953). On television he appeared on *Maverick, The Californians, Leave It to Beaver, National Velvet, Bonanza, The Rifleman, The Andy Griffith Show, Dr. Kildare, Gunsmoke, The Twilight Zone, Dennis the Menace, The Beverly Hillbillies, Green Acres,* and *Love, American Style.*

■ Rick Hurst played Cleaver on *On the Rocks*.

■ Yvonne Wilder played Major Edna Howard on *Operation Petticoat*. She played the Waitress in Episode 37 of *The Partridge Family*.

■ Mitzi Hoag played Essie Gillis on *Here Come the Brides* and Liz Platt on *We'll Get By*. She played Sheila Faber in Episode 13, Mrs. Fergusson in Episode 43, and Miss Farrow in Episode 89 of *The Partridge Family*.

52: Princess and the Partridge

When the Partridges are called upon to have Princess Jennie over for dinner, the princess asks Keith to kidnap her from her hotel room so they can have a typical date, nearly causing an international incident.

Writer: William S. Bickley
Director: Richard Kinon
Cast: Season Hubley as Princess Jennie, Hal Buckley as Ambassador Cecil Turnbow, Laurie Main as Frederic LaForte, John Bernard as Valentine, Sheldon Lee as Photographer
SONG:
■ "Together We're Better," music and lyrics by Tony Romeo and Ken Jacobson (on *Notebook*)
NOTES:
■ Season Hubley played Margit McLean on *Kung Fu* and Salina Magee on *Family*.
■ Hal Buckley played St. John Quincy on *O.K. Crackerby*.
■ Laurie Main replaced Sebastian Cabot as the narrator of Winnie the Pooh cartoons and recordings.

53: Each Dawn I Diet 🐦🐦🐦

Danny bets Mr. Kincaid that he can stick to a diet longer than Mr. Kincaid can quit smoking, requiring the manager to move into Danny's bedroom for the duration of the wager.
Writers: Lloyd Turner and Gordon Mitchell
Director: Richard Kinon
SONG:
■ "It's All in Your Mind," music and lyrics by Johnny Cymbal and Peggy Clinger (on *Shopping Bag*)

54: A Penny for His Thoughts 🐦🐦🐦

When Snake the biker returns to the Partridge Family dejected because his girlfriend Penny Sweetweather turned down his marriage proposal, Shirley intervenes to teach Snake how to pop the question properly.
Writer: Dale McRaven
Director: Bob Claver
Cast: Stuart Margolin as Snake, Judie Stein as Penny Sweetweather, James Beach as Tinker, Henry Olek as Gorgo, Bryan O'Byrne as Father, Helen Kleeb as Mother, Bill Quinn as Minister
SONGS:
■ "Here Comes the Bride (traditional)," solo performed by Laurie
■ "Love Must Be the Answer," music and lyrics by Wes Farrell, Peggy

Clinger, and Johnny Cymbal (on *Notebook*)

NOTES:

■ This episode is a sequel to Episode 28 in which Rob Reiner played the role of Snake.

■ Snake claims his name is Hayman Timothy Goodrow despite the fact that he previously said his name was Harry Murphy in Episode 28.

■ Snake wears the identical denim jacket worn by the redheaded First Biker played by David Jolliffe in Episode 50.

■ See Episode 10 for notes on Stuart Margolin.

■ Henry Olek played Geek in Episode 28 and Skip Radnitz in Episode 88.

■ Bryan O'Byrne played Hodgkins on *Get Smart*. He played Mr. Koolic in Episode 28 of *The Partridge Family*.

■ Helen Kleeb played Miss Claridge on *Harrigan and Son* and Mamie Baldwin on *The Waltons*.

55: You're Only Young Twice

When Shirley, urged by the school psychiatrist, decides to treat Danny like an adult, Danny discovers that he isn't quite ready for adulthood.

Writer: Susan Silver

Director: Lee Phillips

Cast: Charlotte Rae as Dr. Beeder, Maggie Wellman as Molly, Patti Cohoon as Gloria Hicky, Bruce Kimmel as Richard

SONG:

■ "Am I Losing You," music and lyrics by Irwin Levine and L. Russell Brown (on *Shopping Bag*)

■ Mr. Kincaid sits in the Partridge Family's living room, helping Shirley with her quilting, for no apparent business reason.

■ Charlotte Rae starred as Edna Garrett on *Diff'rent Strokes* and *The Facts of Life*. She also played Sylvia Schnauser on *Car 54, Where Are You?*, Mrs. Bellotti on *Hot L Baltimore*, and was a regular on *The Rich Little Show*. She has appeared on *The U.S. Steel Hour*, *The Phil Silvers Show*, *The Ed Sullivan Show*, *The Garry Moore Show*, *The Sid Caesar Show*, *Love, American Style*, *All in the Family*, *Good Times*, *Barney Miller*, *The Love Boat*, *Murder, She Wrote*, and *St. Elsewhere*.

■ Patti Cohoon played Cathy Apple on *Apple's Way*. She played Gloria Hicky on Episode 46 of *The Partridge Family*.

■ Bruce Kimmel was a regular on *Dinah and Her New Best Friends*. He played Laurie's boyfriend Freddy in Episode 32, her boyfriend Marvin in Episode 47, her boyfriend Richard Whipple in Episode 74, and her boyfriend Howard Krump in Episode 81 of *The Partridge Family*.

56: The Mod Father 🐦🐦

After Shirley's parents discover group therapy and try to get the Partridge kids to open up, they decide their marriage isn't working, agree to act as if they were divorced, start dating other people, and wind up renewing their wedding vows before a minister.

Writer: Susan Harris
Director: E. W. Swackhamer
Cast: Ray Bolger as Grandma, Rosemary DeCamp as Grandma, Bill

Zuckert as Dwight, Gordon Jump as Minister, Tonie Berrell as Candy, Ondine Vaughn as Daisy

SONG:

■ "Something New Got Old," music and lyrics by Bobby Hart and Wes Farrell (on *Shopping Bag*)

NOTES:

■ See Episode 3 for notes on Ray Bolger and Rosemary DeCamp.

■ William Zuckert played General Cross on *The Wackiest Ship in the Army* and Chief Sagal on *Captain Nice*. He played the Captain in Episode 81 of *The Partridge Family*.

■ See Episode 1 for notes on Gordon Jump.

■ Ondine Vaughn played Gwen in Episode 68.

57: A Likely Candidate 🐦🐦🐦

When Shirley starts dating Richard Lawrence, a candidate for Congress, who wants the Partridge Family to perform at a campaign rally, Keith tries to break up the romance.

Writer: Martin Cohan

Director: Herb Wallerstein

Cast: Bert Convy as Richard Lawrence, Anne Carol Pearson as Cathy

SONGS:

■ "One Day at a Time," music and lyrics by Terry Cashman and Tommy West (on *Crossword Puzzle*)

■ "Ain't Love Easy," music and lyrics by Carol Hall, produced by Bones Howe

NOTE:

■ See Episode 31 for notes on Bert Convy. Richard Lawrence returns to visit the Partridge Family again in Episode 67.

58: Swiss Family Partridge 🐦🐦

When the Partridge Family and Mr. Kincaid get stranded without any provisions in a secluded cabin in the mountains forty miles from Lake Tahoe during a torrential rainstorm, Keith and Mr. Kincaid try to call for help by hooking the group's amplifier and microphone to the generator on the bus.

Writer: Dale McRaven

Director: Lou Antonio

Cast: Charles Shull as E. J. Whacker
SONG:

■ "It Means I'm in Love with You," music and lyrics by Tony Romeo and Ralph Landis (on *Crossword Puzzle*)
NOTE:

■ While rationing food, Mr. Kincaid questions whether to give his biscuit to Tracy and Chris with the caustic rejoinder, "How important are they to the act?"

59: Ain't Loveth Grand 🐦🐦🐦

When Laurie falls seriously in love with Greg Houser, a childhood sweetheart who is now a minister, Keith and Danny think she will elope.
Writer: William S. Bickley
Director: Herb Wallerstein
Cast: Anthony Geary as Greg Houser, Ta-Tanisha as Mary Lou Trimper
SONG:

■ "Sunshine," music and lyrics by Wes Farrell, Bobby Hart, and Danny Janssen (on *Crossword Puzzle*)
NOTES:

■ The song "Sunshine" sounds remarkably like a combination of "He's Got the Whole World in His Hands" and "The Battle Hymn of the Republic."

■ At the conclusion of this episode, Shirley brings Chris and Tracy upstairs to explain the facts of life.

■ Anthony Geary starred as Luke on *General Hospital*. He also starred on *Bright Promise* and *The Young and the Restless*. He appeared on *Room 222*, *All in the Family*, *Mannix*, *The Streets of San Francisco*, *Marcus Welby, M.D.*, *Barnaby Jones*, and *Murder, She Wrote*.

■ Ta-Tanisha played Pam on *Room 222*.

60: Whatever Happened to Keith Partridge? 🐦🐦🐦🐦

When a talent scout from World International Pictures asks Keith to take a screen test for the part of Vito Gambini (a young man with a pretty face and an evil heart) in the movie *Hitchhike from Death*, Keith wins, then loses, the part.

Writer: Susan Harris
Director: Bruce Bilson
Cast: Shelley Morrison as Mrs. Kornegge, Jim Connell as Gus Gorney, Ray Buktenica as Assistant Director, Robert B. Williams as Otis Butrum, Pat Patterson as Guard, Mark Lambert as Date, Cindy Cassell as Kitty, Claire Wilcox as Cindy

SONGS:
■ "Am I Losing You," music and lyrics by Irwin Levine and L. Russell Brown (on *Shopping Bag*)
■ "Looking Through the Eyes of Love," music and lyrics by Barry Mann and Cynthia Weil (on *Notebook*)

NOTES:
■ When the Partridge Family performs "Looking Through the Eyes of Love," a string section can be heard although no one can be seen playing a violin.
■ Shelley Morrison played Sister Sixto on *The Flying Nun*.
■ Jim Connell played Junior on *Run Buddy Run* and was a regular on *Donny and Marie*. He also played an Orderly in Episode 24 of *The Partridge Family*.
■ Ray Buktenica played Benny Goodwin on *Rhoda*. He played a newsman in Episode 82 of *The Partridge Family*.
■ Cindy Cassell played a girl in Episode 50 and Sally Winkler in Episode 80.
■ Claire Wilcox played Deedee Harris on the short-lived situation comedy *Harris Against the World*. She played Cathy in Episode 6 of *The Partridge Family*.

61: Nag, Nag, Nag

Danny wins a race horse named F. Scott Fitzgerald in a raffle, but when the Partridge Family decides to let the horse run at the San Pueblo County Fair, they discover it has insomnia.
Writer: Steve Pritzker

Director: E. W. Swackhamer
Cast: Slim Pickens as Will Fowler, Lazaro Perez as Pete Navarro, Dick
Balduzzi as Homer Peck
SONGS:

■ "Lullaby" (traditional)

■ "Breaking Up Is Hard to Do," music and lyrics by Neil Sedaka and Howard Greenfield (available as a single recording)

NOTES:

■ Slim Pickens starred as Slim on *The Outlaws*, California Joe Milner on *Custer*, and a regular on *B.J. and the Bear*, *Hee Haw*, *The Nashville Palace*, and *Filthy Rich*. He has appeared on *Death Valley Days*, *Circus Boy*, *Wagon Train*, *Alfred Hitchcock Presents*, *Route 66*, *The Virginian*, *The Man From U.N.C.L.E.*, *Rawhide*, *Mannix*, *Ironside*, *That Girl*, *Medical Center*, *Bonanza*, *The Mary Tyler Moore Show*, *Kung Fu*, *Baretta*, *McMillan and Wife*, and *The Love Boat*.

■ Dick Balduzzi played Marv Fillmore in Episode 78.

62: For Sale by Owner 🐦🐦

The Partridges decide to buy a new house, but they change their minds— only to discover that Mr. Kincaid has sold their house.

Writer: Charlotte Brown

Director: Russ Mayberry

Cast: Bert Freed as George Sharp, Lurene Tuttle as Bea Sharp, Donna Lynne as Girl, Marilyn Childs as Mrs. Gibson, Bobby Baum as Ed Hoffsteader, Maxine Stuart as Gloria Hoffsteader, Gordon Jump as Father, Sari Price as Mother, Susan Neher as Gwen, Robin Raymond as the Woman

SONG:

■ "As Long As You're There," music and lyrics by Adam Miller (on *Notebook*)

NOTES:

■ Bert Freed played Rufe Ryker on *Shane*.

■ Lurene Tuttle played Vinnie Day on *Life with Father*, Doris Dunston on *Father of the Bride*, and Hannah Yarby on *Julia*.

■ Maxine Stuart played Ruth on *Room for One More*, B. J. Clawson on *Slattery's People*, Scotty on *Doctors' Hospital*, and Marge Newberry on *Executive Suite*. She played Mrs. Damion in Episode 43 and Miss Halstead in Episode 92 of *The Partridge Family*.

■ See Episode 1 for notes on Gordon Jump.

■ Sari Price also played the Saleswoman in Episode 36 and the Woman in Episode 73.

■ Susan Neher played Penny Endicott on *To Rome with Love* and Jennifer Conway on *Getting Together*. She also played the Girl in Episode 74 of *The Partridge Family*.

63: Aspirin at 7, Dinner at 8 🐦🐦

When pediatrician Dr. Bernie Applebaum starts getting serious about Shirley, she can't figure out how to break off the relationship.

Writer: Susan Harris
Director: Bob Claver
Cast: Nancy Walker as Mrs. Applebaum, Gerald Hiken as Dr. Bernie Applebaum, Donald Phelps as Maître d'

SONG:

■ "One Day at a Time," music and lyrics by Terry Cashman and Tommy West (on *Crossword Puzzle*)

NOTES:

■ The Partridge Family also performed the song "One Day at a Time" at a campaign rally for congressional candidate Richard Lawrence in Episode 57.

■ No one in the Partridge Family seems to mind that Dr. Bernie Applebaum is Jewish; interfaith marriage apparently poses no problem for Shirley or her children—not even for Laurie who previously professed her love for a minister in Episode 59.

■ Chris and Tracy have the front of the bass drum repainted to read "The Applebaum Family," and add a man to the logo—demonstrating their willingness and eagerness to have their mother remarry.

■ Nancy Walker starred as Ida Morgenstern on *Rhoda* and *The Mary Tyler Moore Show*. She also played Emily on *Family Affair*, Mildred on *McMillan and Wife*, Nancy Kitteridge on *The Nancy Walker Show*, Nancy Blansky on *Blansky's Beauties*, and starred as Rosie in television commercials for Bounty paper towels. She has appeared on dozens of television shows including *The Red Skelton Show*, *The Jack Paar Show*, *The Ed Sullivan Show*, *The Garry Moore Show*, *Love, American Style*, *Medical Center*, *The Carol Burnett Show*, and *Happy Days*.

■ Gerald Hiken also played Dr. Bernie Applebaum in Episode 27.

64: For Whom the Bell Tolls . . . and Tolls . . . and Tolls 🐦🐦🐦

After Mr. Kincaid gives the Partridge Family a brand-new sound (by installing a burglar alarm in their house), an escaped convict breaks in and takes them all hostage.

Writer: Dale McRaven
Director: E. W. Swackhamer
Cast: Arte Johnson as Morris Dinkler, Nelson D. Cuevas as Officer Metscur, Mel Gallagher as Sam Barner
SONG:
- "Sunshine Eyes," music and lyrics by Terry Cashman and Tommy West

NOTES:
- When the Partridge Family sings "Sunshine Eyes," inviting Morris Dinkler to join them on harmonica, violin strings can be heard although no one can be seen playing violin.
- See Episode 44 for notes on Arte Johnson.
- Nelson D. Cuevas played Ernesto Valdez on *Viva Valdez*.

65: Trial of Partridge One

Laurie is falsely accused of stealing a test, so Keith works as her defense attorney, assisted by Danny, but Laurie refuses to identify the real thief: the principal's daughter.

Writers: Steve Zacharias and Michael Leeson
Director: Jerry London
Cast: Dana Elcar as Mr. Felcher, Noah Keen as Principal Brown, Eric Laneuville as Judge, Tannis Montgomery as Cindy Brown, Jim Wakefield as Brad, Michelle Cook as Melinda

SONG:
- "It's You," music and lyrics by Johnny Cymbal and Peggy Clinger (on *Crossword Puzzle*)

NOTES:
- Dana Elcar played Inspector Shiller on *Baretta*, Colonel Lard on *Baa Baa Black Sheep*, and Peter Thornton on *MacGyver*. He has appeared on *The U.S. Steel Hour*, *Car 54, Where Are You?*, *Mannix*, *The F.B.I.*, *Get Smart*, *Medical Center*, *The Virginian*, *Mission: Impossible*, *Room 222*, *The Rockford Files*, *Newhart*, *The A-Team*, and *Hardcastle and McCormick*.
- Noah Keen played Detective Lt. Bone on *Arrest and Trial*.
- Eric Laneuville played Larry on *Room 222*.

66: I Left My Heart in Cincinnati 🐦

During a booking at King's Island Amusement Park in Ohio, Keith falls in love with an older woman, the park's public relations person, Audrey Parson, and Danny tries to make him see the error of his ways.

Writer: Dale McRaven
Director: Bob Claver
Cast: Mary Ann Mobley as Audrey Parson
Cameo: Johnny Bench saying, "Would you care for a drink?"
SONGS:

■ "Girl, You Make My Day," music and lyrics by Tommy Boyce and Bobby Hart (on *Shopping Bag*)
■ "Together We're Better," music and lyrics by Tony Romeo and Ken Jacobson (on *Notebook*)

NOTES:

■ Mary Ann Mobley was Miss America in 1959 and was a regular on *Be Our Guest*, *General Hospital*, and *Diff'rent Strokes*. She has also appeared on *Burke's Law*, *The Man from U.N.C.L.E.*, *The Virginian*, *Love, American Style*, *Police Story*, *Hotel*, and *The Love Boat*.
■ Johnny Bench was the catcher for the Cincinnati Reds for seventeen years and was is a member of the Baseball Hall of Fame.

67: The Eleven-Year Itch 🐦🐦🐦🐦

When Shirley's romantic interest Richard Lawrence returns for a visit with his daughter Julie, the young girl develops a crush on Danny, but the next day, when Danny kisses her, she punches him in the eye.

Writer: William S. Bickley
Director: Richard Kinon
Cast: Jodie Foster as Julie Lawrence, Bert Convy as Richard Lawrence, Dennis Lee Smith as Waiter
SONG:

■ "Like Walking in the Rain," music and lyrics by Barry Mann, Cynthia Weil, and Phil Spector

NOTES:

■ Lawyer Richard Lawrence appeared in Episode 57 with his daughter, Cathy, and never mentioned that he had a second daughter, Julie. In this episode, he never mentions his eldest daughter, Cathy. Enamored with Shirley, Lawrence promises to return soon, but we never see him again.

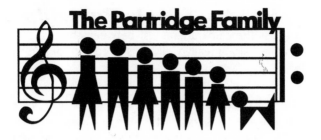

What Is Your Fondest Memory of the Show?

Shirley Jones (Shirley Partridge):

"We did a wonderful show where we filmed in Marineland [Episode 31], and it was one time I was allowed to sing in the show and have my own solo. You know, that was rare. They wrote a beautiful song called 'The Whale Song' with the sounds of the whales. It was such a pretty song. I loved that episode. I loved that moment. I loved the song, I loved being able to sing it. For the most part David was the singing star of the show and sold the records, but that was a nice thing for me."

David Cassidy (Keith Partridge):

"The friends and family that I made for those years, the relationships amongst the cast and some of the creative people."

Susan Dey (Laurie Partridge):

"I had been a model, and the next thing I knew, I was out here, doing a show and having to act grownup. I had to rent a house to live in. I had to rent a car to take me to and from work. I had to pay for someone to stay with me on the set because I was a minor. In addition, everyone was telling me what they wanted me to do. And because I was so afraid of failing, I tried to do it all. I was never easy on myself; I never asked myself what I really wanted. I became a stressoholic who was afraid of everything. The anxiety never showed up on TV, but I was a nervous wreck." (in *Redbook*, August 1987)

Danny Bonaduce (Danny Partridge):

"During [the filming of] one episode, when I was being a particularly jerky kid, Shirley tried to ground me to my room [on the set], and of course, I didn't actually have a room. Her motherly instincts kind of took over, and she yelled out, 'Danny, go to your room!' And everyone just kind of looked at her like 'Man, Shirley has finally flipped out.' It was really funny."

Brian Forster (*Chris Partridge*):

"I would guess the camaraderie just between the cast and everybody. I mean, we all got along really well and shared a lot of laughs and had a lot of fun."

Jeremy Gelbwaks (*Chris Partridge*):

"Riding my bike with Suzanne through the western street on the lot, watching Charlton Heston film *The Omega Man*, and stuff like that. I can remember thinking what a lucky kid I was to meet my musical idol, Bobby Sherman [Episode 25]. I mean, that show was a lot of fun, and I liked being famous, too. You know, fan letters and people crowding me when I went back to school and stuff. Hey, the whole thing was a great time for a kid."

Suzanne Crough (*Tracy Partridge*):

"I think for me especially, because I was the youngest, my fondest memory was just working with all of them on a daily basis and feeling like I was David's little sister and Susan's little sister. From my standpoint, because I wasn't an adult; I wasn't trying to capture a certain amount of the script; I wasn't as stressed out as an adult would be working in that atmosphere. So for me, I felt a closer bond to all of them as their kid sister. And that to me was really important because I felt really close to all of them."

Dave Madden (*Mr. Kincaid*):

"I guess probably the fondest memory I have was the relationship that developed between Danny and me. Danny was having a lot of problems at the time, created by his parents' divorce, a lot of problems with his father. Danny spent a lot of time with me back in those days. I had a beach house in Malibu at the time. There were periods where he spent more time down there than he spent in his own home, and I became a kind of surrogate father to him, before I ever became a real father, because I had never been married at that time. I was still a single man running around. I suppose people who watched the show probably thought that Danny and I really hated each other, but the fact is, we had a very good relationship. I certainly had more of a relationship with Danny off the set than I had with anybody else in the show. I just kind of took to him. I knew he was having problems, and I knew he was basically a good kid, and I wanted to help him in any way that I could. It was nice. That's probably my fondest memory."

Bernard Slade (*Creator*):

"Most of my memories are tied up with the pilot [Episode 1]. The thing is: I was very rarely on the set. I mean, I know all the people involved, but I wasn't heavily involved on a day-to-day basis, so I think it was probably seeing that the pilot worked and that it made me smile. And it was a sweet show. It was one of those pilots that turned out very well and was pretty much what I had in mind."

Bob Claver (Executive Producer):

"I had a good time doing it, and we never, ever had any trouble. I thought it was a very happy show. I enjoyed working on it thoroughly. Shirley would say once in a while, 'Boy, this script isn't very good, is it?' And I would say, 'No, it isn't.' And once you didn't try to pretend, like 'Oh, no, it's really good, Shirley,' she was marvelous. So we just didn't have any great problems."

Paul Witt (Producer):

"It was the first show that I really had a great deal of control. Bob Claver was my mentor, and I did three comedies with him as executive producer and me as producer. And then we did two years of *Here Come the Brides* together, and he gave me a lot of autonomy. So it was the first time I was able to really feel like I was running the show and flex my muscles creatively. It really helped jump-start my whole career. Although I had been in business producing and directing and so forth, this was the first show that I was really able to feel that I was central in producing."

Wes Farrell (Music Producer):

"It was a challenging experience that just kept getting better, as I reflect on it now. When things exceed your expectations and you've sold a lot of records, you just reach another kind of level with the experience. It was a phenomenon. The sales curves on the product were astronomical. We had days where we sold 50 to 75 thousand records a day, statistics which are unheard of, even twenty years later. It was incredible what we experienced, and it was fun.

"It was a very rewarding experience for me for more than one reason. A lot of people I truly believed in creatively really spent and indulged big pieces of their lives at that time. The musicians were the finest musicians that I think have ever come out of any one given period creatively in contemporary music. The same people who played on the hits for the Beach Boys, the Mamas and the Papas, and dozens of other major stars that came out of the West Coast were our musicians. It was one of the greatest studio bands that has ever been assembled, and it was a mixture of certain people, no more than five, six, or seven interchanged. And how it flowed was an amazing experience. When I said we were doing a Partridge Family recording, they took on a certain personality of understanding the project and interpreting where I wanted to go with it."

■ Mr. Kincaid does not appear in this episode. Perhaps he perceives Richard Lawrence as a rival and jealousy keeps him away.

■ When the Partridge Family performs "Like Walking in the Rain," a string section can be heard although no one can be seen playing a violin.

■ Jodie Foster starred in *Napoleon and Samantha* (1972), *Kansas City Bomber* (1972), *Tom Sawyer* (1973), *One Little Indian* (1973), *Alice Doesn't Live Here Anymore* (1975), *Echoes of a Summer/The Last Castle* (1975), *Taxi Driver* (1976), *Bugsy Malone* (1976), *Freaky Friday* (1977), *The Little Girl Who Lives Down the Lane* (1977), *Il Casotto* (1977), *Moi, Fleur Bleue* (1977), *Candleshoe* (1977), and *Ladies of the Valley* (1979) and won an Academy Award for Best Actress for her performance in *The Accused* (1988) and again for *The Silence of the Lambs* (1991). She also directed and starred in *Little Man Tate* (1992) and *Summersby* (1993). On television, she starred as Elizabeth Henderson on *Bob & Carol & Ted & Alice* and as Addie Pray on *Paper Moon*. She appeared on *Mayberry R.F.D.*, *The Courtship of Eddie's Father*, *Gunsmoke*, *Julia*, *Nanny and the Professor*, *My Three Sons*, *Ironside*, *Medical Center*, *The Wonderful World of Disney*, and *Saturday Night Live*.

■ See Episode 31 for notes on Bert Convy.

■ Dennis Lee Smith played Voice #1 in Episode 27 and the First Guy in Episode 41.

68: Bedknobs and Drumsticks 🐦🐦🐦🐦

After Mr. Kincaid arranges for the Partridge Family to star as a wholesome family having a picnic in a commercial for Uncle Erwin's Country Chicken, Erwin insists that the Partridges appear in the commercial wearing feathered chicken suits.

Writers: Lloyd Turner and Gordon Mitchell
Director: Herb Wallerstein
Cast: William Windom as Erwin, Danny Goldman as the Director, Elaine Giftos as Bonnie Kleinschmitt, John Lawrence as Conventioneer, Ondine Vaughn as Gwen

SONGS:

■ "Friend and a Lover," music and lyrics by Wes Farrell, Bobby Hart, and Danny Janssen (on *Notebook*)

NOTES:

■ Mr. Kincaid insists that appearing in a commercial will be good for the Partridge Family's career, despite the fact that almost every successful rock group at the time refused on principle to make commercial endorsements.

■ The song "Friend and a Lover" sounds suspiciously like "Na Na Hey

Hey Kiss Him Goodbye" by Steam.

■ William Windom starred as Congressman Glen Morley on *The Farmer's Daughter* and John Monroe on *My World and Welcome to It*, Dr. Seth Hazlitt on *Murder, She Wrote*,

and Frank on *Parenthood*. He has appeared on hundreds of television shows including *Masterpiece Playhouse, Robert Montgomery Presents, The Donna Reed Show, Surfside Six, Ben Casey, The Twilight Zone, 77 Sunset Strip, The Lucy Show, Gunsmoke, Twelve O'Clock High, The F.B.I., The Wild Wild West, The Fugitive, The Virginian, Mission: Impossible, Star Trek, Bonanza, Mannix, Ironside, Hawaii Five-O, Love, American Style, That Girl, Night Gallery, The Streets of San Francisco, Marcus Welby, M.D., The Flip Wilson Show, McMillan and Wife, S.W.A.T., Barney Miller, Medical Center, Kojak, Quincy, The Love Boat, The A-Team, St. Elsewhere, Simon & Simon*, and *Newhart*. His television movies include *The Homecoming* (1971), *The Day the Earth Moved* (1974), *Blind Ambition* (1979), and *Desperate Lives* (1982).

■ Danny Goldman played Nick Dutton on *The Good Life* and Lester Bellman on *Busting Loose*.

■ Elaine Giftos played Bobbe Marsh on *The Interns*. She also played Bonnie Kleinschmitt in Episodes 40, 79, and 80 of *The Partridge Family*.

■ Ondine Vaughn played Daisy in Episode 56.

69: Everything You Wanted to Know About Sex . . . but Couldn't Pronounce 🐦🐦🐦🐦

America's heartthrob, Keith Partridge, is failing his sex education class in school.

Writer: Dale McRaven
Director: Bob Claver
Cast: Ramon Bieri as Mr. Grisbee

SONG:

■ "It Means I'm in Love with You," music and lyrics by Tony Romeo and Ralph Landis (on *Crossword Puzzle*)

NOTES:

■ Ramon Bieri played Barney Verick on *Sarge*.

70: Forgive Us Our Debts 🐦🐦🐦

After Shirley fails to correct a computer error on a bill from Bartlett's Department Store, Keith, Laurie, and Danny sneak into the store's computer room to reprogram the machine in their favor.

Writer: Skip Webster

Director: Bruce Bilson

Cast: Alan Oppenheimer as Byron Atwater, John David Carson as Tom Baker, Robert F. Simon as Mr. Bartlett, Lou Frizzell as George, Vic Tayback as Harlan Laws, Gary Morgan as Albert

SONG:

■ "Maybe Someday," music and lyrics by Austin Roberts and John Michael Hill (on *Notebook*)

NOTES:

■ When the Partridge Family sings "Maybe Someday," a brass and string section can be heard although no one can be seen playing a horn or a violin.

■ See Episode 16 for notes on Alan Oppenheimer.

■ John David Carson was the finalist competing against David Cassidy for the role of Keith Partridge.

■ Robert F. Simon played Dave Tabak on *Saints and Sinners*, Brig. Gen. Alfred Terry on *Custer*, Uncle Everett on *Nancy*, General Mitchell on *M*A*S*H*, and J. Jonah Jameson on *The Amazing Spider-Man*.

■ Lou Frizzell played Dusty Rhoades on *Bonanza*, Mitch on *Chopper One*, and Murdock on *The New Land*. He also appeared on *Armstrong Circle Theatre*, *Profiles in Courage*, *The F.B.I.*, *Owen Marshall: Counselor at Law*, *Marcus Welby, M.D.*, *Hawaii Five-O*, *Barnaby Jones*, *The Streets of San Francisco*, and *Alice*.

■ See Episode 7 for notes on Vic Tayback.

71: The Partridge Connection 🐦🐦

When Danny is accused of shoplifting a second time from Phelps' Drugstore, he refuses to perform with the Partridge Family on the night

they are to be collectively named "San Pueblo Citizen of the Year."
Writers: Steve Zacharias and Michael Leeson
Director: E. W. Swackhamer
Cast: Henry Jones as Mr. Phelps, Gary Dubin as Punky Lazaar, Joseph Perry as Police Sergeant Donakovsky, Jack Collins as Emcee, Angela Clarke as Myra Fromacher

SONG:
■ "I Don't Care," music and lyrics by Bobby Hart and Wes Farrell

NOTES:
■ Henry Jones starred as Dean Fred Baker on *Channing* and Judge Jonathan Dexter on *Phyllis.*
■ Gary Dubin played Mark Grant on *Brac-*

ken's World. He also played Punky Lazaar in Episodes 30, 89, 91, 92, and 95 of *The Partridge Family.*
■ Joseph Perry played Mr. Jenkins in Episode 21 and the Policeman in Episode 84.
■ Jack Collins was a regular on *The Milton Berle Show* and played Max Brahms on *Occasional Wife.* He played an Investor in Episode 7 of *The Partridge Family.*

72: The Selling of the Partridges

When Keith runs for class president of San Pueblo High School against Phyllis Goldberg, a better qualified candidate (with Laurie as her campaign manager), he decides to back his opponent.
Writers: Steve Zacharias and Michael Leeson
Director: Lee Phillips
Cast: Holly Near as Phyllis Goldberg, Jason Wingreen as Principal, David Dominguez as Ted, Geri Berger as Girl #1, Lori Farrow as Girl #2, Bobby Kramer as Myron, Anne Carol Pearson as Band Member
SONG:
■ "There'll Come a Time," music and lyrics by David Cassidy (on *Shopping Bag*)

■ When the Partridge Family performs "There'll Come a Time," a flute and a string section can be heard although no one can be seen playing those instruments.

■ Holly Near made guest appearances on *Room 222* and *All in the Family*.

■ Jason Wingreen played Harry Snowden on *All in the Family* and *Archie Bunker's Place*. He made guest appearances on *The Twilight Zone*, *The Outer Limits*, *The Fugitive*, *The Man from U.N.C.L.E.*, *The F.B.I.*, *Mannix*, *Columbo*, *Kung Fu*, *Marcus Welby, M.D.*, *Ironside*, *Medical Center*, *Barnaby Jones*, *The Rockford Files*, *Highway to Heaven*, and *Matlock*.

■ Bobby Kramer also played Wally Benton in Episode 80.

73: Diary of a Mad Millionaire 🐦🐦🐦🐦

Reclusive millionaire Sidney Rose befriends the Partridge Family and buys out all the seats at several of their performances so he can be the only person in the audience.

Writers: Steve Zacharias and Michael Leeson
Director: Lou Antonio
Cast: John Astin as Sidney Rose, Jim Antonio as Merl Pearson, Sari Price as a Woman

SONGS:
■ "It Sounds Like You're Saying Hello," music and lyrics by Terry Cashman and Tommy West (on *Crossword Puzzle*)
■ "One Night Stand," music and lyrics by Wes Farrell and Paul Anka (on *Sound Magazine*)

NOTES:
■ John Astin starred as Gomez Addams on *The Addams Family*. He also played Harry Dickens on *I'm Dickens—He's Fenster*, Lt. Commander Matthew Sherman on *Operation Petticoat*, Ed LaSalle on *Mary*, and Buddy, father of Harry Stone, on *Night Court*. He appeared in several motion pictures, most notably *West Side Story* (1961), *That Touch of Mink* (1962), *Candy* (1968), and *Freaky Friday* (1977). He made guest appearances on *Maverick*, *The Twilight Zone*, *The Pruitts of Southampton*, *The Donna Reed Show*, *Route 66*, *The Farmer's Daughter*, *The Wild Wild West*, *Batman*, *The Flying Nun*, *Gunsmoke*, *He & She*, *Bonanza*, *Love, American Style*, *Night Gallery*, *The Odd Couple*, *Police Woman*, *Marcus Welby, M.D.*, *Welcome Back Kotter*, *McMillan and Wife*, *The Love Boat*, *Simon & Simon*, *Diff'rent Strokes*, *The Facts of Life*, *Murder, She Wrote*, *St. Elsewhere*, and *Webster*. His television movies include *Evil Roy Slade* (1972) and *The Dream Makers* (1975).

■ Sari Price also played the Saleswoman in Episode 36 and the Mother in Episode 62.

74: Me and My Shadow

Famous mystery writer Michelangelo Rezo bets the Partridge family he can find them within 24 hours or he'll give $25,000 to their favorite charity.

Writer: Dale McRaven
Director: Jerry London
Cast: Dick Stahl as Michelangelo Rezo, Martin Speer as Lazaar Hannibal, Bruce Kimmel as Richard Whipple, Susan Neher as Girl

SONG:

■ "Storybook Love," music and lyrics by Wes Farrell and Adam Miller (on *Notebook*)

NOTES:

■ Shirley alludes to an unnamed and seemingly clandestine love interest, much to the surprise of her children and Mr. Kincaid.

■ See Episode 41 for notes on Dick Stahl.

■ Martin Speer played the Engineer in Episodes 27, 31, and 34.

■ Bruce Kimmel was a regular on *Dinah and Her New Best Friends*. He also played Laurie's boyfriend Freddy in Episode 32, her boyfriend Marvin in Episode 47, her boyfriend Richard in Episode 55, and her boyfriend Howard Krump in Episode 81 of *The Partridge Family*.

■ Susan Neher played Penny Endicott on *To Rome with Love* and Jennifer Conway on *Getting Together*. She played Gwen in Episode 62 of *The Partridge Family*.

The Partridge Family's home has been redecorated and refurnished. The piano is against a different wall in the living room, the kitchen has new wallpaper, and there's new carpeting on the staircase. Keith is a freshman at San Pueblo College, Mr. Kincaid has grown a mustache and mutton chop sideburns, Danny Partridge has gone through puberty and now parts his red hair down the middle, and a four-year-old next door neighbor, Ricky Stevens, occasionally sings with the Partridges.

75: Hate Thy Neighbor 🦜🦜

When single mother Doris Stevens and her two children move into the house next door to the Partridges, Mrs. Stevens prevents the Partridge Family from rehearsing in their garage—until she sees her four-year-old son, Ricky, perform with the Partridges in concert.

Writers: George Tibbles and William S. Bickley
Director: Richard Kinon
Cast: Nita Talbot as Doris Stevens, Ricky Segall as Ricky Stevens, Ronne Troup as Donna Stevens, Theodore Wilson as Police Officer Sam Mulvaney

SONGS:

■ "I'll Never Get over You," music and lyrics by Tony Romeo (on *Bulletin Board*)

■ "Sooner or Later," music and lyrics by Rick Segall, lead vocal by Ricky Segall (on *Ricky Segall and the Segalls*)

NOTES:

■ This episode marks the first appearance of four-year-old Ricky Segall as Ricky Stevens.

■ When the Partridge Family rehearses "I'll Never Get over You" in their garage, a string section can be heard although no one in the family can be seen playing a violin.

■ When the Partridge Family performs "Sooner or Later," a xylophone can be heard although no one can be seen sounding that instrument.

■ Nita Talbot played Mable Spooner on *Joe & Mabel*, Judy Evans on *Here We Go Again*, and Countess Rivchefski on *Hogan's Heroes*.

■ Ronne Troup played Polly Williams Douglas, wife of Chip Douglas, on *My Three Sons*.

■ Theodore Wilson starred as Phil Wheeler on the short-lived situation comedy *The Sanford Arms* and played Earl on *That's My Mama*.

76: None but the Lonely 🐦🐦

When Laurie refuses to introduce Keith to Dina Firmly, a new girl in school, Keith writes a letter as Mr. Lonely to Laurie's newspaper column and then tries to convince Laurie to set Mr. Lonely up on a date with Dina Firmly.

Writer: Dale McRaven
Director: Charles Rondeau
Cast: Kathleen Cody as Dina Firmly, Mike Rupert as Mark, Gary Morgan as Scotty, Ricky Segall as Ricky Stevens

SONGS:
■ "Alone Too Long," music by Mark James, lyrics by Cynthia Weil (on *Bulletin Board*)
■ "Bicycle Song," music and lyrics by Rick Segall, vocal by Ricky Segall (on *Ricky Segall and the Segalls*)

NOTES:
■ When the Partridge Family performs "Alone Too Long," a string section can be heard although no one in the family can be seen playing a violin.
■ When the Partridge Family performs "Bicycle Song," wood blocks and metal bells can be heard, although no one can be seen playing those percussion instruments.

77: Beethoven, Brahms, and Partridge 🐦🐦🐦🐦

Encouraged by his new girlfriend, Keith composes his first classical concerto and decides to forsake his career as a pop-music songwriter.

Writer: Dale McRaven
Director: Charles Rondeau
Cast: Barbara Sigel as Rachel

Weston, Harold Gould as Walter Yost, Ricky Segall as Ricky Stevens
SONGS:
■ "I Think I Love You," music and lyrics by Tony Romeo (heard on tape deck) (on *Family Album*)
■ "I Think I Love You (classical version)," music and lyrics by Tony Romeo
■ "I'm into Something Good," music and lyrics by Carole King and Gerry Goffin
■ "When I Grow Up," music and lyrics by Rick Segall, vocal by Ricky Segall (on *Ricky Segall and the Segalls*)
NOTES:
■ Harold Gould played Martin Morgenstern on *Rhoda*. He was also a regular on *The Feather and Father Gang*, *Park Place*, *Foot in the Door*, *Spencer*, *Dallas*, and *Singer & Sons*. He appeared in several motion pictures, most notably Woody Allen's *Love and Death* (1975) and Stephen Kessler's *Birch Street Gym* (1991). On television he made guest appearances on *Dennis the Menace*, *Route 66*, *The Twilight Zone*, *Mr. Novak*, *The Virginian*, *The F.B.I.*, *Get Smart*, *The Wild Wild West*, *He & She*, *The Flying Nun*, *Love, American Style*, *The Mary Tyler Moore Show*, *Gunsmoke*, *Hawaii Five-O*, *The Bob Crane Show*, *Police Story*, *Family*, *The Love* Boat, *Lou Grant*, *The Rockford Files*, *Webster*, *St. Elsewhere*, *L.A. Law*, and *Empty Nest*. He also works as a commercial voice-over talent.

78: The Strike-Out King 🦉

When Danny joins a Little League baseball team and becomes the star pitcher, Shirley lectures the coach, reminding him: "It's not whether you win or lose, but how you play the game."
Writer: William S. Bickley
Director: E. W. Swackhamer
Cast: Herb Edelman as Coach Darby Willis, Dick Balduzzi as Marv Fillmore, Gordon Jump as Zack Feldman, Dick O'Shea as Umpire, Jack Haley as Rusty, Ricky Segall as Ricky Stevens
SONGS:
■ "Say, Hey, Willie," music and lyrics by Rick Segall, vocal by Ricky Segall (on *Ricky Segall and the Segalls*)
■ "I Wanna Be with You," music and lyrics by Wes Farrell and Gerry Goffin
NOTES:
■ When Ricky Stevens sings "Say, Hey, Willie," Keith accompanies him

on banjo, an instrument we've never seen him play on the show before.

■ Herb Edelman starred as Bert Gramus on *The Good Guys*, and Stan on *The Golden Girls*. He has appeared on *That Girl*, *It's About Time*, *The Flying Nun*, *The Mothers-in-Law*, *Love, American Style*, *Bewitched*, *The Bill Cosby Show*, *Mission: Impossible*, *Ironside*, *Maude*, *The Streets of San Francisco*, *Happy Days*, *Medical Center*, *Barney Miller*, *Kojak*, *The Love Boat*, *Cagney & Lacey*, *St. Elsewhere*, and *thirtysomething*.

■ Dick Balduzzi played Homer Peck in Episode 61.

■ See Episode 1 for notes on Gordon Jump.

■ Jack Haley emceed *Ford Star Revue* and appeared on *Your Play Time*.

79: Reuben Kincaid Lives 🐦🐦

When Shirley and her children decide to throw a birthday party for Mr. Kincaid to demonstrate their appreciation, inviting his mother and his girlfriend Bonnie Kleinschmitt, the manager convinces himself everyone is displaying kindness because he doesn't have long to live.

Writers: Steve Zacharias and Michael Leeson

Director: E. W. Swackhamer

Cast: Margaret Hamilton as Clara Kincaid, Elaine Giftos as Bonnie Kleinschmitt, Ricky Segall as Ricky Stevens

SONGS:

■ "I Got Your Love All over Me," music and lyrics by Johnny Cymbal and Peggy Clinger (on *Crossword Puzzle*)

■ "Just Loving You," music and lyrics by Rick Segall, vocal by Ricky Segall (on *Ricky Segall and the Segalls*)

NOTES:

■ Mr. Kincaid's mother claims to live 1,500 miles from San Pueblo, yet in Episode 42, Reuben claims that she just moved to Yonkers, NY. Either Mrs. Kincaid moved again, or her son is a terrible judge of distance.

■ Margaret Hamilton is best remembered as the Wicked Witch of the West in *The Wizard of Oz* (1939). She also played Cora in Maxwell House coffee commercials in the 1970s. She appeared in dozens of films, most notably *You Only Live Once* (1937), *Nothing Sacred* (1937), *The Adventures of Tom Sawyer* (1938), *My Little Chickadee* (1940), *The Invisible Woman* (1941), and *The Ox-Bow Incident* (1943). On television, she was a regular on *The Paul Winchell-Jerry Mahoney Show*, *Valiant Lady*, and *As the World Turns*. She also made guest appearances on dozens of shows, including *The U.S. Steel Hour*, *Studio One*, *Playhouse 90*, *Car 54, Where Are You?*, *The Patty Duke Show*, *The Addams Family*, *Gunsmoke*, and *Lou Grant*.

■ Elaine Giftos played Bobbe Marsh on *The Interns*. She also played Bonnie Kleinschmitt in Episodes 40, 68, and 80 of *The Partridge Family*.

80: Double Trouble

When Keith makes two dates to take Johanna Houser and Sally Winkler to the same beach party, he fakes a cold to get out of his obligation to Sally, but the plan backfires.

Writers: Richard Bensfield and Perry Grant
Director: Herb Wallerstein
Cast: Elaine Giftos as Bonnie Kleinschmitt, Bobby Kramer as Wally Benton, Cheryl Ladd as Johanna Houser, Cindy Cassell as Sally Winkler, Ricky Segall as Ricky Stevens

SONGS:

■ "Oh, No, Not My Baby," music and lyrics by Gerry Goffin and Carole King (on *Bulletin Board*)

■ "A Little Bit of Loving," music and lyrics by Rick Segall, vocals by Ricky Segall (on *Ricky Segall and the Segalls*)

NOTES:

■ When the Partridge Family performs "Oh, No, Not My Baby," a string section can be heard although no one can be seen playing a violin. Tracy demonstrates her versatility as a musician by playing the triangle.

■ The broken cuckoo clock Shirley purchased from a department store in Episode 70 is now hanging in the garage.

■ Elaine Giftos played Bobbe Marsh on *The Interns*. She also played Bonnie Kleinschmitt in Episodes 40, 68, and 79 of *The Partridge Family*.

■ Bobby Kramer played Myron in Episode 72.

■ Cheryl Ladd played Kris Munroe on *Charlie's Angels*. She was also a regular on *The Ken Berry "WOW" Show*, and made guest appearances on *Ironside*, *Happy Days*, *Police Woman*, *The San Pedro Beach Bums*, *The Mike*

Douglas Show, *The Tonight Show Starring Johnny Carson*, *General Electric's All-Star Anniversary*, *John Denver and the Ladies*, and *The Presidential Inaugural Gala*. Her television movies include *Satan's School for Girls* (1973), *When She Was Bad* (1979), *Grace Kelly* (1983), *Kentucky Woman* (1983), *A Death in California* (1985), *Romance on the Orient Express* (1985), *Crossings* (1986), *Deadly Care* (1987), *Bluegrass* (1988), and *The Fulfillment of Mary Gray* (1989).

■ Cindy Cassell played a girl in Episode 50 and Kitty in Episode 60.

81: The Last Howard 🐦🐦

The Partridge Family gets booked to perform aboard a cruise ship, the T.S.S. *Fairsea*, and when passenger Howard Wainwright III gives Laurie a fourteenth century bracelet from Madagascar, Keith and Mr. Kincaid suspect he stole the piece of jewelry from another passenger.

Writer: Dale McRaven
Director: Richard Kinon
Cast: Bruce Kimmel as Howard Krump, Bill Zuckert as the Captain, Ruth Gillette as Mrs. Milstead, Stuart Wagstaff as the Head Waiter

SONG:
■ "When Love's Talked About," music and lyrics by Wes Farrell, John Bahler, and Tony Asher

NOTES:
■ This episode marks the first time a television series was ever filmed at sea aboard a cruise ship.
■ When the Partridge Family performs "When Love's Talked About," a string section can be heard although no one can be seen playing a violin.
■ Bruce Kimmel was a regular on *Dinah and Her New Best Friends*. He played Laurie's boyfriend Freddy in Episode 32, her boyfriend Marvin in Episode 47, her boyfriend Richard in Episode 55, and her boyfriend Richard Whipple in Episode 74 of *The Partridge Family*.
■ William Zuckert played General Cross on *The Wackiest Ship in the Army* and Chief Sagal on *Captain Nice*. He played Dwight in Episode 56 of *The Partridge Family*.

82: The Diplomat 🐦

When Ambassador Howard Lipton tries to romance Shirley, she invites him to dinner at her home with her family.

Writers: Paul Lichtman and Howard Storm
Director: Herb Wallerstein
Cast: Richard Mulligan as Howard Lipton, Pat Harrington, Jr., as Roger Harper, Ray Buktenica as Newsman, Florida Freibus as Mrs. Hendleman, and Ricky Segall as Ricky Stevens
SONGS:
■ "How Long Is Too Long," music and lyrics by John Bahler and Tom Asher (on *Bulletin Board*)
■ "What King of Noise Do You Make?," music and lyrics by Rick Segall, lead vocal by Ricky Stevens (on *Ricky Segall and the Segalls*)
NOTES:
■ See Episode 17 for notes on Richard Mulligan.
■ See Episode 7 for notes on Pat Harrington, Jr.
■ Ray Buktenica played Benny Goodwin on *Rhoda*. He also played the Assistant Director in Episode 60 of *The Partridge Family*.

83: Heartbreak Keith 🐦

When Keith teams up with an older woman named Dory to work on a sociology project, he convinces himself Dory has fallen deeply in love with him—only to learn that she is married.
Writer: Bill Manhoff
Director: Charles Rondeau
Cast: Brooke Bundy as Dory, Ivor Francis as Professor Boone, Paul Jenkins as Glenn, Larry Wilcox as Feder, Mwako Cumbuka as Jerry, Maggie Roswell as Lois, Sandi Schrader as Cute Girl, Ricky Segall as Ricky Stevens
SONGS:
■ "I Heard You Singing Your Song," music and lyrics by Barry Mann (on *Bulletin Board*)
■ "A Secret in My Heart," music and lyrics by Rick Segall, vocal by Ricky Segall
NOTES:
■ Brooke Bundy is best known as Diana Maynard on *General Hospital*. She appeared on *The Donna Reed Show*, *The Adventures of Ozzie and Harriet*, *My Three Sons*, *Mr. Novak*, *Gidget*, *The Virginian*, *Dragnet*, *The F.B.I.*, *Medical Center*, *Mission: Impossible*, *The Mod Squad*, *Mannix*, *The Brady Bunch*, *Emergency!*, *Barnaby Jones*, *Simon & Simon*, *Moonlighting*, and *Webster*.
■ Larry Wilcox starred as Officer Jon Baker on *CHiPS*.
■ Sandi Schrader played Fran in Episode 28 and the Third Girl in Episode 33.

84: A Day of Honesty 🐦🐦🐦

When Danny is caught sneaking in the back door of a movie theater, he documents all the white lies being told by his mother and siblings until Shirley proposes that all the Partridges practice total honesty for one full day.

Writers: Lloyd Turner and Gordon Mitchell
Director: Ross Bowman
Cast: Joseph Perry as Policeman, Archie Hahn as Harve, Ricky Segall as Ricky Stevens
SONGS:
■ "If I Were a Monkey," music and lyrics by Rick Segall, vocal by Ricky Segall
■ "Roller Coaster," music and lyrics by Mark James (on *Bulletin Board*)
NOTES:
■ When the Partridge Family performs "Roller Coaster," a horn section can be heard although no one in the family can be seen playing a brass instrument.
■ Joseph Perry played Mr. Jenkins in Episode 21 and Police Sergeant Donakovsky in Episode 71.
■ Archie Hahn played Roger on *The Odd Couple*.

85: Al in the Family 🐦🐦

When Mr. Kincaid's nephew, Alan Kincaid, flies in from New York to work as Reuben's assistant, the Partridge Family encourages him to perform as a standup comedian.

Writer: William S. Bickley
Director: Charles Rondeau
Cast: Alan Bursky as Alan Kincaid, Gino Conforti as Maître d'
SONGS:
■ "That's the Way It Is with You," music and lyrics by Harriet Schoch (on *Bulletin Board*)
■ "I'm into Something Good," music and lyrics by Gerry Goffin and Carole King
NOTES:
■ When the Partridge Family performs "I'm into Something Good," a song originally recorded and popularized by Herman's Hermits, Tracy displays her versatility as a musician by playing the wood blocks.

■ Gino Conforti plays the First Bell Boy in Episode 8 and Logan Mays in Episode 15.

86: Made in San Pueblo 🐦

When Shirley's mother and father have a fight, the Partridges take sides, pitting the males against the females.

Writer: William J. Keenan
Director: Charles Rondeau
Cast: Jackie Coogan as Grandpa Walter Renfrew, Rosemary DeCamp as Grandma Amanda Renfrew, John Dennis as Cop, Ysabel MacCloskey as Mrs. Argyle, Ricky Segall as Ricky Stevens

SONGS:
■ "Workin' on a Groovy Thing," music and lyrics by Neil Sedaka and Chet Atkins
■ "Grandma (We Love You Just the Way You Are)," music and lyrics by Rick Segall, vocal by Ricky Segall

NOTES:
■ Grandpa Walter Renfrew's first name was previously Fred in Episodes 3 and 35.
■ When Ricky Stevens sings "Grandma," we see Danny play the banjo for the first time on the series.
■ See Episode 9 for notes on Jackie Coogan.
■ See Episode 3 for notes on Rosemary DeCamp.

87: Art for Mom's Sake 🐦

When Shirley takes a painting class, her children try to prevent her paintings from being seen at an art show to save her from humiliation.

Writer: Michael Leeson
Director: Ross Bowman
Cast: Alan Oppenheimer as Lorenzo Bernard, Liam Dunn as Mr. Neumeyer, Molly Dodd as Woman #1, Bob Gibbons as Man #2, Gordon Jump as Man #2, Monty Margetts as Mrs. Kleven

SONG:
■ "I'll Never Get over You," music and lyrics by Tony Romeo (on *Bulletin Board*)

NOTES:
■ When the Partridge Family rehearse "I'll Never Get over You" in the

garage, a string section can be heard although no one can be seen playing a violin.

■ Throughout this episode, David Cassidy has bad acne on his right cheek.

■ See Episode 16 for notes on Alan Oppenheimer.

■ Liam Dunn played Mayor Finney on *Captain Nice* and Cap-

tain Washburn on *The Queen and I*. He has appeared on *All in the Family*, *Barney Miller*, *The Girl with Something Extra*, *The Mary Tyler Moore Show*, *The Paul Lynde Show*, *Rhoda*, *Room 222*, and *Sanford and Son*. He played a Salesman on Episode 95 of *The Partridge Family*.

■ See Episode 1 for notes on Gordon Jump.

■ Monty Margetts played Una Fields on *The Tycoon*.

88: Two for the Show

When Mr. Kincaid's new clients, singing identical twins Andy and David Williams, stay with the Partridges, both boys simultaneously get a crush on Laurie, forcing her to decide between thm.

Writer: William S. Bickley
Director: Charles Rondeau
Cast: Andy and David Williams as Andy and David Williams, Henry Olek as Skip Radnitz, Mike Rupert as Mike the Waiter, Rick Gates as Mike Weedback

SONGS:

■ "Crying in the Rain," music and lyrics by Carole King and Howard Greenfield

■ "Say It Again," music and lyrics by Ed Welch, performed by Andy and David Williams

NOTES:

■ Andy and David Williams were fourteen-year-old identical twins who had an extremely brief career as heartthrobs in the pages of *16 Magazine* and *Tiger Beat*.

■ This episode marks the only time a singing group other than the Partridge Family performed on the series.

■ When the Partridge Family rehearses "Crying in the Rain" in their garage, a horn section can be heard although no one can be seen playing a brass instrument.

■ Henry Olek played Geek in Episode 28 and Gorgo in Episode 54.

89: Danny Drops Out 🐦🐦

When Shirley lets Danny drop out of school on the condition that he find a job, Danny decides to become a self-made millionaire.

Writers: Richard Bensfield and Perry Grant

Director: Roger Duchowny

Cast: James Gregory as Claude Tubbles, Mitzi Hoag as Miss Farrow, H. B. Barnum III as Pete, Jamie Lamb as Guy #1, and Gary Dubin as Punky Lazaar

SONG:

■ "Lookin' for a Good Time," music and lyrics by Wes Farrell, Danny Janssen, and Bobby Hart (on *Bulletin Board*)

NOTES:

■ When the Partridge Family rehearses "Lookin' for a Good Time" in their garage and then performs the song in an unnamed venue, horn and string sections can be heard although no one can be seen playing a brass instrument or a violin.

■ James Gregory starred as Barney Ruditsky on *The Lawless Years* and Inspector Frank Luger on *Barney Miller*. He also appeared on *Police Story*, *Studio One*, *The Web*, *All in the Family*, *F Troop*, *M*A*S*H*, and *My Three Sons*. He appeared in over two dozen motion pictures, most notably *The Naked City* (1948), *Al Capone* (1959), *The Manchurian Candidate* (1962), *PT 109* (1963), *The Silencers* (1966), *The Secret War of Harry Frigg* (1968), *Beneath the Planet of the Apes* (1970), and *The Main Event* (1979).

■ Mitzi Hoag played Essie Gillis on *Here Come the Brides* and Liz Platt on *We'll Get By*. She played Sheila Faber in Episode 13, Mrs. Fergusson in Episode 43, and Mrs. Maifussi in Episode 51 of *The Partridge Family*.

■ Gary Dubin played Mark Grant on *Bracken's World*. He also played Punky Lazaar in Episodes 30, 71, 91, 92, and 95 of *The Partridge Family*.

90: Queen for a Minute 🐦🐦🐦🐦

When Laurie's girlfriend Frankie is prohibited from joining the varsity basketball team, Laurie enters the homecoming queen pageant, hoping to use the podium as a venue to voice her feminist views.

Writers: Lloyd Turner and Gordon Mitchell
Director: Ernest Losso
Cast: Tracy Brooks Swope as Frankie, Ken Swofford as Coach, Chris Beaumont as Jerry Bishop, Ty Henderson as Emcee, Melissa O'Mahoney as Judy Brisler, Stuart Getz as Boy #1, Christopher Man as Boy #2, Derrel Maury as Boy #3

SONG:

■ "Money Money," music and lyrics by Wes Farrell, Bobby Hart, and Danny Janssen (on *Bulletin Board*)

NOTES:

■ Keith, who prides himself on being a ladies' man, reveals his double standards by getting visibly upset when Laurie plans to spend the night at the home of a basketball player named Frankie—until he learns that Frankie is a woman.

■ When the Partridge Family rehearses the song "Money Money" in their garage, a horn section and a flute solo can be heard although no one can be seen playing a brass instrument or a flute. The song also seems to have been influenced by "Money (That's What I Want)" by Berry Gordy and Jamie Bradford.

■ Tracy Brooks Swope is daughter of *Partridge Family* producer Mel Swope.

■ Ken Swofford played Lt. Griffin on *Switch*, Al Barber on *Rich Man, Poor Man—Book II*, and J. J. Devlin on *The Eddie Capra Mysteries*. He played Monty in Episode 10 of *The Partridge Family*.

■ Chris Beaumont played Jeff on *Here We Go Again*.

91: Danny Converts 🐦🐦🐦

When Danny skips school to attend a Purim bizarre at Temple Aaron with the Rabbi's daughter, the Rabbi, convinced that the Partridges are Jewish, invites them to perform before the congregation, announces that he is looking forward to Danny's Bar Mitzvah, and invites the Partridge Family to Shabbat dinner at his home.

Writers: Richard Benfield and Perry Grant
Director: Richard Kinon

Cast: Noam Pitlik as Rabbi Ben Stern, Joyce Easton as Mrs. Stern, Lark Gieb as Renee Stern, Judy Farrell as Mrs. Carlysle, Gary Dubin as Punky Lazaar
SONG:
- "I Heard You Singing Your Song," music and lyrics by Barry Mann (on *Bulletin Board*)

NOTES:
- Noam Pitlik played Officer Swanhauser on *Sanford and Son* and Mr. Gianelli on *The Bob Newhart Show*.
- Judy Farrell played various nurses on *M*A*S*H*.
- Gary Dubin played Mark Grant on *Bracken's World*. He also played Punky Lazaar in Episodes 30, 71, 89, 92, and 95 of *The Partridge Family*.

92: Miss Partridge, Teacher

When Laurie gets a job as a student teacher for Danny's class, she treats him exceptionally hard, threatening to fail him and make him attend summer school, which would force the Partridge Family to cancel their European tour.
Writers: Art Baer and Ben Joelson
Director: Roger Duchowny
Cast: Maxine Stuart as Miss Halstead, Gary Dubin as Punky Lazaar, April Flesher as Nancy
SONGS:
- "Workin' on a Groovy Thing," music and lyrics by Neil Sedaka and Chet Atkins

- "I Wouldn't Put Nothing Over on You," music and lyrics by Wes Farrell, Danny Janssen, and Bobby Hart (on *Bulletin Board*)

NOTES:
- When the Partridge Family rehearses "I Wouldn't Put Nothing Over on You" in their garage, a horn section can be heard although no one can be seen playing a brass instrument.
- Maxine Stuart played Ruth on *Room for One More*, B. J. Clawson on *Slattery's People*, Scotty on *Doctors' Hospital*, and Marge Newberry on *Executive Suite*. She played Mrs. Damion in Episode 43 and Gloria Hoffsteader in Episode 62 of *The Partridge Family*.
- Gary Dubin played Mark Grant on *Bracken's World*. He also played Punky Lazaar in Episodes 30, 71, 89, 91, and 95 of *The Partridge Family*.

93: Keith and Lauriebelle

To make Karen Bailey jealous, Keith convinces Laurie to pose as his date, southern belle Lauriebelle Culpepper.

Writers: Richard Bensfield and Perry Grant
Director: Roger Duchowny
Cast: Sherry Miles as Karen, Jack Stauffer as George, Lindsay V. Jones as Betty, Colby Haines as Claire

SONG:
- "How Long Is Too Long," music and lyrics by John Bahler and Tony Asher (on *Bulletin Board*)

NOTES:
- When the Partridge Family plays "How Long Is Too Long" in a nightclub, a horn section can be heard although no one can be seen playing a brass instrument.

94: Morning Becomes Electric

When the Partridge Family volunteers to serve as model citizens by cutting down their electricity consumption by ten percent, Danny accidentally reads the meter wrong, forcing his family to live without electricity for two days.

Writers: Lloyd Turner and Gordon Mitchell
Director: Richard Kinon
Cast: Jack Collins as Mayor Robert Towbin, Maureen Reagan as Photographer

SONG:

- "Sunshine," music and lyrics by Wes Farrell, Bobby Hart, and Danny Janssen

NOTES:

- While trying to explain his mistake to the family, Danny mimics the "Would you believe" gag popularized by *Get Smart*.
- When Keith plays the song "Sunshine," which sounds remarkably like a combination of "He's Got the Whole World in His Hands" and "The Battle Hymn of the Republic," drums, piano, and bass guitar can be heard although Keith is the only family member playing an instrument.
- Jack Collins was a regular on *The Milton Berle Show* and played Max Brahms on *Occasional Wife*.
- Maureen Reagan is the daughter of President Ronald Reagan.

95: Pin It on Danny

For her birthday, Danny gives Shirley a diamond brooch that he found, then discovers it was lost by his English teacher, Mrs. Bullock.

Writers: Art Baer and Ben Joelson
Director: Richard Kinon
Cast: Liam Dunn as Salesman, Kathryn Reynolds as Mrs. Bullock, Gary Dubin as Punky Lazaar, Matilda Calnan as Mrs. Pierson

SONG:

■ "I Wanna Be with You," music and lyrics by Wes Farrell and Gerry Goffin

NOTES:

■ The Partridge kids help Shirley celebrate her birthday by placing eight candles on her cake, claiming each candle represents x years. Since her parents, Fred and Amanada Renfrew, claim to have been married 44 years when we first meet them in Episode 3, Shirley is 40 years old, unless one of the candles is for good luck, in which case she would be 42 years old.

■ See Episode 87 for notes on Liam Dunn.

■ Kathryn Reynolds played Claire on *Soap*.

■ Gary Dubin played Mark Grant on *Bracken's World*. He also played Punky Lazaar in Episodes 30, 71, 89, 91, and 92 of *The Partridge Family*.

96: • • • - - • • • (S.O.S.)

When the Partridges learn that Shirley's high school boyfriend, Captain Chuck "Cuddles" Corwin, is visiting San Pueblo, Laurie invites him over for dinner, but when Keith and Danny suspect that Corwin has a girlfriend in San Francisco, they follow their mother and Corwin to Muldune's Point.

Writers: Richard Bensfield and Perry Grant
Director: Bob Claver
Cast: George Chakiris as Captain Chuck "Cuddles" Corwin

SONG:

■ "Roller Coaster," music and lyrics by Mark James (on *Bulletin Board*)

NOTES:

■ This episode is surprisingly reminiscent of Episode 23 in which Keith and Danny follow Laurie and her date to Muldune's Point.

■ Curiously, Mr. Kincaid seems awfully happy to drive Captain Corwin to the airport and equally reluctant to leave the room so Corwin and Shirley can kiss each other good-bye.

■ When the Partridge Family performs "Roller Coaster," a horn section can be heard although no one can be seen playing a brass instrument.

■ George Chakiris won an Academy Award for Best Supporting Actor for his role as Bernard in *West Side Story* (1961). His motion pictures include *Diamond Head* (1963), *Kings of the Sun* (1963), *The Young Girls of Rochefort* (1967), and *The Big Cube* (1969). He appeared as a dancer in *Gentlemen Prefer Blondes* (1953), *White Christmas* (1954), and *There's No Business Like Show Business* (1954).

DAVID'S TRAGIC ILLNES

HIS DEEP DAR
SECRET REVEALED AT LA

SPEC

35¢

16 JULY 1971 MAGAZINE

COME
SWING
WITH
US!

SNEAK PEEK—
MY NEW
TV SHOW!

MEET THE **REAL** US!

Love
Secrets
we never
told

KISS US GOODBYE

WOULD YOU
MARRY ME?

6

Doesn't Somebody Want to Be Wanted

Doesn't Somebody Want to Be Wanted

I go downtown, and roam all around,
But every street I walk I find another dead end.
I'm on my own, but I'm so all alone,
I need somebody so I won't have to pretend.
I know there's something just waiting somewhere,
I look around for her but she's just not there.
Doesn't somebody want to be wanted like me?
Where are you?
Doesn't somebody want to be wanted like me, just like me?

I'm running free, but I don't want to be,
I couldn't take another day like yesterday.
I'm dead on my feet, from walking the street,
I need somebody to help me find my way.
I've got to get out of this town,
Before I do I'll take a last look around.
Doesn't somebody want to be wanted like me?
Where are you?
Doesn't somebody want to be wanted like me, just like me?

You know I'm no different from anybody else.
I start each day and end each night.
It gets really lonely when you're by yourself.
Now where is love and who is love? I gotta know.
Doesn't somebody want to be wanted like me?
Where are you?
Doesn't somebody want to be wanted like me, just like me?

Wes Farrell-Jim Cretecos-Mike Appel • ©1971 Screen Gems-EMI Music Inc.

Partridgemania swept America in the early 1970s with a mass frenzy not seen since the British invasion. From the first moment the Partridge Family came into our homes, they captured our hearts, and asked for nothing in return but the green paper in our wallets. Love was everywhere, and so was the Partridge Family. Six of their record albums went platinum. Five singles went gold. "I Think I Love You" sold 5 million copies. There were lunchboxes, dolls, bubblegum cards, board games, toys, paperback books, and clothes. David Cassidy released several solo albums, went on concert tour, and appeared on the cover of countless teenybopper magazines, including *16 Magazine*, *Tiger Beat*, and *Teen World*.

Everyone wanted a mother like Shirley Partridge, and no one could get enough of her family's music—and for good reason. The Partridge Family took rock music to an new plateau of innovation and profound lyrical content. To this day, Shirley, Keith, Laurie, Danny, Chris, and Tracy are not merely rock legends, they are cultural gurus who infused bubblegum rock with metaphysical profundities and astute political visions.

What follows are reviews of all the Partridge Family albums and singles, and a collection of Partridge paraphernalia generated by Columbia Pictures Television that gave each member of the Partridge Family a healthy nest egg. You'll also find an invaluable listing of all "The Lost Songs" that the Partridge Family performed on the television series but never released on any record. So *come on get happy!*

The Partridge Family Album

- Brand New Me (Wes Farrell-Eddie Singleton)
- Point Me in the Direction of Albuquerque (Tony Romeo)
- Bandala (Wes Farrell-Eddie Singleton)
- I Really Want to Know You (Barry Mann-Cynthia Weil)
- Only a Moment Ago (Terry Cashman-Tommy West)
- I Can Feel Your Heartbeat (Wes Farrell-Jim Cretecos-Mike Appel)
- I'm on the Road (Barry Mann-Cynthia Weil)
- To Be Lovers (Mark Charron)

- Somebody Wants to Love You (Wes Farrell-Jim Cretecos-Mike Appel)
- I Think I Love You (Tony Romeo)
- Singing My Song (Wes Farrell-Diane Hilderbrand)

Musicians: Hal Blaine (Drums), Mike Melvoin (Keyboard), Larry Knechtel (Keyboard), Joe Osborne (Bass), Max Bennett (Bass), Louie Shelton (Guitar), Dennis Budimir (Guitar), Tommy Tedesco (Guitar)
Vocals: Shirley Jones, David Cassidy
Background Vocals: John Bahler, Tom Bahler, Jackie Ward, Ron Hicklin
Producer: Wes Farrell

REVIEW:

The Partridge Family Album, the group's first LP, immediately catapults the Partridges into the pantheon of prominent existential thinkers, making the principles espoused by Jean-Paul Sartre, Martin Heidegger, Søren Kierkegaard, and Friedrich Nietzsche pale by comparison. From the album's first song, "Brand New Me," the Partridge Family revels in the realization that existential authenticity results from the conscious awareness and brave acceptance of the true character of the human situation— namely that individuals are, as Sartre professes in *Being and Nothingness*, ultimately whatever they chose to be, readily acknowledging Sartre's doctrine that "existence precedes essence."

On the surface, "Point Me in the Direction of Albuquerque" appears to be a ballad about a runaway girl headed for Albuquerque, but this transcendent sequel to the Beatles' "She's Leaving Home" takes Karl Jaspers' insistence that freedom is necessarily accompanied by responsibility to a higher plane; alienation from society forces the young girl to the brink of her existential authenticity, requiring philosophical direction. "I Really Want to Know You," noticeably missing David Cassidy's lead vocals and layered with ersatz Fifth Dimension harmonies, finds the Partridges yearning for a meaningful "I and Thou" relationship with greater intensity than anything Martin Buber could have ever imagined. Similarly, "Only a Moment Ago" expresses dissatisfaction with the inescapable anxiety and dread that, as Nietzsche insists, accompanies the realization of the ultimate futility and absurdity of life.

"I Can Feel Your Heartbeat," with its reverberating bass notes imitating the beat of a heart, ambitiously addresses the issue of death and the shadow it casts on life, with greater insight than Albert Camus in *The Myth of Sisyphus*. The song's abrupt ending represents the abruptness with which life ends, a chilling addendum to Camus' argument that people hang on to life even though it has no purpose to justify it and is thus absurd.

"I'm on the Road," another tune sorely missing the benefit of David Cassidy's riveting vocals and saturated with lulling harmonies reminiscent of the Association, glorifies the promise of philosophical fulfillment on the road toward self-discovery, making Sartre's *The Roads of Freedom* look like Jack Kerouac's *On the Road*. "Somebody Wants to Love You" implores listeners to notice the love all around, despite the difficulty of maintaining satisfactory relationships with other people. "Stop, stop, look around," the Partridge Family urges with a passion surpassing Nikolai Berdyaev's insistence that creative acts bridge the chasm between the material world and the spiritual world, setting the stage for the Partridge Family to reveal their succinct manifesto in the album's core song.

"I Think I Love You," the Partridge Family's ingenious metaphysical anthem, while subtly parodying the philosophical vacuousness of the Beatles' "I Feel Fine," not only voices trepidation toward proclaiming love for another, but elevates Rene Descartes' axiom, "I think, therefore I am," to a new plateau: "I think, therefore I love you." Existence does not merely precede essence; existence *requires* essence. The dynamic bass playing throughout and the free-spirited harpsichord interlude rebel against the traditional philosophies of Immanuel Kant and Georg Wilhelm Friedrich Hegel, as does the imperfect rhyme: "I'm afraid that I'm not sure of/A love there is no cure for." Anxiety accompanies freedom, acknowledges the Partridge Family, but to live meaningfully and authentically, the individual must reject self-deception and accept conscious thought as a prerequisite for Being-in-Love as such.

The album closes with "Singing My Song," an exuberant tune that renounces philosophy's traditional attempt to grasp the ultimate nature of the world in abstract systems of thought. Instead, the Partridge Family urges listeners to investigate what it is like to be an individual human being living in the world. The subjective nature of human choices are the predicament of the human condition, but unlike Voltaire's Candide, the Partridges refuse to find refuge in cultivating one's own garden—unless that garden is a public venue from which they can proclaim their existential doctrine.

The Partridge Family Up to Date

- I'll Meet You Halfway (Wes Farrell-Gerry Goffin)
- You Are Always on My Mind (Tony Romeo)
- Doesn't Somebody Want to Be Wanted (Wes Farrell-Jim Cretecos-Mike Appel)

- I'm Here, You're Here (Wes Farrell-Gerry Goffin)
- Umbrella Man (Wes Farrell-Jim Cretecos-Mike Appel)
- Lay It on the Line (Wes Farrell-David Cassidy)
- Morning Rider on the Road (Tony Romeo)
- That'll Be the Day (Tony Romeo)
- There's No Doubt in My Mind (Wes Farrell-Gerry Goffin)
- She'd Rather Have the Rain (Terry Cashman-Tommy West)
- I'll Leave Myself a Little Time (Steve Dossick)

Musicians: Hal Blaine (Drums), Mike Melvoin (Keyboard), Joe Osborne (Bass), Louie Shelton (Guitar), Dennis Budimir (Guitar)
Vocals: Shirley Jones, David Cassidy
Background Vocals: John Bahler, Tom Bahler, Jackie Ward, Ron Hicklin
Producer: Wes Farrell

REVIEW:

As the title suggests, *Up to Date*, the Partridge Family's second album, is more timely than the group's first album. *Up to Date* not only explores the constant change implicit in the nature of physical time, but takes issue with rapid modernization and mankind's subsequent alienation in a transient technocracy, adding new dimensions to the theories and themes put forth by Alvin Toffler in *Future Shock*, Aldous Huxley in *Brave New World*, and Upton Sinclair in *The Jungle*.

On one level, "I'll Meet You Halfway," like the Beatles' "We Can Work It Out," advocates compromise as a means of settling a romantic misunderstanding, but more in-depth analysis suggests the Partridge Family is more concerned with the compromise necessary to strike the proper balance between individual dignity and rapid technological indus-trialization. Similarly, "You Are Always on My Mind" seems to be about a young man yearning for reconciliation with his girlfriend, yet the haunting "my-my-my-my-mind" harmonies warn the astute listener against surrendering individual liberty to a totalitarian state backed by Thought Police and the omnipresent Big Brother of George Orwell's *1984*. Not surprisingly, this provocative Partridge tune apparently inspired Willie Nelson to record his own version of "Always on My Mind."

In "Doesn't Somebody Want to Be Wanted," the Partridges simulta-neously wonder where a lovelorn individual can find a like-minded soul mate, while stressing the need for individuality in the labyrinth of faceless bureaucrats. "You know, I'm no different than anybody else," David Cassidy talk-sings. "I start each day, and I end each night," he adds, reiterating R. Buckminster Fuller's repudiation of conformity as a means

of coping with a society where technology advances exponentially. The Partridge Family recognizes the existential angst that accompanies the transience and constant change of a burgeoning industrial oligarchy, and in "I'm Here, You're Here," they urge listeners to reclaim their humanity before we are all transformed into Eugene Ionesco's rhinoceri.

While "Umbrella Man" appears to be a subtle parody of "Raindrops Keep Fallin' on My Head" by Burt Bacharach and Hal David, the Partridges aren't simply longing for a father figure to act as their "umbrella"; the song, satirically idealizing the Umbrella Man seen in the Zapruder film of President Kennedy's assassination, attacks the antispiritual forces the Partridge Family sees signaling the assassination of the human spirit. Indeed, the Partridge Family is ready to "Lay It on the Line," as the title of the next song suggests, and with more verve and panache than the Rolling Stones' "All Down the Line."

"Morning Rider on the Road," like the Byrds' "Ballad of Easy Rider," advocates a return to Henry David Thoreau's *Walden* so we may better achieve the ideal society outlined in B. F. Skinner's *Walden Two*. Similarly, in "That'll Be the Day," the Partridge Family aligns the messianic vision of Martin Luther King's "I Have a Dream" speech with Alvin Toffler's demand for a humanistic government, insisting that such a society is attainable in the next song, "There's No Doubt in my Mind." "She'd Rather Have the Rain" cleverly combines two songs by the Turtles ("She'd Rather Be with Me" and "You Don't Have to Walk in the Rain") to gently mock cynics who doubt the potential of the human spirit.

Appropriately, the album concludes with "I'll Leave Myself a Little Time," in which the Partridges "see the time to go a different way," illustrating their deep commitment to creating a future filled with alternatives and giving a subtle nod to Albert Einstein's theory of relativity—making the Partridge Family visionaries who are not only "up to date" but way ahead of their time.

The Partridge Family Sound Magazine

- One Night Stand (Wes Farrell-Paul Anka)
- Brown Eyes (Wes Farrell-Danny Janssen)
- Echo Valley 2-6809 (Kathy Cooper-Rupert Holmes)
- You Don't Have to Tell Me (Tony Romeo)
- Rainmaker (Wes Farrell-Jim Cretecos-Mike Appel)
- I'm on My Way Back Home (Bobby Hart-Jack Keller)
- Summer Days (Tony Romeo)
- I Would Have Loved You Anyway (Tony Romeo)
- Twenty-Four Hours a Day (Wes Farrell-Danny Janssen)
- I Woke Up in Love This Morning (Irwin Levine-L. Russell Brown)
- Love Is All That I Ever Needed (Wes Farrell-David Cassidy)

Musicians: Hal Blaine (Drums), Mike Melvoin (Piano), Larry Knechtel (Piano), Joe Osborne (Bass), Louie Shelton (Guitar), Dennis Budimir (Guitar)
Vocals: Shirley Jones, David Cassidy
Background Vocals: John Bahler, Tom Bahler, Jackie Ward, Ron Hicklin
Producer: Wes Farrell

REVIEW:

Sound Magazine, with its graphic cover parodying teenybopper magazines like *16*, *Tiger Beat*, and *Teen World*, courageously criticizes the hollow ethics of tabloid and pulp magazines, boldly examining the neces-

sity and relevance of the truth in both personal relationships and society as a whole. Aside from offering a multifaceted discourse on ethics, *Sound Magazine*, as the title suggests, also delivers a dazzling kaleidoscope of eclectic sounds.

In "One Night Stand" the Partridge Family attacks the tabloids for depicting them as one-dimensional showbiz performers rather than gleaning any depth of character, courageously rejecting the dichotomy between the medium and the message first observed by Marshall McLuhan. On the surface, "Brown Eyes" appears to be a love song to a brown-eyed girl, but when the Partridge Family insists upon a honest relationship, they become proponents of the truth in all situations—and with more vigor than both Socrates and Hippocrates.

"Echo Valley 2-6809," apparently inspired by the Andrews Sisters' "Pennsylvania 6-5000," tells the story of a young man who telephones his girlfriend hoping to discover her true feelings, only to learn that her number has been disconnected—a disturbing metaphor for the pain that truth can sometimes inflict. Appropriately, the next song, "You Don't Have to Tell Me," finds the Partridge Family acknowledging that although the truth may hurt, deception is far more painful. The listener is immediately reminded of the works of Herman Hesse.

"Rainmaker" allegorically alludes to the unfeeling yellow journalist who ruthlessly peddles vicious gossip as authentic news, single-handedly destroying an individual's reputation and inflicting the melancholy of metaphorical rain. "I'm on My Way Back Home," while a lyrical nod to the Beatles' "Two of Us," celebrates the total honesty that can only be found within our authentic selves, a personal integrity so pure it can only stem from love. "Summer Days" starts off sounding like the Rolling Stones' "Paint It Black" to refute sardonically negativity before shifting into a perky optimism that implores the listener to reach a higher moral ground, where absolute truth reigns supreme.

"I Would Have Loved You Anyway," filled with stunning harpsichord work, lyrically illustrates the Partridge Family's disdain for superficiality. "Twenty-Four Hours a Day" tells the story of a man who longs to be with his girlfriend twenty-four hours a day, but now finds himself alone twenty-four hours a day—a clever twist worthy of François Rabelais to convey the Rousseauism that unless you're honest with yourself, you won't be able to live with yourself. "I Woke Up in Love This Morning," the album's most exuberant number, celebrates a brash and intuitive revelation of emotional bliss resulting from a passionate pursuit of truth on both a conscious and subconscious level worthy of John Locke.

The album culminates with "Love Is All That I Ever Needed," a highly imaginative synthesis of the Box Tops' "The Letter" and the Beatles' "All You Need Is Love," delineating the interdependent relationship between love and truth. Love is the impetus for truth, the Partridges proclaim, because truth is, after all, an act of love. And the truth is, you can't help but love *The Partridge Family Sound Magazine*.

The Partridge Family Shopping Bag

- Girl, You Make My Day (Tommy Boyce-Bobby Hart)
- Every Little Bit o' You (Irwin Levine-L. Russell Brown)
- Something New Got Old (Wes Farrell-Bobby Hart)
- Am I Losing You (Irwin Levine-L. Russell Brown)
- Last Night (Wes Farrell-Tony Romeo)
- It's All in Your Mind (Johnny Cymbal-Peggy Clinger)
- Hello, Hello (Wes Farrell-Tony Romeo)

- There'll Come a Time (David Cassidy)
- If You Ever Go (Wes Farrell-Tony Romeo)
- Every Song Is You (Terry Cashman-Tommy West)
- It's One of Those Nights (Yes Love) (Tony Romeo)

Musicians: Hal Blaine (Drums), Mike Melvoin (Keyboards), Joe Osborne (Bass), Max Bennett (Bass), Louie Shelton (Guitar), Dennis Budimir (Guitar), Tommy Tedesco (Guitar), Larry Carlton (Guitar)
Vocals: Shirley Jones, David Cassidy
Background Vocals: John Bahler, Tom Bahler, Jackie Ward, Ron Hicklin
Producer: Wes Farrell

REVIEW:

Shopping Bag satirically implores listeners to view consumerism as a powerful economic tool to transform our egocentric capitalistic society swiftly and smoothly into a utopian Marxist state, brilliantly elevating adolescent bubblegum music into the realm of radical politics. The *Shopping Bag* album is cleverly designed as a shopping bag (with a free shopping bag included inside) as a scathing indictment of the false values of the bourgeoisie and the social waste of the capitalist system. Instead, the Partridge Family urges listeners to renounce materialistic predilections and shop for a new set of values.

The first song, "Girl, You Make My Day," shares the elation inherent in the establishment of the classless and communal societies depicted in Plato's *Republic* and Thomas More's *Utopia*, and when David Cassidy sings, he trajects the feeling of liberation and empowerment that indubitably accompanies the dictatorship of the proletariat envisioned by Karl Marx. "Something New Got Old" attacks planned obsolescence, reiterating Marx's insistence in *Das Kapital* that "Capitalist production begets, with the inexorability of a law of nature, its own negation." The poignant lyric "something warm got cold" alludes to the icy sting of the cold war that inhibited the free exchange of ideas, a prerequisite to bringing about the classless society imagined by Karl Marx, Friedrich Engels, and V. I. Lenin.

Before elaborating further on their ideological doctrine, the Partridge Family pauses to sing "Am I Losing You," to make certain the listener is following the intricate ideas outlined thus far. In "Last Night" the Partridges yearn for a meaningful dialectic before launching into "It's All in Your Mind," a boppy tune that urges listeners to embrace dialectical materialism, the philosophic basis for communism, and eliminate archaic institutions in favor of a more progressive economy.

Side two begins with "Hello, Hello" (an intriguing synthesis of the Beatles' "Hello Goodbye" and Elton John's "Harmony"), welcoming the listener to a new realm of economic consciousness, a utopian bliss achieved through a velvet revolution of unprecedented proportions. "There'll Come a Time" acknowledges the spiritual attributes of rational empiricism, advocating that humanistic elements be incorporated into the new economic order, brilliantly integrating ideas elucidated by Thomas Hobbes with Karl Marx's basic tenet "From each according to his abilities, to each according to his needs." "If You Ever Go" rejects Marx's insistence that government be ultimately eliminated, urging instead that it be elected through democratic methods. Still, "Every Song Is You" dogmatically advocates the abolition of private property. The album concludes with "It's One of Those Nights," apparently the inspiration for the Eagles' "One of These Nights," in which the group admits the difficult challenge we face in implementing the Partridge Manifesto without simultaneously unleashing social upheaval, making *Shopping Bag* a revolutionary album of unparalleled depth and social insight.

A Partridge Family Christmas Card

- My Christmas Card to You (Tony Romeo)
- White Christmas (Irving Berlin)
- Santa Claus Is Coming to Town (J. Fred Coots-Haven Gillespie)
- Blue Christmas (Billy Hayes-Jay Johnson)
- Jingle Bells (Traditional, arranged by Wes Farrell)
- The Christmas Song (Mel Torme-Robert Wells)
- Rockin' Around the Christmas Tree (Johnny Marks)
- Winter Wonderland (Felix Bernard)
- Frosty the Snowman (Steve Nelson-Jack Rollins)
- Sleigh Ride (Leroy Anderson-Mitchell Parish)
- Have Yourself a Merry Little Christmas (Hugh Martin-Ralph Blane)

Musicians: Hal Blaine (Drums), Mike Melvoin (Piano), Max Bennett (Bass), Louie Shelton (Guitar), Dennis Budimir (Guitar)
Vocals: Shirley Jones, David Cassidy
Background Vocals: John Bahler, Tom Bahler, Jackie Ward, Ron Hicklin
Producer: Wes Farrell

REVIEW:

On *Christmas Card* the Partridge Family brings their unique sound to a collection of traditional Christmas songs, giving these holiday standards a contagious enthusiasm, a dynamic rock beat, and exuberant harmonies as only the Partridge Family can. From the opening song (and the one original composition on the album), "My Christmas Card to You," the Partridges telegraph their holiday greetings in the best way they know how: with song. Although the group covers ten traditional songs, they consciously excluded "The Twelve Days of Christmas," containing the familiar lyric "And a partridge in a pear tree." By steering away from such an obvious selection, *Christmas Card* subtly delivers an important secondary message, encouraging listeners to avoid predictability at all costs.

Partridge Family Notebook

- Friend and a Lover (Wes Farrell-Danny Janssen-Bobby Hart)
- Walking in the Rain (Barry Mann-Phil Spector-Cynthia Weil)
- Take Good Care of Her (Danny Janssen-Bobby Hart)
- Together We're Better (Tony Romeo-Ken Jacobson)
- Looking Through the Eyes of Love (Barry Mann-Cynthia Weil)
- Maybe Someday (Austin Roberts-John Michael Hill)
- We Gotta Get Out of This Place (Barry Mann-Cynthia Weil)
- Storybook Love (Wes Farrell-Adam Miller)
- Love Must Be the Answer (Wes Farrell-Peggy Clinger-Johnny Cymbal)
- Something's Wrong (Wes Farrell-Danny Janssen-Bobby Hart)
- As Long As You're There (Adam Miller)

Musicians: Hal Blaine (Drums), Mike Melvoin (Keyboards), Larry Knechtel (Keyboards), Joe Osborne (Bass), Max Bennett (Bass), Louie Shelton (Guitar), Dennis Budimir (Guitar), Tommy Tedesco (Guitar), Larry Carlton (Guitars)
Vocals: David Cassidy, Shirley Jones
Background Vocals: John Bahler, Tom Bahler, Jackie Ward, Ron Hicklin
Producer: Wes Farrell

The Partridge Family Notebook

Name: The Partridge Family
Starring: Shirley Jones
Featuring: David Cassidy

Subject: Music
Class: Bell 111
Year: 1972

REVIEW:

As the title and design of *The Partridge Family Notebook* suggests, the topic is school. But the compositions in *Notebook* offer a scathing indictment of the American educational system.

The Partridge Family begins by lauding education as both a "Friend and a Lover," siding with Epictetus in his astute observation that "only the educated are free." But the group considers the American educational system a stagnant institution, and "Walking in the Rain" emerges as a brilliant allegory for students whose academic aspirations are dashed by uninspired educators. In "Take Good Care of Her," the group laments that most teachers and administrators fail to take greater responsibility for shaping young minds, making this LP far more than a simple collection of irrelevant musical doodles with a back to school theme.

"Together We're Better" urges parents and students to dismantle the archaic educational system and champion the progressive and experimental curricula envisioned by Alexander Meiklejohn. Educators must view academic freedom as if they were "Looking Through the Eyes of Love," sings the idealistic Partridge Family. In "Maybe Someday," the group revels in the possibility that maybe someday all educators will share the passion of Horace Mann, Nicholas Murray Butler, and Elizabeth Peabody. Until that day, they join in with the Animals' "We Gotta Get Out of This Place," urging students to rebel against mediocrity, conformity, and sterility.

The Partridge Family opposes dropping out of school; instead, they urge students to take responsibility for their own educations. "Storybook Love" advocates literacy while simultaneously labeling the current educational system a fairy tale. In "Love Must Be the Answer," they urge students to be motivated by their love for knowledge.

In "Something's Wrong," the Partridge Family continues to hammer away at the American school system, surpassing the indignation of John

Holt's *How Children Fail*. Despite their infuriation at the state of public education, the Partridge Family ends with "As Long as You're There," urging students to get the most out of the school while working to revolutionize the obsolete educational system. Not surprisingly, *The Partridge Family Notebook* contains some excellent notes.

The Partridge Family Crossword Puzzle

- One Day at a Time (Terry Cashman-Tommy West)
- Sunshine (Wes Farrell-Danny Janssen-Bobby Hart)
- As Long as There's You (Tony Romeo)
- It's a Long Way to Heaven (Mark James)
- Now That You Got Me Where You Want Me (Wes Farrell-Danny Janssen-Bobby Hart)
- It Means I'm in Love with You (Tony Romeo)
- Come on Love (Terry Cashman-Tommy West)
- I Got Your Love All over Me (Johnny Cymbal-Peggy Clinger)
- Let Your Love Go (Wes Farrell-Danny Janssen)
- It Sounds Like You're Saying Hello (Terry Cashman-Tommy West)
- It's You (Johnny Cymbal-Peggy Clinger)

Musicians: Hal Blaine (Drums), Mike Melvoin (Keyboard), Larry Knechtel (Keyboards), Joe Osborne (Bass), Max Bennett (Bass), Louie Shelton (Guitar), Dennis Budimir (Guitar), Tommy Tedesco (Guitar), Larry Carlton (Guitar)
Vocals: Shirley Jones, David Cassidy
Background Vocals: John Bahler, Tom Bahler, Jackie Ward, Ron Hicklin
Producer: Wes Farrell

REVIEW:

The very title of *The Partridge Family Crossword Puzzle* is a clever metaphor for the group's overly ambitious attempt to solve the grand puzzle of the universe. But when the Partridge Family fails to provide any cosmic insights on this LP, they begin a banal exploration of phenomenology and predestination—letting this potentially daring concept album spiral uncontrollably into a black hole.

The album opens with "One Day at a Time," elucidating Nicolaus Copernicus's principle that the earth revolves on its axis over a twenty-four-hour period and simultaneously explaining that any attempt to

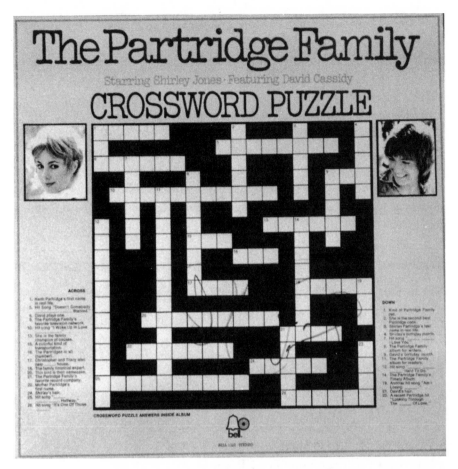

unravel the mystery of the universe requires methodic study. "Sunshine" acknowledges the life-giving force of our sun, but rather than delving into thermonuclear fusion, the song, sounding like a combination of "He's Got the Whole World in His Hands" and "The Battle Hymn of the Republic," deteriorates into a spiritual number, as if the Partridge Family were worshipping the sun as a god.

In "As Long as There's You" the Partridges forsake astrophysics again, choosing instead to glorify a benevolent force controlling the universe. While "It's a Long Way to Heaven" acknowledges the infinite nature of the universe, the song fails to propose any new ideas to advance Albert Einstein's theory that the universe is expanding. Instead, the Partridge Family seems to accept the doctrine of predestination in "Now That You Got Me Where You Want Me"; they then precede to embrace phenomenology, insisting that human perception of reality derives solely from our consciousness, severely limiting mankind's ability to ever understand the mysteries of the universe.

While "It Means I'm in Love with You" is a catchy tune, the Partridge Family now suggests that love is the basis of the universe, forsaking any further scientific exploration. The remaining songs on the album ignore astronomy; "Come on Love," "Let Your Love Go," and "It Sounds Like You're Saying Hello" are all pathetic pleas for the universe to unveil its mysteries so the Partridges don't have to think anymore.

The album closes with "It's You," in which the Partridge Family, fully embracing phenomenology and disregarding all science, concludes that each individual listener holds the key to understanding the universe since all acts of perception are personal. With this album, the Partridge Family only succeeds in leaving the *Crossword Puzzle* unsolved and the listener completely puzzled.

The Partridge Family Bulletin Board

- Money Money (Wes Farrell-Danny Janssen-Bobby Hart)
- Roller Coaster (Mark James)
- Lookin' for a Good Time (Wes Farrell-Danny Janssen-Bobby Hart)
- Oh, No, Not My Baby (Gerry Goffin-Carole King)
- I Wouldn't Put Nothing Over on You (Wes Farrell-Danny Janssen-Bobby Hart)
- Where Do We Go from Here (Mark James)
- How Long Is Too Long (Tom Bahler-Tony Asher)
- I'll Never Get over You (Tony Romeo)
- Alone Too Long (Mark James-Cynthia Weil)
- I Heard You Singing Your Song (Barry Mann)
- That's the Way It Is with You (Harriet Schoch)

Musicians: Hal Blaine (Drums), Max Bennett (Bass), Larry Carlton (Guitar), Chuck Findley (Horns), Tom Bahler (Horns), Lou McCreary (Trombone), George Bohanon (Trombone), Bill Perkins (Saxophone), Jackie Kelso (Saxophone), Bob Hardaway (Saxophone), Richard Bennett (Guitar), Ben Benay (Guitar), Dean Parks (Guitar), Gary Coleman (Percussion), Joe Porcaro (Percussion), Jim Hughart (Bass), Michael Omartian (Keyboards), Larry Muhoberac (Keyboards)
Vocals: Shirley Jones, David Cassidy
Background Vocals: John Bahler, Tom Bahler, Jackie Ward, Ron Hicklin
Producer: Wes Farrell

REVIEW:

Bulletin boards remain the simplest form of posting notices and communicating publicly within a small community. Not surprisingly, the Partridge Family uses their *Bulletin Board* LP to advocate political, social, and economic freedom for all—with more passion than the Magna Carta, the Declaration of Independence, and the Bill of Rights rolled into one.

"Money Money" glorifies the freedoms that form the basis of capitalism. Economic freedom, the Partridge Family sings, makes the pursuit of happiness possible. The group's joie de vivre emerges in "Roller Coaster," a buoyant tribute to the pursuit of happiness, and "Lookin' for a Good Time," an exuberant attack on the limits on social freedom reminiscent of Montesquieu, Jean Jacques Rousseau, and Voltaire at their best.

The Partridge Family advocates freedom of speech with equal passion. While "Oh, No, Not My Baby" concerns the troubling rumors circulating about a girlfriend's alleged infidelity, the Partridges are actually reiterating

Voltaire's statement "I disapprove of what you say, but I will defend to the death your right to say it." Similarly, "I Wouldn't Put Nothing Over on You," while arguably nothing more than a fun little ditty about a girl who catches her boyfriend kissing her best friend, is actually a formidable demand for due process of law to protect individuals against unjust accusations, thus safeguarding personal freedom. One can't help but be reminded of John Locke's *Two Treatises on Government*.

In "Where Do We Go from Here," the Partridge Family flirts with anarchism, pondering whether systems of government and laws destroy liberty, and in "How Long Is Too Long," they question whether the time will ever be ripe for the individualistic anarchism envisioned by Pierre Joseph Proudhon.

The Partridge Family returns their attention to the pursuit of happiness in "I'll Never Get over You" and "Alone Too Long" before leaping into "I Heard You Singing Your Song," a wonderfully harmonic celebration of the right of every person to speak freely and publicly, reiterating the philosophic treatises of both John Locke and Thomas Jefferson. The album culminates with "That's the Way It Is with You," triumphantly reprising the Partridge Family's advocacy of political, social, and economic freedom—making *Bulletin Board* an album exceptionally worthy of public notice.

The Partridge Family Greatest Hits

- Come On Get Happy (Wes Farrell-Danny Janssen)
- I Think I Love You (Tony Romeo)
- Doesn't Somebody Want to Be Wanted (Wes Farrell-Jim Cretecos-Mike Appel)
- I'll Meet You Halfway (Wes Farrell-Gerry Goffin)
- I Woke Up in Love This Morning (Irwin Levine-L. Russell Brown)
- Cherish (David Cassidy solo) (Terry Kirkman)
- It's One of Those Nights (Tony Romeo)
- I Can Feel Your Heartbeat (Wes Farrell-Jim Cretecos-Mike Appel)
- Am I Losing You (Irwin Levine-L. Russell Brown)
- Could It Be Forever (David Cassidy solo) (Wes Farell-Danny Janssen)
- Point Me in the Direction of Albuquerque (Tony Romeo)
- Echo Valley 2-6809 (Kathy Cooper-Rupert Holmes)

Musicians: Hal Blaine (Drums), Mike Melvoin (Keyboard), Larry Knechtel (Keyboard), Joe Osborne (Bass), Max Bennett (Bass), Louie Shelton

(Guitar), Dennis Budimir (Guitar), Tommy Tedesco (Guitar), Larry Carlton (Guitar)
Vocals: Shirley Jones, David Cassidy
Background Vocals: John Bahler, Tom Bahler, Jackie Ward, Ron Hicklin
Producer: Wes Farrell

REVIEW:

This album is, quite simply, a collection of the Partridge Family's greatest hits. All the selections are undoubtedly the group's most memorable songs, and the inclusion of two songs that David Cassidy recorded independently of the group make this album an exceptional anthology. Like previous Partridge Family efforts, *Greatest Hits* is a brilliant concept album; each song on the LP shares the distinction of being one of the Partridge Family's finest tunes, proving beyond any shadow of a doubt that the album's catchy title, *The Partridge Family Greatest Hits*, is anything but an oxymoron.

The Singles

- **I Think I Love You** (Tony Romeo). *Released October 31, 1970, rose to number one on the* Billboard *chart, where it remained for sixteen weeks.*
- **Doesn't Somebody Want to Be Loved** (Wes Farrell-Jim Cretecos-Mike Appel). *Released February 2, 1971, rose to number six on the* Billboard *chart, where it remained for eleven weeks.*
- **I'll Meet You Halfway** (Wes Farrell-Gerry Goffin). *Released May 15, 1971, rose to number nine on the* Billboard *chart, where it remained for eight weeks.*
- **I Woke Up in Love This Morning** (Irwin Levine-L.Russell Brown). *Released August 21, 1971, rose to number thirteen on the* Billboard *chart, where it remained for ten weeks.*
- **It's One of Those Nights** (Tony Romeo). *Released January 1, 1972, rose to number 20 on the* Billboard *chart, where it remained for six weeks.*
- **Breaking Up Is Hard to Do** (Neil Sedaka-Howard Greenfield). *Released July 29, 1972, rose to number 28 on the* Billboard *chart, where it remained for four weeks.*
- **Looking Through the Eyes of Love** (Barry Mann-Cynthia Weil). *Released January 27, 1973, rose to number 39 on the* Billboard *chart, where it remained for two weeks.*

The Lost Songs

The Partridge Family sang the following songs on the television series, but none of these songs ever appeared on any album.

- "Ain't Love Easy" [Episode 57]
- "All of the Things" [Episode 9]
- "Baby I Love Love I Love You" [Episodes 3 and 15]
- "Bye Bye Blackbird," vocal by Grandpa Fred Renfrew [Episode 3]
- "Crying in the Rain" [Episode 88]
- "Find Peace in Your Soul," performed by Red Woodloe [Episode 14]
- "God Bless You, Girl" [Episode 50]
- "Good Times Are Coming to Me" [Episode 9]
- "Here Comes the Bride (traditional)," solo performed by Laurie Partridge [Episode 54]
- "I Don't Care" [Episode 71]
- "I Think I Love You (Classical Version)" [Episode 77]
- "I Wanna Be with You" [Episodes 78 and 95]
- "I'm Into Something Good" [Episodes 77 and 85]
- "It's Time That I Knew You Better" [Episode 39]
- "Let the Good Times In" [Episode 1]
- "Like Walking in the Rain" [Episode 67]
- "Listen to the Sound" [Episode 28]
- "The Love Song" [Episode 16]
- "Lullaby (traditional)" [Episode 61]
- "My Best Girl" [Episode 35]
- "Stephanie" [Episode 25]
- "Sunshine Eyes" [Episode 64]
- "Together" [Episodes 1, 3, 35, and 41]
- "The Whale Song" [Episode 31]
- "When Love's Talked About" [Episode 81]
- "Workin' on a Groovy Thing" [Episodes 86 and 92]

David Cassidy Albums

Cherish

- Being There (Tony Romeo)
- I Just Want to Make You Happy (Wes Farrell-Bobby Hart)
- Could It Be Forever (Wes Farrell-Danny Janssen)
- Blind Hope (Adam Miller)
- I Lost My Chance (Adam Miller)
- My First Night Alone Without You (Kin Vassy)
- We Could Never Be Friends ('Cause We've Been Lovers Too Long) (Tony Romeo)
- Where Is the Morning (Adam Miller)
- I Am a Clown (Tony Romeo)
- Cherish (Terry Kirkman)
- Ricky's Tune (David Cassidy)

Musicians: Hal Blaine (Drums), Mike Melvoin (Piano), Max Bennett (Bass), Louis Shelton (Guitar), Dennis Budimir (Guitar), Tommy Tedesco (Guitar), Larry Carlton (Guitar), Reinie Press (Bass)
Vocals: David Cassidy
Producer: Wes Farrell

Rock Me Baby

- Rock Me Baby (Johnny Cymbal-Peggy Clinger)
- Lonely Too Long (Felix Cavaliere-Eddie Brigati)
- Two Time Loser (David Cassidy)
- Warm My Soul (Joerey Ortiz)
- Some Kind of Summer (Dave Ellingson)
- (Oh No) No Way (Wes Farrell-Johnny Cymbal-Peggy Clinger)
- Song for a Rainy Day (David Cassidy-Kim Carnes)
- Soft as a Summer Shower (Adam Miller)
- Go Now (Milton Bennett-Larry Banks)
- How Can I Be Sure (Felix Cavaliere-Eddie Brigati)
- Song of Love (Adam Miller)

Musicians: Hal Blaine (Drums), Mike Melvoin (Keyboards), Max Bennett (Bass), Louis Shelton (Guitar), Larry Carlton (Guitar), Jim Gordon (Drums), Dean Parks (Guitar), Joe Osborn (Percussion), Gary Coleman (Percussion), Alan Estes (Percussion), Gene Estes (Percussion), Carl Fortina (Accordion), Ollie Mitchell (Trumpet), Chuck Findley (Trumpet), Slyde Hyde (Trombone), Tom Scott 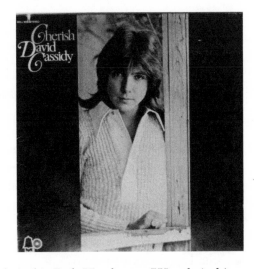 (Woodwinds), Jim Horn (Woodwinds), Bob Hardaway (Woodwinds)
Vocals: David Cassidy
Producer: Wes Farrell

Dreams Are Nuthin' More Than Wishes

- Daydream (John Sebastian)
- Sing Me (Tony Romeo)
- Bali Ha'i (Richard Rodgers-Oscar Hammerstein II)
- Mae (Gary Montgomery)
- Fever (Davenport-Cooley)
- Summer Days (Tony Romeo)
- The Puppy Song (Harry Nilsson)
- Daydreamer (Terry Dempsy)
- Some Old Woman (Gibson-Silverstein)
- Can't Go Home Again (David Cassidy-Kim Carnes-Dave Ellingson)
- Preyin' on My Mind (David Cassidy-Kim Carnes-Dave Ellingson)
- Hold on Me (Mike McDonald)

Musicians: Larry Knechtel (Bass, Mouth Organ), Max Bennett (Bass), Louie Shelton (Electric Guitar, Accoustic Guitar), Larry Carlton (Guitar), James Burton (Dobro, Acoustic Guitar), John Guerin (Drums), Michael O'Martian (Tack Piano), Milt Holland (Percussion), Mike McDonald (Electric Piano), Bobbye Hall (Conga), Al Casey (Ukulele), Emory Gordy (Bass), Ron Tutt (Drums), Victor Feldman (Vibes), David Cassidy (Guitar), Richard Bennet (Guitar), Dave Ellingson (Acoustic

Guitar), Chad David (Acoustic Guitar)
Vocals: David Cassidy
Producer: Rick Jarrard

Cassidy Live

- Preyin' on My Mind (David Cassidy-Kim Carnes-Dave Ellingson)
- Some Kind of Summer (Dave Ellingson)
- Breakin' Up Is Hard to Do (Neil Sedaka-Howard Greenfield)
- Bali Ha'i (Richard Rodgers-Oscar Hammerstein II)
- Mae (Gary Montgomery)
- I Am a Clown (Tony Romeo)
- Delta Lady (Leon Russell)
- Please Please Me (John Lennon-Paul McCartney)
- Daydreamer (Terry Dempsy)
- How Can I Be Sure (Felix Cavaliere-Eddie Brigati)
- For What It's Worth (Stephen Stills)
- C.C. Rider Blues/Jenny Jenny ("Ma" Rainey/Max Freedman-Jimmy DeKnight)
- Rock Medley: Blue Suede Shoes (Carl Perkins), Rock Around the Clock (Max Freedman-Jimmy DeKnight), Jailhouse Rock (Jerry Leiber-Mike Stoller), Rock and Roll Music (Chuck Berry), Rock Me Baby (Peggy Clinger-Johnny Cymbal)

Musicians: Not listed
Vocals: David Cassidy
Producer: David Cassidy and Barry Ainsworth

The Higher They Climb, the Harder They Fall

- When I'm a Rock 'n' Roll Star (David Cassidy)
- Be-Bop-a-Lula (Gene Vincent-Tex Davis)
- I Write the Songs (Bruce Johnston)
- This Could Be the Night (Harry Nilsson-David Cassidy)
- Darlin' (Brian Wilson-Mike Love)
- Get It Up for Love (Ned Doheny)
- Fix of Your Love (David Cassidy-Dave Ellingson)

- Massacre at Park Bench (David Cassidy-Phil Austin)
- Common Thief (Bill House)
- Love in Bloom (David Cassidy-Richie Furay)
- When I'm a Rock 'n' Roll Star (Reprise) (David Cassidy)

Musicians: David Cassidy (Rhythm Guitar, Lead Guitar, Piano), John Hobbs (Organ, Piano, Pumping Piano), Bill House (Electric Guitar, Rhythm Guitar, Steel Guitar), Curtis Stone (Bass), Jimmie Seiter (Tambourne, Percussion), Stan House (Drums), Leland Sklar (Bass), Ron Tutt (Drums), Steve Douglas (Saxophone), Bruce Johnston (Electric Guitar), Jim Gordon (Drums), Emory Gordy (Bass), Danny Kootch (Electric Guitar), Willie Weeks (Bass), Jim Keltner (Drums), King Errisson (Congas), Ned Doheny (Acoustic Guitar), Jesse Ed Davis (Guitar), David Kemper (Drums), Tom Henseley (Piano), Homer Diltz (Harp), John Raines (Percussion)
Vocals: David Cassidy
Producers: David Cassidy and Bruce Johnston
Notes: "Massacre at Park Bench" is a dialogue performed with Phil Austin of the Firesign Theatre, a comedy group that achieved cult status with several comedy albums in the 1970s.

Home Is Where the Heart Is

- On Fire (David Cassidy-Bill House)
- Damned If This Ain't Love (David Cassidy)
- January (David Paton)
- A Fool in Love (David Cassidy-Bill House)
- Tomorrow (Paul and Linda McCartney)
- Breakin' Down Again (David Cassidy-Bill House)
- Run and Hide (David Cassidy-Bill House)
- Take This Heart (David Cassidy-Gerryy Beckley)
- Goodbye Blues (Ronnie S. Wilkins)
- Half Past Our Bedtime (David Cassidy-Gerry Beckley-Ricky Fataar)

Musicians: Bryan Garofalo (Bass), Ricky Fataar (Drums, Congas, Tambourine), King Errisson (Drums, Congas), John Hobbs (Electric Piano, Keyboards), Jimmie Seiter (Tamborine), David Cassidy (Accoustic Guitar, Electric Guitar, Piano), Bruce Johnston (Elecric Piano), Harry Robinson (Bongo), Bill House (Rhythm Guitar), Gary Malsbar (Drums), Steve Ross (Guitar), Jon Joyce (Cello)

Vocals: David Cassidy
Producers: David Cassidy and Bruce Johnston

Gettin' It in the Street

- Gettin' It in the Street (David Cassidy-Gerry Beckley)
- Cruise to Harlem (David Cassidy-Gerry Beckley-Wilson)
- I'll Have to Go Away (Chater-Armand)
- The Story of Rock and Roll (Harry Nilsson)
- I Never Saw You Coming (David Cassidy-Jay Gruska)
- Living a Lie (David Cassidy-Gerry Beckley)
- Rosa's Cantina (David Cassidy-Bryan Garofalo)
- Love, Love the Lady (David Cassidy-Gerry Beckley)
- Junked Heart Blues (David Cassidy)

Musicians: Gerry Beckley (Piano), Jay Gruska (Keyboards), Mick Ronson (Lead Guitar), Bryan Garofalo (Bass), David Kemper (Drums), Steve Ross (Guitar), Ernie Watts (Saxophone), David Cassidy (Rhythm Guitar)
Vocals: David Cassidy
Background Vocals: Gerry Beckley
Producers: David Cassidy and Gerry Beckley
Executive Producer: Alan Abrahams

Romance

- Romance (Alan Tarney-David Cassidy)
- Touched by Lightning (Alan Tarney-David Cassidy)
- The Last Kiss (Alan Tarney-David Cassidy)
- Thin Ice (Alan Tarney-David Cassidy)
- Someone (Alan Tarney-David Cassidy-Sally Boyden)
- The Letter (Alan Tarney-David Cassidy)
- Heart of Emotion (Alan Tarney-David Cassidy)
- Tenderly (Alan Tarney)
- She Knows All About Boys (Dan Merino)
- Remember Me (Alan Tarney)

Musicians: Not listed
Vocals: David Cassidy
Producer: Alan Tarney

David Cassidy—His Greatest Hits Live

- Could It Be Forever (Wes Farrell-Danny Janssen)
- Tenderly (Alan Tarney)
- Darlin' (Brian Wilson-Mike Love)
- Thin Ice (Alan Tarney-David Cassidy)
- Someone (Alan Tarney-David Cassidy-Sally Boyden)
- She Knows All About Boys (Dan Merino)
- I'll Meet You Halfway (Wes Farrell-Gerry Goffin)
- I Am a Clown (Tony Romeo)
- Daydreamer (Terry Dempsy)
- Get It Up for Love (Ned Doheny)
- How Can I Be Sure (Felix Cavaliere-Eddie Brigati)
- Please Please Me (John Lennon-Paul McCartney)
- Romance (Alan Tarney-David Cassidy)
- Touched by Lightning (Alan Tarney-David Cassidy)
- I Think I Love You (Tony Romeo)
- I Write the Songs (Bruce Johnston)
- Cherish (Terry Kirkman)
- Looking Through the Eyes of Love (Barry Mann-Cynthia Weil)
- When I'm a Rock 'n' Roll Star (David Cassidy)
- Rock Me Baby (Johnny Cymbal-Peggy Clinger)
- Breakin' Up Is Hard to Do (Neil Sedaka-Howard Greenfield)
- I'm Still Standing (Elton John-Bernie Taupin)
- The Last Kiss (Alan Tarney-David Cassidy)

Musicians: Ian Wherry (Keyboards), Geoff Dunn (Drums), Ruari McFarlane (Bass), Alan Coates (Guitar), Keith Atak (Guitar), Tim Atak (Keyboards)
Vocals: David Cassidy
Producer: David Cassidy

David Cassidy

- Labor of Love (David Cassidy-Sue Shifrin-Michael Dan Ehmig)
- You Remember Me (David Cassidy-Sue Shifrin-Michael Dan Ehmig)
- Lyin' to Myself (David Cassidy-Sue Shifrin)
- Boulevard of Broken Dreams (David Cassidy-Sue Shifrin)
- Hi-Heel Sneakers (Robert Higginbotham)

- Message to the World (David Cassidy-Sue Shifrin)
- Living Without You (David Cassidy-Sue Shifrin-Rick Neigher)
- Stranger in Your Heart (David Cassidy-Mark Spiro-Mike Reno)
- Prisoner (David Cassidy-Sue Shifrin-John Wetton)
- All Because of You (Sue Shifrin-Jon Lind)

Musicians: Jeff "Skunk" Baxter (Guitar), Ron Komie (Guitar), Ralph Carter (Bass), Jim Heins (Drums), C. J. Vanston (Keyboards), Michael Thompson (Guitar), David Cassidy (Guitar), Bradford Cobb (Bass), Denny Fongheiser (Drums), Ken Savigar (Keyboards), Brandon Fields (Saxophone), Tim McGovern (Guitar, Drums), Hurricane Jay (Harp), Myron Grumbacher (Drums), Michael Landau (Guitar), John Pierce (Bass), Charles Judge (Keyboards), Mike Spiro (Keyboards), Jeff Silverman (Guitar), Jack White (Drums), Paca Thomas (Keyboards)
Vocals: David Cassidy
Producers: E. T. Thorngen (except "Labor of Love," which was produced by Phil Ramone and E. Thorngren; and "Hi-Heel Sneakers," which was produced by Clams Casino and Carter)

The Best of David Cassidy

- All I Want Is You (Unknown)
- Crazy Love (Unknown)
- Half Heaven Half Heartache (Unknown)
- I Can See Everything (Unknown)
- I Never Saw You Coming (David Cassidy-Jay Gruska)
- Save Me Save Me (Unknown)
- Dirty Work (Unknown)
- You Were the First One (Unknown)
- Strengthen My Love (Unknown)
- Junked Heart Blues (David Cassidy)
- Once a Fool (Unknown)
- Hurt So Bad (Unknown)
- It Should've Been Me (Unknown)

Musicians: Not listed
Vocals: David Cassidy
Producer: Not listed
Note: This limited edition LP was issued by MCA Curb Records in Japan in 1991. This album is not a collection of greatest hits; most of the tracks

were recorded in 1979 for an album that was never released, with the exception of two tracks from *Gettin' It in the Street*: "I Never Saw You Coming" and "Junked Heart Blues." David Cassidy was apparently upset by the release of this album since he purportedly felt it no longer represented his music.

Didn't You Used to Be . . .

- Raindrops (Dee Clark-David Cassidy-Sue Shifrin)
- For All the Lonely (David Cassidy-Sue Shifrin)
- Treat Me Like You Used To (David Cassidy-Sue Shifrin-Mark Spiro)
- Somebody to Love (David Cassidy-Sue Shifrin)
- I'll Never Stop Loving You (David Cassidy-Sue Shifrin-John Wetton)
- Soul Kiss (David Cassidy-Sue Shifrin)
- Tell Me True (David Cassidy-Sue Shifrin)
- Like Father, Like Son (David Cassidy-Sue Shifrin-Steve Diamond)
- It's Over (Sue Shifrin-K. Gold)
- One True Love (David Cassidy-Sue Shifrin

Musicians: Vaughn Johnson (Keyboards, Drum Programming), Ron Komie (Guitars), David Cassidy (Guitars), Kevin Wyatt (Bass), Denny Fongheiser (Drums, Percussion), Chuckii Booker (Synth Bass), Derek Nakamoto (Strings, Organ), Dick McIlvery (Organ), Luis Conte (Percussion), Steve Diamond (Drum Programming, Keyboards), Bill Bergman (Tenor Saxophone), Scott Page (Baritone Sax), Dennis Farias (Trumpet), Nick Lane (Trombone)
Vocals: David Cassidy
Producer: E. T. Thorngren

David Cassidy Singles

- **Cherish** (Terry Kirkman). *Released November 11, 1971, rose to number nine on the* Billboard *chart, where it remained for eleven weeks.*
- **Could It Be Forever** (Wes Farrell-Danny Janssen). *Released March 25, 1972, rose to number 37 on the* Billboard *chart, where it remained for two weeks.*
- **How Can I Be Sure** (Felix Cavaliere-Eddie Brigati). *Released June 10, 1972, rose to number 25 on the* Billboard *chart, where it remained for five weeks. Released in the United Kingdom on September 16, 1972, the single rose to number one on the* Billboard *chart, where it remained for eleven weeks.*
- **Rock Me Baby** (Johnny Cymbal-Peggy Clinger). *Released October 14, 1972, rose to number 38 on the* Billboard *chart, where it remained for two weeks.*
- **Daydreamer** (Terry Dempsy). *Released in the United Kingdom on October 13, 1973, rose to number one on the* Billboard *chart, where it remained for fifteen weeks.*
- **Frozen Noses** (Unknown)/**If I Didn't Care** (Unknown). *1974, European release.*
- **Hurt So Bad** (Unknown)/**Once A Fool** (Unknown). *1979.*
- **The Last Kiss** (Alan Tarney-David Cassidy). *Released in the United Kingdom on February 23, 1985, rose to number six on the* Billboard *chart, where it remained for nine weeks.*
- **Romance** (Alan Tarney-David Cassidy). *Released in the United Kingdom on May 11, 1985, rose to number 54 on the* Billboard *chart, where it remained for six weeks.*
- **Lyin' to Myself** (David Cassidy-Sue Shifrin). *Released October 27, 1990, rose to number 27 on the* Billboard *chart, where it remained for five weeks.*

Danny Bonaduce Album

Dreamland

- I'll Be Your Magician (Levine-Brown)
- Save a Little Piece for Me (Bruce Roberts)
- Turn-Down Day (Keller-Blume)
- Blueberry You (Bergen-Barkan)
- You're Old Enough to Fall in Love (Bruce Roberts)
- The 59th Street Bridge Song (Feelin' Groovy) (Paul Simon)
- Dreamland (Bruce Roberts)
- A New Kind of Me (Bruce Roberts)
- Colors of Love (Barkan-Bergen)
- Fortune Lady (Oriolo-Barkan-Bergen)
- All the Time in the World (Bruce Roberts)

Musicians: Ben Benay (Guitar), David Cohen (Guitar), Norman Bergen (Keyboards), John Conrad (Bass), Ed Greene (Drums), Bruce Roberts (Percussion), Jimmy Sedlar (Heading the Horns), Eliot Rosoff (Heading the Strings)

Vocals: Danny Bonaduce

Producers: Steve Metz, Norman Bergen, Bruce Roberts

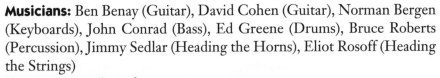

Ricky Segall Album

Ricky Segall and the Segalls

- Say, Hey, Willie
- Just Loving You
- Mr. President
- Bicycle Song
- When I Grow Up
- What Kind of Noise Do You Make?
- Sooner or Later
- What Would You Like to Be?
- All I Want to Ask Santa Claus
- A Little Bit of Love

All selections written by Rick Segall

Musicians: Hal Blaine (Drums), Jim Gordon (Drums), Ben Benay (Guitar), Dennis Budimir (Guitar), Richard Bennett (Guitar), Gary Coleman (Percussion), Larry Muhoberac (Keyboards), Tom Hensley (Keyboards), Michael Omartian (Keyboards), Jackie Kelso (Woodwinds), Bill Perkins (Woodwinds), Ernie Watts (Woodwinds), Plaz Johnson (Woodwinds), Ray Pizzi (Bassoon)
Vocals: Ricky Segall
Producer: Wes Farrell

Lost Songs

Four-year-old Ricky Segall sang the following songs on the television series, but none of these appeared on any album.

- "Grandma (We Love You Just the Way You Are)" [Episode 86]
- "If I Were a Monkey" [Episode 84]
- "A Secret in My Heart" [Episode 83]

Collectibles

Compact Discs and Cassette Tapes

Available at your local record store or:

■ The '70s Preservation Society in conjunction with Razor & Tie Music offers five Partridge Family albums on compact disc or cassette. The following titles are available:

The Partridge Family Album—CD (#390) Cassette (#391)

The Partridge Family Up to Date—CD (#388) Cassette (#389)

The Partridge Family Sound Magazine—CD (#386) Cassette (#387)

The Partridge Family Shopping Bag—CD (#384) Cassette (#385)

A Partridge Family Christmas Card—CD (#293) Cassette (#294)

To order, call **1-800-872-1233**. For a free '70s Preservation Society catalog, write to: '70s Preservation Society, P.O. Box 585, Cooper Station, Dept. PFB, New York, NY 10276.

■ Arista Records offers *The Partridge Family Greatest Hits* album on compact disc or cassette, available in record stores.

"SINGING MY SONG"   THE PARTRIDGE FAMILY

Bubblegum Cards

Topps issued three series of Partridge Family bubblegum cards:
- Partridge Family Series I—55 cards with yellow border (1971).
- Partridge Family Series II—55 cards with blue border (1971).
- Partridge Family Series III—88 cards with green border (1971).

Bubblegum cards and other collectibles are available through Baseball Cards-Movie Collectibles, 4619 Lakeview Canyon Road, Westlake Village, CA 91361. Tel: (818)-707-2273.

Toys

- **Lunch Box.** *The Partridge Family lunch box was featured on the cover of* The Partridge Family Greatest Hits *album.*
- **The Partridge Family Toy Bus**
- **The Partridge Family Game.** *Milton Bradley.*
- **The Partridge Family View Master Reels**
- **The Partridge Family Talking Viewmaster**

- The Partridge Family Coloring Book
- The Partridge Family Fun Book
- The Partridge Family Activity Book
- David Cassidy Notebook
- The Partridge Colorforms
- David Cassidy Colorform Dress-up Set
- The Partridge Family Paper Dolls. *Three different boxed sets.*
- Susan Dey Paper Dolls
- Laurie Partridge Doll
- Patti Partridge Doll
- David Cassidy Toy Guitar
- David Cassidy Jigsaw Puzzle
- The Partridge Family Tree Flicker Badge Set

- Cereal Boxes. *General Foods featured the Partridge Family kids' faces on their cereal boxes.*
- David Cassidy Love Kit. *Contains, according to the advertisements in 16 Magazine, "a life-size, full length portrait, an autographed maxi-poster three times life-size, a complete biography and childhood photo album, 40 wallet-size photos, a secret love message from David, and a lovers' card with his name and yours."*
- David Cassidy Choker Luv Beads
- David Cassidy's Super Luv Stickers

Clothing

- Kate Greenway "Partridge Collection." *A press release, issued to publicize the collection, reads: "Fashions from the collection are frequently worn by Suzanne Crough and Susan Dey . . . Jeans, dresses, and jumpers are printed with the bus which the family uses to travel."*
- David Cassidy Beach Towel

Comic Books

Charlton Comics published 21 *Partridge Family* comic books between March 1971 and December 1973. In mint condition, issue 1 is valued at $15, issue 5 (Summer Special) is valued at $18, and the remaining issues are

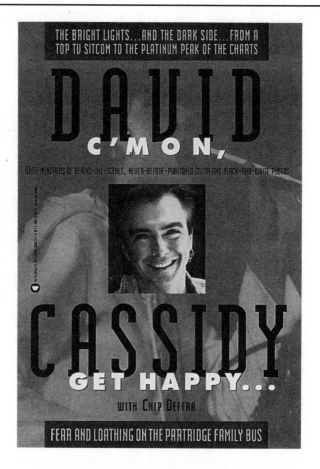

THE BRIGHT LIGHTS...AND THE DARK SIDE...FROM A
TOP TV SITCOM TO THE PLATINUM PEAK OF THE CHARTS

DAVID
C'MON,

WITH HUNDREDS OF BEHIND-THE-SCENES, NEVER-BEFORE-PUBLISHED COLOR AND BLACK-AND-WHITE PHOTOS

CASSIDY
GET HAPPY...
WITH CHIP DEFFAA

FEAR AND LOATHING ON THE PARTRIDGE FAMILY BUS

C'mon, Get Happy. . .
Fear and Loathing on the Partridge Family Bus
By David Cassidy with Chip Deffaa

Throughout the first half of the '70s, he was the highest paid solo performer in the world—even bigger than Elvis, the Rolling Stones, or the Beatles. Now David Cassidy tells his own story, an irreverent, unflinchingly honest saga of what life was like as Keith Partridge—working with his real-life stepmother, the endless cavalcade of groupies that invaded his bed, his tempestuous relationships with Susan Dey and Meredith Baxter, revealing encounters with John Lennon, Paul McCartney, Elvis, and the Beach Boys, the concerts, the singing career that sold over 20 million albums, and the desolation after the fans went home.

Available through bookstores or directly from Warner Books by calling **1-800-759-0190.**

valued at $8 each, according to *The Overstreet Guide to Comic Books* (1993). Comic books are available through Rick's Comics, (310)-527-7185.

Other Books

■ *Shirley and Marty: An Unlikely Love Story* by Shirley Jones and Marty Ingels (New York: William Morrow, 1990)

■ *The David Cassidy Story* (New York: Reese Publishing Company, 1971)

■ *9 Lives of David Cassidy* (New York: *Spec Magazine*, 1972)

■ *David David David* by James Gregory (New York: Curtis Books, 1972)

■ *For Girls Only* by Susan Dey

■ *Boys, Beauty & Popularity: How to Have Your Share of Each* by Susan Dey

■ *Growing Up with the Partridge Family* (booklet)

■ *The Private Lives of the Partridge Family* (booklet)

■ *David's Private Photo Album* (booklet)

■ *Dynamic David Cassidy* (booklet)

Teenybopper Magazines

The following magazines ran stories on The Partridge Family *from 1970 through 1974*:

■ *16 Magazine*

■ *Fave*

■ *Tiger Beat*

■ *Teen World*

■ *The Official Partridge Family Magazine*

Mad Magazine Parody

"The Putrid Family" orginally appeared in *Mad* Issue Number 150, April 1972, and was reprinted in *Mad Super Special* Number 94, July 1994 (*See* pages 115-119). For subscription information, write to: *Mad Magazine*, 485 Madison Avenue, New York, NY 10022-5852.

TV Appearances

■ *This Is Your Life, Shirley Jones*, 1971. Opens with the Partridge Family lip-syncing to "I Think I Love You" for a filmed promo.

■ *Thanksgiving Reunion*, 1977. Features a reunion of the casts of *The Partridge Family* and *My Three Sons*, with clips from past episodes and several musical numbers. David Cassidy sings "Strengthen My Love" and "As Time Goes By." Shirley Jones sings "He Touched Me."

■ "Child Actors," *Geraldo*, 1990. A panel discussion with Danny Bonaduce, Danielle Briseboits (Stephanie Mills on *All in the Family*), Jon Provost (Timmy on *Lassie*), Jeannie Russell (Margaret Wade on *Dennis the Menace*), Susan Olsen (Cindy Brady on *The Brady Bunch*), Butch Patrick (Eddie Munster on *The Munsters*), and Johnnie Whitaker (Jody Davis on *Family Affair*).

■ *Instant Recall*, 1990. Retrospective on *The Partridge Family*.

■ "'Lyin' to Myself,'" 1990. David Cassidy's video for the Top Twenty single of the same name.

■ *Entertainment Tonight*, 1991. Features Danny Bonaduce, his wife, and his mother.

■ "David Cassidy: Life After the Partridge Family," *Geraldo*, September 23, 1991. Features David Cassidy, Danny Bonaduce, Dave Madden, and a telephone linkup with Shirley Jones and David's real mother, Evelyn Ward. Cassidy sings "Cherish" and "I'll Meet You Halfway."

■ *Then and Now*, 1992. Retrospective on David Cassidy.

■ *Saturday Night Live*, 1992. Host Susan Dey played Laurie Partridge, Dana Carvey played Keith Partridge, and Mike Myers played Danny Partridge in a sketch featuring a battle of the bands between the Partridge Family and the Brady Bunch.

■ *Idols*, 1993. Documentary on what it's like to be a teen idol, featuring David Cassidy.

■ *The Arsenio Hall Show*, July 1993. Guests include Shirley Jones, David Cassidy, and Danny Bonaduce. Cassidy sings "I Woke Up in Love This Morning."

Photographs

Available through:

- Cinema Collector's, 1507 Wilcox Avenue, Hollywood, CA 90028
- Howard Frank Archives, PO Box 50, Midwood Station, Brooklyn, NY 11230
- Jerry Ohrlinger's, 242 West 14th Street, New York, NY 10011

Scripts

Available through: Script City, 8033 Sunset Boulevard, Box 1500, Hollywood, CA 90046. *(Send $2 for catalog.)*

Paperback Books

Curtis Books published seventeen Partridge Family paperback mystery books between 1970 and 1974.

The Partridge Family by Michael Avallone—"Can America's top rock group prevail against an evil enemy agent without blowing its cool?"

The Partridge Family #2: The Haunted Hall by Michael Avallone—"It's a real spook out when rock's coolest supergroup invades a mansion filled with ghosts and deadly danger!"

The Partridge Family #3: Keith the Hero by Michael Avallone—"The rock clan's future hangs in the balance when Keith is forced to make an impossible choice."

The Partridge Family #4: The Ghost of Graveyard Hill by Paul Fairman—"Would you believe the Partridge clan staging a rock concert for a Nevada desert town full of nothing but ghosts?"

The Partridge Family #5: Terror by Night by Vic Crume—"Somebody or something is out to get them, and when Keith tries to find out why, the rock star's vacation becomes a nightmare."

The Partridge Family #6: Keith Partridge, Master Spy by Vance Stanton—"Something clicked in Keith's head and enter Keith Partridge, master spy."

The Partridge Family #7: The Walking Fingers by Vance Stanton—"Keith and sidekick in big trouble with deadly characters and a gold mine."

The Partridge Family #8: The Treasure of Ghost Mountain by Paul Fairman—"The curse of Ghost Mountain haunts rock's first family."

The Partridge Family #9: The Fat and Skinny Mystery by Vance Stanton—"A frantic, far-out sleighride in Manhattan, Kansas, for rock's first family."

The Partridge Family #10: Marked for Terror by Vic Crume—"Danny's look-alike moves into the gloomy old mansion next door."

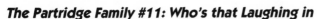

The Partridge Family #11: Who's that Laughing in the Grave? by Vance Stanton—"Theodora Moon, the witchiest of the west, goes Partridge hunting with her satanic disciple, Brother George, and an oozy blob-like thing called the All-Destroying Hex."

The Partridge Family #12: The Phantom of the Rock Concert by Lee Hays—"When Mr. Kincaid books the Partridge Family to perform in a haunted house, an unknown phantom wants to stop the show."

The Partridge Family #13: The Mystery of the Mad Millionairess by Edward Fenton—"Flying high in society lands rock's first family in deep and deadly terror."

The Partridge Family #14: Thirteen at Killer Gorge by Vic Crume—"A missing skyjacker and a stolen fortune bring danger to America's first family of rock."

The Partridge Family #15: The Disappearing Professor by Lee Hays—"Shirley is swept off her feet by a professor, and rock's first family learns a lesson in terror."

The Partridge Family #16: The Stolen Necklace by Lee Hays—"Rock's first family sails into mystery and danger when the theft of a necklace turns a trip into a bummer."

The Partridge Family #17: Love Comes to Keith Partridge by Michael Avallone—"Keith finds that romance can be dangerous when he blows his cool over an extraordinary girl."

7

I'll Meet You Halfway

I'll Meet You Halfway

Will there come a day when you and I can say,
We can finally see each other?
And will there come a time when we can find the time,
To reach out for one another?
We've been traveling in circles,
Such a long, long time trying to say hello, oh!
And we can just let it ride,
But you're someone that I'd like to get to know.
I'll meet you halfway, that's better than no way.
There must be some way to get it together.
And if there's some way, I know that some day,
We just might work it out forever.

Will there come a day when you and I can say,
We can finally see each other?
And will there come a time when we can find the time,
To reach out for one another?
We've been traveling in circles,
Such a long, long time trying to say hello, oh!
And we can just let it ride,
But you're someone that I'd like to get to know.
I'll meet you halfway, that's better than no way.
There must be some way to get it together.
And if there's some way, I know that some day,
We just might work it out forever.

Wes Farrell-Gerry Goffin • ©1971 Screen Gems-EMI Music Inc.

ow well do you really know the Partridge Family? We all know that Shirley was a widow, but who took her to the high school senior prom? Sure, Keith blow-dried his hair and wore a pukka-shell necklace, but can you name three girls he took to Muldune's Point? Everyone remembers when Laurie got braces on her teeth, but how long did she have to wear them? Danny Partridge had a big black bank safe in his room, but what was the combination? Yes, Mr. Kincaid was the Partridge Family's manager, but can you name one other act he represented?

Here's your chance to test your intimate knowledge of Partridge Family lore. The questions that follow span the spectrum of Partridge trivia. As for the above questions, well, they're part of the essay exam. Because as you'll see, this is one trivia quiz that is truly for the birds.

Partridge Family Pop Quiz

1. What is the name of the Partridge Family's original lead singer?
   - (A) Betty Jo Bradley
   - (B) Patty Lane
   - (C) Penny Robinson
   - (D) Gloria Steinman
   - (E) Cindy Brady

2. What was the late Mr. Partridge's first name?
   - (A) Steve
   - (B) Harry
   - (C) Max
   - (D) Sidney
   - (E) Never revealed

3. What is the license plate number of the Partridge Family's bus?
   - (A) P-FMLY
   - (B) 869913
   - (C) ABC-123
   - (D) NLX-590
   - (E) Never revealed

JUST DAVID!

4. What is the Partridge Family's home address?
   - (A) 698 Sycamore Road
   - (B) 77 Sunset Strip
   - (C) 650 West End Avenue
   - (D) 1313 Mockingbird Lane
   - (E) Never revealed

5. What is Keith's favorite food?
   - (A) Hot dogs
   - (B) A toss-up between steak and meat loaf
   - (C) Chile Relleño and refried beans
   - (D) Corned beef and cabbage
   - (E) Pizza

6. At what hotel are the Partridges mistaken for robbers?
   - (A) Howard Johnson's
   - (B) Hotel Florida
   - (C) Hotel Splendid
   - (D) The Sunshine Motor Haven
   - (E) Club Med

7. When Laurie gets braces on her teeth, she hears the music of what rock 'n' roll band being broadcast in her mouth?
   - (A) The Rolling Stones
   - (B) The Partridge Family
   - (C) The Archies
   - (D) Sly and the Family Stone
   - (E) Peter and Gordon

8. Who is the Partridge family's pediatrician?
   - (A) Dr. David Rosenberg
   - (B) Dr. Steven Gilman
   - (C) Dr. Scott Press
   - (D) Dr. Jeff Gorodetsky
   - (E) Dr. Ted Michaels

9. Where do runaway Maggie Newton's grandparents live?
   - (A) Idaho
   - (B) Kentucky
   - (C) Tennessee
   - (D) Nebraska
   - (E) Oklahoma

10. What color luggage does the Partridge Family have?
    - (A) Blue
    - (B) Brown
    - (C) Red
    - (D) Yellow
    - (E) Tangerine

11. When Shirley decides to enroll in a college course, what course does she take?
    - (A) Creative Writing 101
    - (B) Psychology 1A
    - (C) Economics 100

(D) Music Appreciation 3B

(E) Art History 102

12. When Danny is convinced that he will not survive a tonsillectomy operation, he leaves his one share of AT&T stock to whom?

(A) Keith

(B) Laurie

(C) Chris

(D) Tracy

(E) Mr. Kincaid

13. What is Keith's middle name?

(A) Douglas

(B) Philip

(C) David

(D) Michael

(E) Glenn

PEACE LOVING DANNY!

14. Where does Shirley Partridge keep her savings account?

(A) The First National Bank

(B) San Pueblo Savings and Loan

(C) The Bank of Boston

(D) San Pueblo National Bank

(E) None of the above

15. When Keith ran away from home as a child, how long did it take for him to come back home?

(A) 21 minutes

(B) 47 minutes

(C) 52 minutes

(D) 1 hour

(E) 3 hours

16. When Danny ran away from home as a child, how long did it take for him to come back home?

(A) 21 minutes

(B) 47 minutes

(C) 52 minutes

(D) 1 hour

(E) 3 hours

17. When Keith makes a movie starring all the members of his family, what does he title the film?
    (A) *16 ½*
    (B) *Dial P for Partridge*
    (C) *One Flew Over the Partridge's Nest*
    (D) *Partridge Knowledge*
    (E) *The Partridge and the Pussycat*

18. What does Keith claim is the message of his film?
    (A) It's easier for movie stars to get dates
    (B) Wet birds don't fly at night
    (C) The more things change, the more they stay the same
    (D) People are ridiculous
    (E) Too much of everything is never enough of anything

19. After English teacher Mrs. Damion reads in the newspaper that Keith has a crush on her, what poem does she read to him?
    (A) "The Carpenter, the Mouse, and the Plumber" by Lewis Carroll
    (B) "To His Coy Mistress" by Andrew Marvell
    (C) "To George Sand: A Desire" by Elizabeth Barrett Browning
    (D) "Résumé" by Dorothy Parker
    (E) "Howl" by Allen Ginsberg

20. What color is Shirley's bathrobe?
    (A) Pink
    (B) Yellow
    (C) Red
    (D) Plaid
    (E) A and B

21. What does Danny steal from Shirley and Laurie's backpack when they go wilderness camping?
    (A) A tube of toothpaste
    (B) Five dollars
    (C) Mosquito repellent
    (D) A flashlight
    (E) A can of beans

LEARNING THEIR LINES!

22. When Keith and Danny attempt to break into the high school newspaper office to steal back Laurie's diary, what are their code names?
    (A) Siegfried and Shtarker
    (B) Gilligan and Skipper
    (C) Antigone and Clytemnestra
    (D) Bluejay and Redwing
    (E) Wally and Beaver

23. When the Partridge Family performs a benefit concert at the Papago Indian Fair, where is the Papago Indian Reservation?
    (A) Twenty miles from Albuquerque
    (B) Forty miles from Piedmont
    (C) Fifty miles from San Pueblo
    (D) Sixty miles from King's Island Amusement Park
    (E) Seventy miles from Clarksville

24. Where does psychic Max Ledbetter live?
    (A) 1232 NE 176 Terrace
    (B) 1313 Mockingbird Lane
    (C) Highway 73
    (D) 312 Elm Street
    (E) On the Papago Indian Reservation

25. Where does Shirley get ticketed for speeding while driving the family in the bus?
    (A) Crater City
    (B) Albuquerque
    (C) San Pueblo
    (D) Mayfield
    (E) Ojus

26. When a foreign princess is coming to dinner, what topic of conversation does Keith assign to his sister Laurie?
    (A) Rust: The Real Red Menace
    (B) The Helman Theory on Helmanivity
    (C) The Treaty of Versailles: Why Did It Fail?
    (D) The Common Market: Pros and Cons
    (E) The Rise and Fall of the United States of America

27. When Snake's biker friends park their motorcycles all over the Partridges' front lawn, what type of flowers do they ruin?
    (A) Chrysanthemums
    (B) Tulips
    (C) Roses
    (D) Azaleas
    (E) Carnations

28. What are Shirley's parents' first names?
    (A) Jeffrey and Amy Sue
    (B) Douglas and Suzanne
    (C) Michael and Audrey
    (D) Fred and Amanda
    (E) Robert and Barbara

FEELING GROOVY!

29. After Shirley's parents reaffirm their wedding vows in a wedding ceremony, who catches the bouquet?
    (A) Laurie Partridge
    (B) Gloria Hicky
    (C) Shirley Partridge
    (D) Tracy Partridge
    (E) Simone, the dog

30. Keith likes his eggs poached, Danny likes his eggs boiled for 4.5 minutes, Tracy likes her eggs sunny-side up, and Chris likes his eggs with the yoke broken. How does Laurie like her eggs?
    (A) Scrambled
    (B) Cooked into an omelet
    (C) Sunny-side down
    (D) She doesn't like eggs
    (E) Never revealed

31. When Laurie dates a minister, where do they go on their first date?
    (A) The Royale Theatre to see *Gone with the Wind*
    (B) A Three Dog Night concert
    (C) The San Pueblo Public Library
    (D) Hotel Peer Gynt
    (E) Muldune's Point

32. When Danny wins a race horse in a raffle, what is the horse's name?
    (A) Affirmed
    (B) Swifty Schwartzberg
    (C) Lionel
    (D) Smokey
    (E) F. Scott Fitzgerald

33. When the Partridge Family puts their house up for sale, who offers to buy it?
    (A) George and Bea Sharp
    (B) Mr. Kincaid
    (C) Mike and Carol Brady
    (D) Bobby Sherman
    (E) Darrin and Samantha Stephens

34. When the Partridge Family gets taken hostage by escaped convict Morris Dinkler, what does Morris have in his pocket that he calls Bertha?
    (A) A parakeet
    (B) A gun
    (C) A harmonica
    (D) A chipmunk
    (E) A photograph of his wife

35. When Keith, Laurie, and Danny sneak into the computer room at Bartlett's Department Store to reprogram the machine in Shirley's favor, what do they nickname their mission?
    (A) Operation Catapult
    (B) Mission Improbable
    (C) Mission Megabyte
    (D) Operation Goo-goo
    (E) Operation Partridge

36. What is the name of the sleuth in mystery writer Michelangelo Rezo's books?
    (A) Floyd Lawson
    (B) Major Anthony Nelson
    (C) Major Hockstedder
    (D) Wynwood Baines
    (E) Inspector Sparrow

37. When Keith composes a classical concerto, what does he title his work?
    (A) "Partridge Concerto"
    (B) "First Concerto for Cello in D Major"
    (C) "Unfinished Concerto Number 1"
    (D) "Come on Get Classical"
    (E) "Symphony in B Minor"

38. What baseball team does Danny Partridge pitch for?
    (A) Dodgers
    (B) Orioles
    (C) Red Jays
    (D) Gargoyles
    (E) Cowsills

AMERICA'S FAVORITE GROUP

39. What is Mr. Kincaid's middle name?
    (A) Clarence
    (B) Edgar
    (C) Sandwich
    (D) Wilbur
    (E) Leonard

40. When the Partridge Family attends a costume party aboard the T.S.S. *Fairsea*, Shirley dresses as a clown, Keith goes as a bunny rabbit, Danny disguises himself as a garbage can, and Laurie wears a witch costume. What does Mr. Kincaid dress up as?
    (A) A skunk
    (B) A good fairy
    (C) Ringo Starr
    (D) The Pope
    (E) He doesn't

41. Who gave the Partridge Family the New Zealand azaleas planted in their front yard?
    (A) Queen Elizabeth
    (B) Mayor Henry White
    (C) Ambassador Howard Lipton
    (D) Governor Alan Salzman
    (E) Mr. Kincaid

42. What is the license plate number on the blue Ford Mustang Keith sells to Harve?
   - (A) KEITH
   - (B) LMW 28IF
   - (C) TQP 534
   - (D) PF 1974
   - (E) 2-6809

LAURIE'S GOT A DATE TONIGHT

43. What is Shirley Partridge's mother's maiden name?
   - (A) Partridge
   - (B) Hollinger
   - (C) Douglas
   - (D) Casey
   - (E) Clampett

44. When Keith has Danny plagiarize a published author's work to find out whether Laurie, as his student teacher, is biased against him, what short story does Danny put his name to?
   - (A) "The Judgement of Matterfield" by Ernest Hemingway
   - (B) "The Strange Life of Walter Mitty" by James Thurber
   - (C) "The Nose" by Nicolai Gogol
   - (D) "Metamorphosis" by Franz Kafka
   - (E) "The Waltz" by Dorothy Parker

45. What does Mr. Kincaid give Shirley as a present for her birthday?
   - (A) A framed photo of himself
   - (B) A four-slice toaster
   - (C) A gold record of the Partridge Family *Shopping Bag* album
   - (D) A new car
   - (E) A diamond engagement ring

46. What is Shirley Partridge's high school yearbook entitled?
   - (A) *Genesis*
   - (B) *Pueblonian*
   - (C) *Falcon*
   - (D) *Ceralbus*
   - (E) *Crusader*

47. Three actresses who later starred on *Charlie's Angels* guest starred on *The Partridge Family*. Which one did not?
    (A) Jaclyn Smith
    (B) Cheryl Ladd
    (C) Kate Jackson
    (D) Farah Fawcett
    (E) None of the above

48. Which two characters from *The Wizard of Oz* guest starred on *The Partridge Family*?
    (A) Dorothy and Toto
    (B) Scarecrow and the Wicked Witch of the West
    (C) Tin Woodsman and Cowardly Lion
    (D) Dorothy and Scarecrow
    (E) Aunt Em and Glenda the Good Witch of the North

49. The daughter of one of the Partridge Family's session musicians is a famous musician in her own right. Who is she?
    (A) Chrissie Hynde of the Pretenders
    (B) Tina Weymouth of Talking Heads
    (C) Wendy Melvoin of Prince and the Revolution
    (D) Edie Brakell of the New Bohemians
    (E) Natalie Merchant of 10,000 Maniacs

50. Which of the following street signs cannot be seen hanging in the Partridge Family's garage?
    (A) US 40
    (B) Ohio 73
    (C) Texas 73
    (D) Florida Turnpike
    (E) Pennsylvania Interstate 76

(ANSWERS ON PAGE 319)

8

Hello, Hello

Hello, Hello

Hello, hello, I love you so,
Yet it all began when I ran into you not so long ago.
And since that day I've wanted to say hello.
Hello, hello, would you like to go,
To a place with me where we can watch the hours go by,
Cause you're someone I'd like to get to know.
I still don't know your name and I couldn't care less,
I like what I already see.
Whatever sign you are or what's your address
Don't really matter much to me.
I just want to say:

Hello, hello, I love you so,
Yet it all began when I ran into you not so long ago.
And since that day I've wanted to say hello.
I still don't know your name and I couldn't care less
I like what I already see.
Whatever sign you are or what's your address
Don't really matter much to me.
I just want to say:

Hello, hello, I love you so,
Yet it all began when I ran into you not so long ago.
And since that day I've wanted to say hello.
Hello, hello.

Wes Farrell-Tony Romeo • ©1972 Screen Gems-EMI Music Inc.
All rights reserved. International copyright secured. Used by permission.

ike the Beatles, the individual members of the Partridge Family went their own separate ways after the series went off the air. They're all still traveling along with a song that they're singing, though now on different allegorical buses on different metaphorical roads. The cast members all achieved varying degrees of success after the disintegration of the group, but the fame and notoriety they achieved as the Partridge Family never faded.

Though none of the former Partridges married an avant-garde Japanese dragon lady, the comparisons with the Beatles certainly aren't far-fetched. David Cassidy, like Paul McCartney, had the most successful solo career as a musician, even though he never joined another family or recorded a duet with Stevie Wonder. Susan Dey became Grace Van Owen on *L.A. Law*, not unlike Ringo Starr, who gave acting a try. Danny Bonaduce works as a popular radio deejay at WLUP in Chicago, was arrested for drug possession, and was once charged with punching a transvestite; similarly, John Lennon was often interviewed on the radio, arrested for drug possession, and charged for punching a photographer. Brian Forster races cars as does George Harrison, and Suzanne Crough owned and operated a bookstore where several books on the Beatles were sold. Jeremy Gelbwaks, the first Chris, has gone down in history as the Pete Best of the Partridge Family.

The most obvious similarity between the Partridge Family and the Beatles is that neither group ever reunited after their break-up. A Partridge Family reunion is, however, within the realm of possibilities, and to see the Partridges reunite to lip-sync to a recording of "I Think I Love You" would undoubtedly be the most remarkable event in the annals of music history.

Where Are They Now?

Shirley Jones *(Shirley Partridge)*

Born on March 31, 1934, in Smithton, Pennsylvania, Shirley Mae Jones was the daughter of the local brewer. Her father ran Jones Brewing Company, makers of Stoney's Beer. After her graduation from high school in 1952, she entered the Miss America contest, became Miss Pittsburgh and was runner-up for Miss Pennsylvania. With the scholarship she won, she enrolled at the Pittsburgh School of Drama and sang with the Pittsburgh Civic Light opera productions of *Lady in the Dark* and *Call me Madam*. A year later she met Richard Rodgers and Oscar Hammerstein, who put her in the chorus of *South Pacific* on Broadway and then in the lead of their movie production of *Oklahoma!* (1955) at the age of twenty, launching a long movie career. She married actor Jack Cassidy, became stepmother to seven-year-old David Cassidy (who was still living with his mother, actress Evelyn Ward), and between film roles had three children: Shaun, Patrick, and Ryan.

Her films include *Oklahoma!* (1955), *Carousel* (1956), *April Love* (1957), *Never Steal Anything Small* (1959), *Elmer Gantry* (1960), for which she won an Academy Award for her performance as prostitute Lulu Baines, *Bobbikins* (1960), *Pepe* (1960), *Two Rode Together* (1961), *The Music Man* (1962), *The Courtship of Eddie's Father* (1963), *A Ticklish Affair* (1963), *Dark Purpose* (1964), *Bedtime Story* (1964), *Fluffy* (1965), *The Secret of My Success* (1965), *The Happy Ending* (1966), *the Cheyenne Social Club* (1970), *Beyond the Poseidon Adventure* (1979), and *Evening in Byzantium* (1979). She also appeared in plays including *Maggie Flynn* with her husband, the late Jack Cassidy. After *The Partridge Family*, Shirley starred on the short-lived television series *Shirley* on NBC from 1979 to 1980.

On television, she has appeared on *Fireside Theatre, Gruen Guild*

Theatre, *Ford Star Jubilee*, *Playhouse 90*, *Lux Video Theatre*, *The U.S. Steel Hour*, *Pat Boone Chevy Showroom*, *The Frank Sinatra Show*, *The Du Pont Show of the Month*, *The Voice of Firestone*, *The Eddie Fisher Show*, *The Danny Thomas Show*, *The Garry Moore Show*, *The Bell Telephone Hour*, *The Dinah Shore Chevy Show*, *Bob Hope Presents the Chrysler Theatre*, *The Danny Kaye Show*, *The Smothers Brother Comedy Hour*, *Out of the Blue*, *The Mike Douglas Show*, *Alan King Special*, *This Is Tom Jones*, *The Name of the Game*, *This Is Your Life*, *Hollywood Squares*, *Dinah!*, *McMillan and Wife*, *The Love Boat*, *Hotel*, and *Murder, She Wrote*. She also appeared in the television movies *Silent Night, Lonely Night* (1969), *But I Don't Want to Get Married!* (1970), *The Girls of Huntington House* (1973), *The Family Nobody Wanted* (1975), *Winner Take All* (1975), *The Lives of Jenny Dolan* (1975), *Yesterday's Child* (1977), *Who'll Save Our Children?* (1978), *Evening in Byzantium* (1978), *The Children of An Lac* (1980), and *Inmates: A Love Story* (1981). Shirley performs symphony concerts worldwide. She is also a member of the board of directors of Jones Brewing Company.

Shirley is married to comedian Marty Ingels, and the couple live in Beverly Hills. Her autobiography, *Shirley and Marty: An Unlikely Love Story*, was published by William Morrow and Company in 1990.

David Cassidy *(Keith Partridge)*

Born on April 12, 1950, in New York City, David Bruce Cassidy, the son of actor Jack Cassidy and singer-actress Evelyn Ward, was raised in West Orange, New Jersey. His parents were divorced when he was five, and he moved to Hollywood with his mother when he was eleven. He was expelled from two high schools before completing his education at the private Rexford School in Los Angeles. He lasted one semester at Los Angeles City College, then played guitar and drums, wrote songs, and performed with the Los Angeles Theater Group. He decided to try acting, moved to New York, and landed a co-starring role in Alan Sherman's Broadway production of *The Fig Leaves Are Falling*. After moving back to Los Angeles, he appeared on *Ironside*, *Marcus Welby*, *The FBI*, *Bonanza*, and *Medical Center*. He was also a regular on *The Survivors*.

His role as Keith Partridge on *The Partridge Family* launched his career as a bona fide teen idol. His photograph appeared on the cover of *16 Magazine* twenty-four issues in a row, and his surging popularity lead to several concert tours, solo albums, and hit singles. In 1972, in an attempt to change his teen idol image, Cassidy did a candid interview in *Rolling Stone*, complete with a partially undraped photograph of himself. In 1974, at the height of his popularity, he walked away from it all at the age of 24.

After *The Partridge Family*, David took refuge from show business, bred horses in England, and, in 1977, he married actress Kay Lenz. He returned to television in May 1978 as the star of a two-hour *Police Story* in which he played a rookie cop who goes undercover at a high school to crack a narcotics ring, receiving an Emmy nomination for his performance.

He starred as Officer Dan Shay in the television series *David Cassidy—Man Undercover* on NBC from 1978 to 1979. He also appeared in the

television movie *The Night the City Screamed* (1980). His marriage dissolved in 1981, and in 1984, he married horse breeder Meryl Tanz. His second marriage lasted less than a year. On Broadway, David starred in *Joseph and the Amazing Technicolor Dreamcoat*, and in 1987 he began five years of psychoanalysis. His motion pictures include *Instant Karma* (1990) and *The Spirit of '76* (1991), and he has guest starred on *The Love Boat, Fantasy Island*, and *Alfred Hitchcock Presents*.

In 1991, Cassidy hit the concert circuit for the first time in more than fifteen years with a 35-city tour, performing updated versions of his old hits along with new material, including his 1990 Top Twenty hit, "Lyin' to Myself." In July 1993, Nick at Night broadcast four episodes of the series every night for a week, culminating with David Cassidy hosting his four favorite *Partridge Family* episodes. After touring seven cities with the Partridge Family bus to promote the series, Cassidy hosted sixteen episodes of *The Partridge Family* on MTV on Sunday, July 23, 1993. That same week, Shirley Jones, David Cassidy, and Danny Bonaduce appeared together as guests on *The Arsenio Hall Show*. In 1993, he costarred with his half-brother Shaun Cassidy in the Broadway production of *Blood Brothers*. His autobiography, *C'mon, Get Happy: Fear and Loathing on the Partridge Family Bus*, was published by Warner Books in 1994.

The trademark ring he wears on the pinkie finger of his right hand features his family crest and was given to him before he turned 21 by his father, Jack Cassidy. He has never taken it off.

David is married to songwriter Sue Shifrin, has a son, Beau Devon, and lives in Los Angeles, California.

Susan Dey (Laurie Partridge)

Born on December 10, 1952, in Pekin, Illinois, Susan Hallock Dey is the daughter of a newspaper journalist who moved his family to Mount Kisco, New York, when Susan was three months old. Her mother died of pneumonia when Susan was eight, and her father remarried a few years later. She has two sisters, Leslie, older, and Elizabeth, who is younger, and a brother. When she was fifteen, her step-mother took her to a modeling agency and Susan was soon modeling for *Vogue*, *McCall's*, and *Mademoiselle*. Within a year, her picture had appeared on the covers of *Glamour*, *Bride's*, and *Seventeen*. The next year she flew to Los Angeles to audition for *The Partridge Family*, and moved to Los Angeles alone to take the part. During the first year of the series, Susan lived with the family of Danny Bonaduce. She completed her courses at Fox Lane High in Bedford, New York, by mail. During the first

two years of the series, Susan was anorexic and bulimic, which she overcame on her own.

While *The Partridge Family* was still on the air, Susan appeared in the motion picture *Skyjacked*, starring Charlton Heston (1972). After *The Partridge Family*, she starred as Jane on the short-lived comedy series *Love Me, Loves Me Not*, Grace Van Owen on *L.A. Law*, and Wally on *Love and War*. Susan has guest starred on *This Is Your Life*, *Circle of Fear*, *Born Free*, *The Rookies*, *S.W.A.T.*, *The Quest*, *The Streets of San Francisco*, *Barnaby Jones*, *Late Night with David Letterman*, *A Place on the Table*, and *Saturday Night Live*. She has starred in the television movies *Terror on the Beach* (1973), *Cage Without a Key* (1975), *Mary Jane Harper Cried Last Night* (1977), *Little Women* (1978), *The Comeback Kid* (1980), *Malibu* (1983), *Sunset Limousine* (1983), *Love Leads the Way* (1984), *The Trouble with Dick* (1986), *Angel in Green* (1987), *L.A. Law* (1987), and *I Love You Perfect* (1989). Her motion pictures include *First Love* with William Katt (1977), *Looker* with Albert Finney and James Coburn (1981), and *Echo Park* (1986).

Susan is married to TV Producer Bernard Sofronski and has a daughter, Sarah, from her first marriage to agent Leonard Hirshan.

What Makes You Most Proud of The Partridge Family?

Shirley Jones (Shirley Partridge):

"I think the fact that it was a family-oriented show. It was good for everybody to watch. You know, there are so few of those kinds of shows today. That's why I'm happy that it's now being shown on Nickelodeon because my grandchildren are watching it for the first time. It's a real kick, and it's nice to see eight- and nine- and ten-year olds watching me on 'Nick at Night' or seeing my movies now on television, which is nice, too, *The Music Man* and so on. So that part of it was nice. It was nice to be associated with that kind of show where everybody said, 'Oh, how wonderful,' and 'Isn't it nice to have a show that the whole family can sit down together on a Friday night and watch.' And let's face it. It was a hit. It's nice to be associated with a hit of any kind. I don't care what it is. To run almost five years, even at that time was pretty good. That in itself is a reason to be proud."

David Cassidy (Keith Partridge):

"That it's sustained. That it's maybe as big now as it's ever been. And it has a tremendously loyal following amongst a vast demographic from kids to people in their eighties. And that means a lot, you know, nearly twenty-five years later."

Susan Dey (Laurie Partridge):

"The show was fun and a good experience, and David [Cassidy] and I had a marvelous relationship. When the show was canceled, I lost a person out of my life. Of course, I had a nice relationship with Shirley, too, but David and I were of the same age group. I started playing a fourteen-year-old and grew up very slowly. In fact, when the show finished, I was 21 and still playing a sixteen-year-old." (in *Family Weekly*, October 23, 1977)

Danny Bonaduce (Danny Partridge):

"The lasting power. I mean, there have been a lot of series since and before, but I would say my favorite thing about the show is that it's become Americana. It's become important to American society somehow. There are some shows that just do it, and some shows that don't. *The Brady Bunch* became part of Americana, whereas *Nanny and the Professor* did not. You know, it's weird. I don't know why some do and some don't, but this one did."

Brian Forster (Chris Partridge):

"I think being on that show was really fun, it was really an accomplishment. I guess I was just proud of being on the show at all because it was one of the top shows of its time. Also people come up to me and tell me I was a real part of their life growing up. I never really could believe it, but now enough people have told me that, I guess it's true. I mean, to be a part of people's life growing up is really something special."

Jeremy Gelbwaks (Chris Partridge):

"That I did it, and that it's made a lasting impression. Let's face it, this show was not brain surgery, but a lot of people liked it. In fact, it seems like *The Partridge Family* is referenced in half the Generation X stuff that's being written now. And as small as my role was, I still get people saying that I touched them, or influenced them to learn to drum, or made them jealous, or whatever. You know, my friends' kids watch the show and think it's pretty funny that I was in it. So I guess the answer is that I had my fifteen minutes, and it was in something that made an impact."

Suzanne Crough (Tracy Partridge):

"Probably the mere fact that it's still around today. There's so many shows that go by, and I've done a lot that get filed away and you never see them again. I am glad that for a long time now *The Partridge Family* hasn't really been overexposed. Had I been on *The Brady Bunch*, I would have really felt like I was overexposed. You know, *The Partridge Family* has kind of been hiding away somewhere for a while, which makes me pretty happy. But all in all, it's a classic television show, and that's something to also be proud of."

Dave Madden (Mr. Kincaid):

"I guess that we lasted four years. The fact that it survived. The fact that for its time it was a pretty good show. I was very happy with the fact that we got along as well as we did. It was a fun set to go to work on. From my point of view, we all got along very well and we had fun on the set. Danny and I used to be the official greeters of guests who would come on the set. We had our little routine that we would do for guests. Danny would explain that my nose was shot off in Korea and I had a rubber nose, and he would offer to show them by rubbing my nose. And then I would take out a half dollar and say, 'I have developed the ability to take Danny's face'—because he had a very pliable, Silly Putty face—'and I can squeeze the features, the two eyes, the nose, and the mouth, just by kneading his skin, down almost to the size of a half dollar. And I would explain I was working on eventually being able to get all of his features down to the size of a dime. We just had fun."

Bernie Slade (Creator):

"It was a perfectly good-natured family show, nothing to be ashamed of, and it was on for four years. I guess we were kind of in competition with *The Brady Bunch*. We always figured that we were a classier show and that we had better scripts. And I think we did, actually, to tell you the truth."

Bob Claver (Executive Producer):

"I just thought it was a very well done show. It was very well produced. And it was edited well. And just overall, I thought it was a good show. I mean, I don't think it's in a class with *The Mary Tyler Moore Show* or *The Phil Silvers Show*. It wasn't meant to be. My ex-wife said it very well: 'If our daughter Nancy'—who was very young at the time—'was watching the show, I would watch it with her.' I think that was her way of saying, it was a very pleasant show, unlike a lot of others oriented for youngsters. We never did a show that wasn't about something [moral]. I don't think you'll find one."

Paul Witt (Producer):

"A couple of things. I think we combined wholesomeness with a pretty strong level of comedy. And I think given that we worked with such young kids, we did remarkably little damage to them. Also the level of production was really good, it was a great looking show from the design of the bus to the sets. It was a very well produced show. It was well acted, well directed. It was well mounted. A lot of care went into it. It was not haphazard or sloppy in any way. For its time, I thought we were pretty intelligent and reasonably honest and funny. And it was a really well mounted, classy little show."

Wes Farrell (Music Producer):

"That we were the success we had planned for it to be, and it lived up to my expectations. I think that's a very important thing. A lot of times you live up to a project's expectations, but it doesn't live up to yours. So it empties you out. And you feel less than pleased with all of your efforts. I think *The Partridge Family* lived up to my expectations. I think it became everything we planned for it to be."

Danny Bonaduce *(Danny Partridge)*

Born on August 13, 1959, in Los Angeles, Dante Daniel Bonaduce acted in commercials and made guest appearances on *Mayberry RFD, Bewitched, My World and Welcome To It, The Ghost and Mrs. Muir,* and *Accidental Family* before he landed the part of Danny Partridge. He has also

appeared on *Police Story, Hollywood Television Theater,* in the television movie *Murder on Flight 502* (1975), and in the motion picture *H.O.T.S.* (1979). Danny worked as a bartender, a security guard, a restaurant manager, and then, in 1988, he became a radio deejay by accident, having become a self-proclaimed "guest freak" on radio shows. He soon became the highest paid nighttime radio deejay in local radio history. He was a disc jockey at KKFR-FM in Phoenix, WEGX-FM in Philadelphia, and is now a deejay on WLUP-FM in Chicago. "I have a tattoo on my butt of the radio station's logo, the names of two other disc jockeys and my boss," admits Danny. "I get fired a lot, and I thought it would be harder for me to get fired if I had their names indelibly tattooed on my ass. So I did that on my very first show on my very first day on the air."

Danny studied martial arts under Chuck Norris for twenty years and appeared in eight episodes of *CHiPS* as a martial artist. He holds a fourth degree black belt in Okinawan Chinan Ryu, a first degree black belt in Tae Kwon Do, a first degree black belt in Tokyo, and a first degree black belt in Shorin Ryu. He won the 1980 and 1981 International Championships.

Danny also performs as a standup comedian once a month in clubs around Chicago, occasionally tours America and Canada, and hosts *The Tonight Show* in Australia one week a year.

Danny made controversial headlines when he was arrested for attempting to buy cocaine in Daytona Beach, Florida, in March 1990 and was sentenced to fifteen months probation. He was arrested again for cocaine possession in Beverly Hills and was bailed out of jail by *The National Enquirer.* In 1991, he was charged with assaulting a transvestite prostitute in a liquor store in Phoenix, Arizona. The only crime he was found guilty of was reckless endangerment, speeding away from the scene of the crime at 125 miles per hour in a 25-mile-per-hour zone.

Danny married Gretchen Hilmer on their first date on November 4, 1990, because Gretchen refused to sleep with him until they were married. The happy couple live in Chicago, Illinois.

Brian Forster *(Chris Partridge)*

Born in Los Angeles, California, Brian Forster appeared in twenty television commercials and made guest appearances on *My Friend Tony, The Brady Bunch, The Survivors*, and *Family Affair* before filling the role of Chris Partridge after Jeremy Gelbwaks left the series in 1971. Brian is the great-great-great-grandson of Charles Dickens and the grandson of Alan Napier, the actor who played Alfred the Butler on *Batman*. His step-father was actor Whit Bissell (*I Was a Teenage Werewolf, Creature from the Black Lagoon, Birdman of Alcatraz, Hud*, and *Seven Days in May*).

"The fame from the Partridge Family really got old," admits Brian. "It got boring to be out in public in a restaurant and have people staring at you and pointing at you. I mean there were so many times I felt like just saying, 'Yes, I was on *The Partridge Family*, come over and talk to me or stop pointing at me.' I really wanted to be a normal kid."

Brian received a degree in zoology from Humboldt State University and considered pursuing a career in veterinary medicine or physical therapy before he discovered the thrills of high performance automobile racing. He is a race car driver and instructor, and he has won 25 percent of the races he has entered. Brian won the San Francisco Regent Championship in 1988, the Northern Pacific Division National Championship in 1989, and the Pacific Coast Road Racing Championship in 1989 and 1992. He raced professionally in the American City Racing League for Team Los Vegas in 1990 and is currently seeking sponsorship. Brian lives in Sebastopol, California.

Jeremy Gelbwaks *(Chris Partridge)*

Born on May 22, 1963, Jeremy Gelbwaks played the role of Christopher Partridge for the first season of the show, and his mysterious disappearance from the series prompted rumors that he had been killed,

died of a drug overdose, or simply been forced to leave the show as a result of antagonism between him and Danny Bonaduce. In actuality, his father had been transferred, forcing the family to move to Reston, Virginia, leaving the role of Chris empty. The Gelbwaks moved from Virginia to Connecticut to London, England, and finally to a dairy farm on the St. Lawrence Seaway in Upstate New York. Jeremy majored in chemistry at SUNY Potsdam and considered a career in veterinary medicine. After a short stint at the University of California at Berkeley, he turned to computers. A job brought him to New York in 1986, and he was soon taking acting classes and performing in amateur productions. In 1989, he left the corporate world to work as a production assistant on feature films, including *Enemies—A Love Story*, *Funny About Love*, *Q&A*, *Alice*, *Awakenings*, and *Bonfire of the Vanities*. After his marriage to Patricia Polander in 1990, he moved to New Orleans, where he works as a consultant for EDS, specializing in digital new media and interactive television. He also continues to act, having completed a series of educational videos for children. Once in a while, he is still recognized as the first Chris Partridge, which he "sort of enjoys."

Suzanne Crough *(Tracy Partridge)*

Born on March 6, 1963, in Fullerton, California, Suzanne Crough is the youngest of eight children. She appeared in several commercials before she was cast as Tracy Partridge. After *The Partridge Family*, Suzanne played Stevie Friedman on the short-lived comedy series *Mulligan's Stew* on NBC in 1977. She also appeared in *Teenage Father* (a short film that won an Academy Award), several television movies (*Children of Divorce*, *Dawn: Portrait of a Teenage Runaway*, starring Eve Plumb, in 1976, and *When the Whistle Blows*), several television pilots, commercials for Hostess and Pontiac, and a stage production of *The Bad Seed*. Suzanne is a graduate of Pierce College, and until 1993 she owned and operated a bookstore. She lives with her husband William Condray and their two daughters, Samantha and Alexandra, in Temecula, California.

David Madden *(Reuben Kincaid)*

Born on December 15, 1933, in Sarnia, Ontario, Dave Madden, the youngest of four children, was sent to live with an aunt and uncle in Terre Haute, Indiana, after his father died. Immobilized by a bicycle accident, he took up magic and later added comedy to his act. He graduated from Otter Creek High, attended Indiana State Teachers College for one semester, and then worked in a bakery. In 1951, he joined the Air Force, was assigned to Special Services, and was stationed in Tripoli, Libya, where he once performed before the king of Libya. After his discharge, he majored in

communications at the University of Miami and performed his comedy routine at fraternity parties and clubs on Miami Beach. After graduation, Dave played the Southern night-club circuit for two years, and then finally moved to Los Angeles. After several club engagements, he was discovered by Frank Sinatra, who called Ed Sullivan and got him booked for three shows.

Dave played Pruett on the short-lived situation comedy *Camp Runamuck*, did voice-overs in commercials, and made guest appearances on several television shows, including *Bewitched* and *Hogan's Heroes*. After touring one summer with a comedy troupe headed by Dan Rowan and Dick Martin, he was hired as a regular in the first season of *Rowan & Martin's Laugh-In*, appearing as the guy who threw confetti in the air.

After starring as Reuben Kincaid on *The Partridge Family* for four years, Dave played Earl Hicks on *Alice*. Dave has also appeared on *The Ed Sullivan Show*, *Bewitched*, *Love, American Style*, *Happy Days*, *Starsky and Hutch*, and *Barney Miller*. His television movies include *The Girl Who Came Gift-Wrapped* (1974) and *More Wild Wild West* (1980), and he appeared in the motion picture *Eat My Dust* (1976). He currently works as a commercial voice-over talent. He lives in Los Angeles.

Bernard Slade *(Creator)*

Born in Toronto, Canada, Bernard Slade spent thirteen years of his youth in England, attended grammar school in Caernarvon in North Wales, and then returned to Canada, where he worked as an actor for ten years before

writing some twenty one-hour television shows for the Canadian Broadcasting Corporation. In 1964, he moved to Los Angeles with his wife, Jill, and his two children, Laurel and Christopher, and began his career there by writing for *Bewitched*. Bernard has written extensively for film and television and is the creator of seven television series: *Love on a Rooftop*, *The Partridge Family*, *The Flying Nun*, *Mr. Deeds Goes to Town*, *The Girl with Something Extra*, *Getting Together*, *Heaven Help Us*, and *Bridget Loves Bernie*. He made his Broadway debut as a playwright with *Same Time Next Year*, which ran for four years in New York and subsequently has been performed in almost every country, in over forty different languages, all over the world, including the Chekhov Theatre in Moscow. His screenplay for the movie that starred Alan Alda and Ellen Burstyn (1978) was nominated for an Academy Award. The play received a Tony nomination and won the Drama Desk award. His next play, *Tribute*, starred Jack Lemmon on both the stage and screen (1980). His other plays include *Romantic Comedy*, *Special Occasions*, *Fatal Attraction*, *An Act of the Imagination*, *Return Engagements*, *Every Time I See You*, and *You*

Say Tomatoes. Bernard is presently working on a sequel to *Same Time Next Year* called *Same Time, Another Year*.

Bernard and his wife Jill divide their time between a house in Malibu and a flat in London. When not writing, he can usually be found avoiding writing by having excessively long lunches with friends or trying to work off the result of those lunches on the tennis court. He is a member of the Dramatists Guild of America.

Bob Claver *(Executive Producer)*

Born on May 22, 1928, in Chicago, Illinois, Bob Claver majored in journalism at the University of Illinois. Claver was producer and director of *Here Come the Brides* starring Bobby Sherman, and directed episodes of *Mork & Mindy*, *Welcome Back, Kotter*, *Newhart*, *Rhoda*, *Out of This World*, *The Farmer's Daughter*, *All's Fair*, *House Calls*, *Charles in Charge*, *Gloria*, *Doc*, *The Facts of Life*, *Gidget*, *The Dukes of Hazard*, *The Girl with Something Extra*, and *The New Leave It to Beaver*. He now lives in Chicago, Illinois, and is currently seeking a publisher for his first novel.

Paul Witt *(Producer)*

Born on March 20, 1941, in New York City, Paul Junger Witt majored in English at the University of Virginia and attended the London School of Film Technique. He joined Screen Gems in 1965 and was named assistant to producer Bob Claver on *The Farmer's Daughter* in 1966. He was associate producer on *Occasional Wife* for NBC in 1967, and he made his directorial debut on an episode of that series. He served as associate producer on *The Second Hundred Years* and directed several episodes. He was a producer and director on *Here Come the Brides*, and developed new series for Screen Gems, producing *The Girl with Something Extra* and *One Big Family*.

Paul produced the Emmy Award-winning television movie *Brian's*

Song (1971), working for the first time with associate producer Tony Thomas. The two joined Danny Thomas Productions in 1972 as president and vice president, respectively.

As a partner with Thomas in Witt-Thomas Productions and Thomas and Susan Harris in Witt-Thomas-Harris Productions, Paul is one of

Hollywood's most successful television producers. He and his companies had more shows on television for the 1991–92 season than any other independent production company.

Witt-Thomas Productions produced the series *Beauty and the Beast* for CBS and the television movies *No Place to Run*, *A Cold Night's Death*, *Home for the Holidays*, and *The Letter*. The company currently produces in association with Touchstone Television the hit NBC comedy series *Blossom* and the innovative Fox series *Herman's Head*.

Witt-Thomas-Harris Productions has been responsible for *Soap, Benson, Fay, Hail to the Chief, I'm a Big Girl Now, It Takes Two*, the Emmy Award-winning *The Golden Girls*, the Top Ten hit *Empty Nest*, the NBC series *The Nurses*, and *The John Larroquette Show*.

Paul entered the feature film arena with partner Tony Thomas in 1984 with *Firstborn*, starring Teri Garr and Peter Weiler, and also produced *The Dead Poets Society*, which won an Academy Award for Best Screenplay, and *Final Analysis*, starring Richard Gere and Kim Basinger.

Paul lives with his family in Brentwood, California.

Wes Farrell *(Music Producer)*

Wes Farrell produced and wrote the music that catapulted David Cassidy and the Partridge Family to stardom and resulted in the sale of 56 million records in less than four years. His own compositions include "Boys" (recorded by the Beatles), "Hang on Sloopy" (recorded by the McCoys), "Come a Little Bit Closer" and "Let's Lock the Door" (recorded by Jay and the Americans), "I'll Meet You Halfway" and "Doesn't Somebody Want to Be Wanted" (recorded by the Partridge Family), and

"Come On Down to My Boat" (recorded by Every Mother's Son). In 1966, he formed the Wes Farrell Organization, nurturing hundreds of aspiring songwriters under contract to his companies, including Neil Diamond, Barry Manilow, the Rascals, and Irwin Levine and L. Russell Brown. The hit list of songs he published over the years includes "Candida" and "Knock Three Times" (recorded by Tony Orlando and Dawn), "Groovin'," "How Can I Be Sure," "People Got to Be Free," "Lonely Too Long," and "What a Beautiful Morning" (recorded by the Rascals), "Danke Schoen" (recorded by Wayne Newton), "Spanish Eyes" (recorded by Al Martino), "Indian Lake" (recorded by the Cowsills), "I Like Dreaming" (recorded by Kenny Nolan), "I'm Going to Make You Mine" (recorded by Lou Christie), and "The Night Chicago Died" (recorded by Paper Lace). Wes has more than one hundred gold records to his name.

After *The Partridge Family*, Wes founded Chelsea Records, producing albums for a diverse range of artists, including Wayne Newton, New York City, Lulu, Austin Roberts, Disco-Tex and His Sex-o-lettes, William DeVaughn, James Gilstrap, Dee Clark, and Rick Springfield. He also founded Coral Rock Commercials, the Clio-winning music house responsible for creating advertising jingles for Ford Motor Company, Coca-Cola, General Motors, and Kellogg.

Wes also scored several motion pictures, most notably the Academy Award-winning *Midnight Cowboy* (1969). Since 1966, the Farrell publishing, production, and manufacturing companies have been responsible for worldwide sales figures of over 300 million records, dozens of gold records, Emmy and Grammy nominations, and many other national and international awards.

Wes lives in Coconut Grove, Florida, and New York City with his wife, Jean, and their two children.

Pop Quiz Answers

1. D [Episode 1] 2. E 3. D 4. E 5. B [Episode 6] 6. D [Episode 8] 7. A [Episode 16] 8. E [Episode 17] 9. D [Episode 22] 10. A [Episode 22] 11. B [Episode 29] 12. D [Episode 30] 13. A [Episode 32] 14. D [Episode 39] 15. B [Episode 40] 16. C [Episode 40] 17. A [Episode 41] 18. D [Episode 41] 19. B [Episode 43] 20. C [Episode 44] 21. E [Episode 45] 22. D [Episode 47] 23. B [Episode 48] 24. D [Episode 49] 25. A [Episode 51] 26. C [Episode 52] 27. A [Episode 54] 28. D [Episode 56] 29. D [Episode 56] 30. E [Episode 57] 31. E [Episode 59] 32. E [Episode 61] 33. A [Episode 62] 34. C [Episode 64] 35. C [Episode 70] 36. D [Episode 74] 37. B [Episode 77] 38. A [Episode 78] 39. A [Episode 79] 40. A [Episode 81] 41. C [Episode 83] 42. C [Episode 84] 43. D [Episode 86] 44. A [Episode 92] 45. A [Episode 95] 46. D [Episode 96] 47. C [Episodes 2, 5, and 80] 48. B 49. C 50. D

the birth of music television

The Partridge Family.
In heavy rotation on

Acknowledgments

I am gratefully indebted to the cast, creators, and producers of *The Partridge Family* who generously opened their hearts and memories to spread a whole lot of lovin': Shirley Jones, David Cassidy, Danny Bonaduce, Brian Forster, Jeremy Gelbwaks, Suzanne Crough, Dave Madden, Bernard Slade, Bob Claver, Paul Witt, and Wes Farrell.

Susan Dey's publicist, agent, and manager all claimed that Susan refused to grant an interview for this officially authorized book, apparently hoping to disassociate herself from the television show that launched her acting career—at the risk of disappointing her fans. Go figure.

My editor, Chris McLaughlin, championed the Partridge Family crusade at HarperCollins, and my agent, Jeremy Solomon, proved once again that his skills and savvy far outshine those of Reuben Kincaid. Joseph Montebello hired a brilliant book designer, Doreen Louie masterminded the cover design, Karen Malley oversaw the production, and Jeff Smith copyedited into the wee hours of the night.

I am also indebted to Marty Ingels, Kevin McShane, Karen Kelly, Gretchen Bonaduce, Melanie Green, Barbara Gale, Gina Rugolo, Herb Tannen, Marc Kleiner, Craig Balsam (at Razor & Tie Music), Paul Ward and Tom Hill (at *Nick at Night*), Elizabeth Moran (author of *Bradymania*), Steve Cox (author of *Here on Gilligan's Isle*, *The Hooterville Handbook*, and *Here's Johnny*), Michele Morris, Anne Gaines, Marc Bego, Glen Salzman, Ken Fitzgerald, Barbara Pazmino, Katy Leuty, Randell Kirsch, Karen J. Smith, Doug Hochstadt, Lisa Sutton, Duane Dimock, David Jolliffe, Glorya Lord, Judy Nierman, Alan Eskew, Bill Aichison, John Fiore Pucci, Mark Blechman, Susan Pandes, David Nickel, Julie Pedace, Ginny Westcott, Stacy Westrum, Alice Tabor, Alan Bezozi, David Wild, John Lee Wong, Brian Boyd, Melissa Webber, and Jeremy Wolff.

Thanks to Stephen Bishop, "Weird Al" Yankovic, Annie Callingham, and Norma Bishop for their terrific quotes on page 114.

Columbia Pictures Television graciously opened *The Partridge Family* files for this project, and thanks go out to Lester Borden, Susan B. Christison, Ron Rubin, Donna Schneiderman, Karen Witte, and Michael Fox. I am also grateful to Peter Murray and Ann Ferrell (at Capital Cities/ABC), Michael Ochs and Helen Ashford (at Michael Ochs Archives),

Howard Frank (at Personality Photos), Fred Seibert and Joe LoCicero (at Hanna-Barbera), and Scott Abrams (at EMI Music Publishing).

I never could have assembled such an extensive collection of Partridge Family memorabilia without the help of Cindy Press, Rick Polizzi (coauthor of *Spin Again*), Scott Bruce, (author of *The Official Price Guide to Lunch Box Collectibles*), Rick Waugh of Rick's Comics, and Dan Schwartz of Baseball Cards-Movie Collectibles.

Above all, thanks to Debbie and Ashley for the inspiration. I think I love you.

Photo Credits

Photos courtesy of Michael Ochs Archives/Venice, CA—pages *xvi*, 50, 60, 67, 73, 75, 104, 127, 129, 131, 135, 162, 166, 167, 175, 177, 184, 185, 190, 192, 195, 197, 198, 201, 205, 213, 215, 220, 225, 228. © 1994 Michael Ochs Archives/Venice, CA. Used with permission.

Photos courtesy of Capital Cities/ABC, Inc.—pages 36, 88, 133, 137, 151, 153, 160, 164, 165, 181, 183, 189, 202, 211, 217. © 1994 Capital Cities/ABC, Inc. Used with permission.

Photos courtesy of Personality Photos, Inc.—pages *xviii*, 78, 97, 142, 149, 169, 173.

Photo courtesy of Hanna-Barbera Productions—page 33. © 1994 Hanna-Barbera Productions, Inc. Used with permission.

Photos courtesy of Nick at Night—pages 35, 311, 312. © 1994 Nick at Night. Used with permission.

Photos courtesy of Ginny Westcott—pages 11, 21, 22, 23, 24, 29, 30, 108, 232, 275 (bottom three).

Photos courtesy of Joey Green—pages 4, 34, 43, 44, 45, 51, 53, 54, 58, 59, 63, 64, 65, 71 (both), 77, 79, 80, 85, 86, 99, 111, 120, 163, 170, 171, 178, 187, 230, 239, 243, 245, 247, 249, 251, 253, 255, 257, 261, 269, 270, 273, 275 (top only), 278 (all), 279 (all), 280, 286, 288, 289, 291, 293, 294, 296, 306.

Photo courtesy of Scott Bruce—page 271.

Photo courtesy of David Cassidy—page 274. © 1994 David Cassidy. Used with permission.

Photo courtesy of Shirley Jones—pages *x*, *xiii*, 13, 19, 303.

Photo courtesy of David Cassidy Fan Club—page 305. © 1993 David Cassidy Appreciation Society. Used with permission.

Photo courtesy of Danny Bonaduce and WLUP-FM—page 310.

Photo courtesy of Suzanne Crough—page 313 (top).

Photo courtesy of Dave Madden—page 313 (bottom).

Photo courtesy of Bernard Slade—page 314.

Photo courtesy of Bob Claver—page 315.

Photo courtesy of Paul Witt—page 316.

Photo courtesy of Wes Farrell—page 317.

Photo courtesy of Debbie Green—page 331.

Fan Clubs

For information on how to join a fan club to stay on top of all the latest Partridge Family news and paraphernalia, send a self-addressed stamped envelope to either:

DAVID CASSIDY FAN CLUB
c/o Barbara Pazmino
979 East 42 Street
Brooklyn, NY 11210
or
c/o Rene Burdick
1447 Twinridge Road
Santa Barbara, CA 93111

Or send two international reply coupons (available for purchase at any post office) and a self-addressed envelope to:

DAVID CASSIDY APPRECIATION SOCIETY
c/o Katy Leuty
The Old Post House
The Street
Litlington, East Sussex
BN26 5RD, England

or

DAVID CASSIDY FAN CLUB
c/o Tina Funk
Bueltbek #20
22962 Siek
Germany

Index

CAST AND GUEST STARS

SONGS

WRITERS

About the Author

Joey Green was a contributing editor to *National Lampoon* until he wrote an article in *Rolling Stone* on why *National Lampoon* isn't funny anymore. A native of Miami (where he was awarded *The Miami Herald* Silver Knight), Green was almost expelled from Cornell University for selling fake football programs at the 1979 Cornell-Yale homecoming game. He was editor of the *Cornell Lunatic*, president of the National Association of College Humor Magazines, and has authored several books, including *Hellbent on Insanity* (with Bruce Handy and Alan Corcoran), *The Unofficial Gilligan's Island Handbook*, and *The Get Smart*

Handbook. Green worked at J. Walter Thompson in New York and Hong Kong, where he wrote television commericals for Burger King, the launch campaign for the Grand Hyatt Hotel, and won a Clió for a print ad he created for Eastman Kodak. He spent two years backpacking around the world on his honeymoon, wrote television commercials for Walt Disney World in Florida, and currently lives in Los Angeles.